The
COP
Cookbook

The COP Cookbook

*Arresting Recipes from the
World's Favorite Cops, Good Guys,
and Private Eyes*

Greta Garner-Hewitt,
Ken Beck,
and Jim Clark

RUTLEDGE HILL PRESS

Nashville, Tennessee

Published in Nashville, Tennessee by Rutledge Hill Press, Inc., 211 Seventh Avenue North, Nashville, Tennessee 37219. Distributed in Canada by H. B. Fenn & Company, Ltd., 34 Nixon Road, Bolton, Ontario, L7E 1W2. Distributed in Australia by Lothian Books, 11 Munro Street, Port Melbourne, VIC 3207. Distributed in New Zealand by Tandem Press, 2 Rugby Road, Birkenhead, Auckland 10. Distributed in the United Kingdom by Verulam Publishing, Ltd., 152a Park Street Lane, Park Street, St. Albans, Hertfordshire AL2 2AU.

Typography by Roger A. DeLiso, Nashville, Tennessee
Design by Harriette Bateman

Library of Congress Cataloging-in-Publication Data

Garner-Hewitt, Greta, 1958–
      The cop cookbook / Greta Garner-hewitt, Ken Beck, and Jim Clark.
          p. cm.
      Includes index.
      ISBN 1-55853-536-5 (paperback)
      1. Cookery, American. 2. Motion picture actors and actresses—
      United States—Miscellanea.
I. Beck, Ken, 1951–   . II. Clark,
Jim, 1960–   . III. Title.
TX715.G226   1997
641.5—dc21   97-16046
                                                    CIP

Printed in the United States of America
1 2 3 4 5 6 7 8 9 — 00 99 98 97

This book is dedicated

to the courageous men and women
who unselfishly risk their lives daily
to protect and serve others
and to the memory of the fallen heroes
who have paid the ultimate price
in the line of duty.

In Honor of Law Enforcement's Finest

The third week of May each year marks National Police Week, and the centerpiece is the annual National Peace Officers' Memorial Day Service in Washington, D.C., which is sponsored by the National Fraternal Order of Police's Grand Lodge Auxiliary.

On this day, thousands gather at the west front of the U.S. Capitol to honor the police officers who have given their lives during service the previous year. From its beginning in 1981, when 120 survivors and supporters of law enforcement met, the event has now grown to over 8,000 participants and observers.

During the ceremonies, medals of honor are presented to the officers' surviving family members, and their names are placed on the memorial's "Wall of Remembrance."

In 1995, Gilbert G. Gallegos, president of the Fraternal Order of Police, the largest law enforcement organization in the country, introduced President Bill Clinton, who gave the keynote address to the survivors, co-workers, and concerned citizens who honored the officers and families who had given their all.

The authors of *The Cop Cookbook* are pleased to share a portion of the earnings from this book with the Fraternal Order of Police, which sponsors Concerns of Police Survivors (COPS) scholarships. These scholarships are available to survivors whose states do not provide tuition-free education benefits to surviving spouses or children and to survivors who are no longer eligible for assistance. The money can be used for tuition, registration fees, and textbooks.

The Lineup

An Officer's Grace

Lord, please bless this food before me,
Shimmering in speckled grease,
To be washed down with scalding coffee;
That's powerful, to say the least.

My doctor said don't eat it,
Because it's bad for my stomach and heart,
But the health food places all close before
The grueling night watch starts.

He says I'll shorten my life span,
That I won't get my three score and ten,
And it's true cops average just fifty-eight years
To get all their living in.

But the job I do is *important,*
Standing between the savage and the weak,
Though I often wonder where we warriors will go
When you give the earth to the meek.

I love healthy food same as any
With loved ones at a *real* table,
But usually—what with my extra jobs—
I just really am not able.

So Lord, bless this food before me;
I'm thankful for what I've got.
And if it's not too much trouble, God,
Just once, I'd like to eat it hot.

David Hunter
Author and former police officer

Foreword

IT HAS BEEN NEARLY FORTY years since I tried on the hat of Eliot Ness, a federal officer of the law in *The Untouchables*, at the old Desilu Studios. I guess it turned out to be a pretty good fit, even if those were some tough shoes to fill.

Over the years I have always held great respect for Eliot Ness and what he stood for. In fact, when I have come to a crossroads in my life, I've often wondered, "How would Eliot Ness have handled this?"

As actors, we play all kinds of roles, but it is a special honor to portray a police officer, detective, or solver of crimes, since it is a tribute to all those who do it for real and make our world a safer place.

This book pays homage to those who have played cops on the big and small

screen, and there are dozens of wonderful photographs inside that will revive great memories for the fans as well as for those of us who portrayed cunning sleuths and gumshoes. These memories are a form of saying "thank you" to America's finest, the men and women in blue who give their best every day for us citizens.

The Cop Cookbook, of course, has many terrific recipes. You see, cops have to eat, because pounding a beat from eight to sixteen hours a day is no small feat. I think you'll enjoy trying the various dishes and will have just as much fun reading and cooking with this book as you have had watching the movies and the television shows.

Robert Stack

Informants

WE WOULD LIKE TO THANK EVERYONE who helped this book come into being. Countless people gave their time and energy helping us acquire recipes, photographs, and information. We received a great deal of support from chiefs of police and other law enforcement officials throughout the country as well as from their spouses, secretaries, and executive assistants. For working above and beyond the call of duty, we thank you.

We are grateful to all of the actors, their spouses and families, agents, managers, assistants, and publicists who took time out of their busy lives to share their recipes and photographs with us.

For undercover investigation, we would especially like to thank Gil Gallegos, Jim Pasco, Lt. Jerry Atnip, Deborah Richardson, Susan Superczynski, Jesse Bushman, Fred Dowdle, David and Cheryl Hunter, Tom Williams, Sgt. Jerry Hallenger, Jean Miles, Steve Cox, Jesse Wayne, Chief and Mrs. Emmett Turner, Assistant Chief and Mrs. Charles Smith, Sheriff Gayle Ray, Sue and D. C. Woods, Margie Smith, Det. Sgt. Brook Schaub, Mike Canning, Barbara Hale Delgado, the whole Helmick family, Shirlee Fonda, Julie Savalas, Terry McQueen, Sara Karloff, Iris Frederick, Dani Janssen, Ginny Mancini, Barbara Morgan, Rosemarie Stack, Paula Steiger, Shawna Trabert, Mrs. Ben Click, Alexa Hamilton, China Soul, Ruth Thompson, Diana Douglas, Ethel Longnecker, Anna Lazlo Kerlikowske, Dorothy Best, Suzanne Woolsey, Alice Sessions, Lynda Webster, Carolyn Whipple, Tracey Glaser, Luisa Moore, Lucinda Bridges Cunningham, Ida Prosky, Susan Robertson, Anne Douglas, Claire Boone, Julia Hingle, Mary Cox, Crystal Thomas, Clara Burrell, Tippy Conrad, Laura Peppard, Mollie Birney, Elizabeth Shayne, Linda Lee Caldwell, Monica Mancini, Gail Davis, Pauline Pusser, Dwana Pusser, Theresa Repp, W. P. Davis, Grace Curio, Martha Dixon, Martha Selleck, Lyn Burke, Georgia Luisi, Marilyn Taylor, Gerry Weaver, Colleen Carey, Jayni Chase, Pamela Boothe, La Velda Conrad, Mona Malden, Myrna Colley-Lee, Ruth Rodriguez, Jeanne Philippus, Dr. Herbert Tanney, Mary Ann Rea, Dom DeLuise, Martha Dixon, Joan Kellogg, Jennifer Allen at PMK, Tracie Dean, Carol Safir, Judy Ciani, Officer Kevin Grandalski, Sgt. Jay Gribbon, Cynthia Snyder and Det. Gene Peterson, Darice O'Mara, Jimmy McDonald, Millie Bickford, and Sue Barley, thank you so much!

For providing backup, we would like to thank Karen Tabara, Glenda Washam, Frank Sutherland, Marilyn Atlas, Randall Franks, Cliff Smith, Johnny Western, Martha Moore, Ron Goodwin, Pat Embry, Angee Hudgens, Lt. Lewis E. Reed, Sherwin Bash, Randy Bash, Ken Hofer, Ray Simmons, David Valenzuela, Rosemary Shad, Vivian Stanley, Cal Lynn, De Lois Brown, Karen Smith, Sharon Manifold, Anna Kingery, Linnie Winters. Charlotte Jackson, Ruth Ann Presley, Shelly Cusick, Lt. Zora Lykken, Kim Cavanaugh, Angie Steenberg, Florence Bilecki, Becky Knudson, Virginia Fischer, Teresa Sagel, Sandra Talbot, Renee Wegschlaidler, Roxanne Archuleta, Kim Dettwiller, and Scherr Lillico.

For aiding and abetting, we thank Michele Graves, Dolores Carman, Toni Chesworth, Pat Lally, Darellyn Kiser, Audry Crisp, Pam Manion, Capt. Randy Tate, Maj. Fred White, Ken Murphy, Barbara Whitaker, Rick Guzman, Anita Ramirez, Robin Sloan, Mary Eres, Steve Miessner, Sue Roebuck, Beverly Magid, Ron Leis, Jeff Hardwick, Linda Zeisman, N. A. M. Butler, Jo Montgomery, Jeannie Potts, Dr. Larry and Linda Burrell, Vicky Gill, Bruce Holiday, Margaret Harris, Angela Bray, Ann Kaiser, Mary Steelsmith, Arthur Toretzky, Nancy Cain, Vanessa Gilbert, Junko Takeya, Amy Guenther, the Tisherman Agency, Wilma Wheeler, Amy Seipp, Valerie Thompson, Ethan Tyler, and Rod Sadler.

For assistance on the scene, we thank Teresa Morley, Katherine Wallace, Karen Holmstrom, Rosanne Carlton, Judith Lovejoy, Pat Walton, Jackie Taylor Zortman, Geri Kelley, Chris Sambain, Linda Robertson, Officer Debbie Abdur-Rasheed, Roberta Smith, Dale C. Olson and Associates, Bonnie Shaffner, Marjorie Schicktanz, Jack Jason, Robert Malcolm, David Shapiro and Associates, Arlene Dayton, Marit Blake, Green/Siegel Management, Jan McCormack, Richard Sindell Management, Elise Konalian, Mary Erickson, Patrick Wayne, Stephen McChesney, Phyllis DeFranco, Lt. Joseph Eddy, Shannon Hulzebos, Marcia Toma, and Frankie Stuart.

For their quick response to our calls for assistance, we wish to thank Sgt. John McDonald, Helen and Sgt. Jay Gribbin, Nancy Taber, Lt. Calvin Moss, Scott and Mary Deal, Janie Warshaw, April Raynell, Michele Roberge, Jo An Kincaid, Fonda St. Paul, Paul Reed Jr., Lori De Waal, Simon Hall, Christopher Gustafson, Nancy Sherman, Kim Grabowski, and Merilee Mahoney.

Providing additional backup were Ken Stovitz, Dick Guttman, Jennnifer Price, the Lippen Group, Mahmoudah Young, Terrie Williams, Rachel Noerdlinger, Mark Mack, Jason Weinberg, Michael Karg, Carol Lupton, Jan Taylor, Patrick McMinn, Michael Hartig, Denis Selinger, Christine Jardine, Lieutenant Freeman, Don Pitts, Sandra Trotter, the Blake Agency, Melissa and Tom Rooker, Kathy Bartels, Renee Young, Diane Passarelli, and Gino Alfonso.

At Rutledge Hill Press we would like to thank Publisher Chief Larry Stone; Editorial Vice Squad Commander Peaches Yeilding Scribner; Editorial Jailer Jennifer Greenstein; Recipe Sharpshooters Teri Mitchell and Laurin Stamm; Sketch Artists Harriette Bateman, Roger DeLiso, and Tim Holland; Undercover Detective Mike Towle; Marksman of Marketing Bryan Curtis; SWAT Team Leader of Publicity Kath Hansen; and the rest of the fine Rutledge Hill forces both at the precinct and patrolling the streets.

We especially want to thank our families for their support and patience while we compiled this book. Greta gives her heartfelt gratitude to her loving husband, Steve (a detective sergeant and SWAT team member in Nashville), her very supportive parents, Lois and James Garner, and also Justin, Gavin, Evan, Katie, and Angus Hewitt. Ken thanks his wife, Wendy, and daughter and son, Kylie and Cole. Jim thanks his wife, Mary.

Thank you all for your help!

Rookie Orientation

IN THE WORLD OF ENTERTAINMENT, FEW genres, if any, have provided storytelling that's more riveting than crime fighting, mystery solving, and good old-fashioned whodunits. Good guys stand up to bad guys, law and order defeat crime and chaos, right battles wrong—these are themes that consistently make movies and television shows about cops and detectives among the most compelling for audiences everywhere. From tough guys to cartoon characters, 911-call shows to unsolved mysteries, cop culture is pop culture.

Part of what makes these movies and television shows so interesting is that we do not have to look any further than the morning paper or the evening news to see how real the stories are. Sometimes, we have to look only through the windows of our own homes. We see real-life cops on the streets every day risking their lives to keep our communities safe. Hundreds of thousands of people in law enforcement put their lives on the line to protect and serve us. Thousands more are working to unravel mysteries and solve crimes that have already occurred. It is exhausting, often dangerous, work. Too often it is also a thankless job. Therefore, one of our main goals in compiling this cookbook is to thank those working in law enforcement across the country.

Why a cookbook? With hard work comes a hearty appetite! While not all cops are known for their skills in the kitchen, all cops do know where and how to find good food. They know the best places to have a big steak dinner, and they know which greasy spoon serves the best meat and three. We thought that the food real cops and detectives all across the country enjoy the most would be interesting. Let's just call it the "eat beat."

We also believed a cookbook could provide an enjoyable and appropriate way to remember some of our best-loved television and movie cops. Dozens of actors and writers have entertained us with cop and detective stories during the last five decades or so, and we have collected some of their tastiest recipes for you to enjoy.

Compiled here are special recipes from seven dozen chiefs of police and other top cops representing all fifty states and recipes from your favorite cop and detective actors and writers. Clint Eastwood's Dirty Harry, Peter Falk's Columbo, Richard Roundtree's Shaft, Hal Linden's Barney Miller, Don Knotts's Barney Fife, and Dennis Franz's Andy Sipowicz are just a few of the dozens of entertainment cops who share their best dishes and culinary secrets. We have not forgotten female sleuths, including stars Tyne Daly and Sharon Gless, Angie Dickinson, Cheryl Ladd, Frances McDormand, and Angela Lansbury.

The result is a comprehensive cookbook with everything from appetizers to desserts. To spice things up a little, you can feast your eyes on two hundred photographs of cops from the entertainment world. More than a cookbook, this collection will please movie and television fans with dozens of trivia quizzes as well as a compendium of Emmy and Academy Award winners to satisfy your appetite for interesting tidbits about television and movie cops and detectives.

We have created a cookbook that is enjoyable both to cook with and to read. The icing on the cake is that a portion of the proceeds from the sale of *The Cop Cookbook* is being donated to the National Peace Officers' Memorial Service Fund, which honors police officers who have paid the ultimate price in the line of duty. So along with the delicious food and good fun that this cookbook provides, it also supports a worthy cause.

You've heard enough from us. Your own investigation awaits. Take a 10-95!* Now, 10-4 and out!

The Los Angeles Police Historical Society and the Annual Jack Webb Awards

The Los Angeles Police Historical Society began as the dream child of retired LAPD detective Richard E. Kalk in 1988. The primary goal of the historical society is the creation of a nonprofit historical museum and community education center. Its aim is to organize and supervise the conversion of the historic Highland Park police station into a state-of-the-art center for police and community communication. The Los Angeles Police History and Community Education Center will serve as a museum, community center, and police substation. Furthermore, it is designed as a place for young people to gather and explore the LAPD's proud 128-year history.

In 1994 the Los Angeles Police Historical Society created the Jack Webb Award in perpetual honor of Jack Webb for his devotion and volunteer service to law enforcement. The award also pays tribute to those who continue that tradition. Each year the award is presented at the historical society's major fund-raising event, the Jack Webb Awards Gala, which is held every fall to benefit the Los Angeles Police History and Community Education Center.

This festive, black-tie event includes fabulous silent and live auctions, a gourmet dinner, and headline entertainment. It is here that real cops are honored by the countless actors who have played "reel" cops, and thus cast members of shows such as *NYPD Blue, Hill Street Blues, CHiPs, Law & Order, Police Story*, and many more participate in the festivities.

Dan Cook, who retired in 1988 after thirty-five years of service with the LAPD, wrote: "Jack Webb died of a heart attack on December 23, 1982, at sixty-two years of age. The LAPD gave him a farewell worthy of an officer killed in the line of duty. Chief of Police Darryl Gates retired Joe Friday's sergeant badge #714 on the day he died."

The famous "What Is a Cop?" monologue (from the February 9, 1967, episode of *Dragnet)* was read at the ceremony. "There are over five thousand men in this city who know that being a policeman is an endless, thankless job that must be done. I know it too. And I'm damned glad to be one of them."

The Los Angeles Police Historical Society is proud to present the Jack Webb Awards in his honor and to salute his memory at its annual anniversary gala.

*Police officers' ten-code for a meal break.

The lawman's lawman of television land, Jack Webb was the creative force behind *Dragnet, Adam-12,* and *Emergency.*

Robert Stack as Eliot Ness on *The Untouchables*.

Fingerprints

APPETIZERS

CHiPs Patrol Party Mix

Much better than plain old chips!

■ Dedicated to the memory of my brother, Lt. John Helmick, who was killed in the line of duty.

12 cups popped popcorn
 4 cups fresh, pitted cherries
 4 cups Crispix or other Chex cereal
 2 cups walnuts, peanuts, almonds, or cashews
 2 sticks margarine
 1 16-ounce box brown sugar
 ½ cup light corn syrup

In a large roasting pan, mix together the popcorn, cherries, cereal, and nuts. In a saucepan, combine the remaining ingredients and bring to a boil over medium heat to form a syrup. Pour the syrup over the popcorn-cereal mixture. Bake in a 250° oven for 1 hour. Stir every 15 minutes.

Makes about 22 cups.

Dwight "Spike" Helmick
Commissioner
California Highway Patrol

Larry Wilcox (left) and Erik Estrada portrayed Jon Baker and Ponch Poncherello, members of the California Highway Patrol, when *CHiPs* debuted in 1977.

Tommy Lee Jones won an Oscar for his performance as the federal marshal (Sam Gerard) who doggedly pursued Harrison Ford in the 1993 movie *The Fugitive*. He also played a big-city gumshoe in *Gotham*.

Sam Gerard's San Saba Red Salsa

■ This is popular on my ranch in San Saba County, Texas.

4 or 5 jalapeño peppers
½ large white onion
1 large spoonful of minced garlic
  Salt to taste
9 canned, peeled whole tomatoes
  with juice
  Lots of fresh cilantro leaves
  Tortilla chips

Combine all the ingredients except tortilla chips in a blender or food processor and blend to the consistency preferred. Taste with one of the tortilla chips. If your blend is too spicy, add more tomatoes and juice. Serve with tortilla chips.

Makes about 4 cups.

Tommy Lee Jones

Chile Verde Sacramento

2 pounds lean pork
3 7-ounce cans Herdez green chile sauce
  Eggs, cooked to taste
  Refried beans (optional)
  Spanish rice (optional)
  Fried potatoes (optional)
  Tortillas, corn or flour (optional)

Cube the pork and brown the cubes well. Drain off excess fat (we want to stay healthy!). Pour the green chile sauce over the meat and stir for 3 to 5 minutes, not allowing it to evaporate. Serve over eggs cooked to your taste and complement with refried beans, Spanish rice, or fried potatoes (or all three, depending on how hungry you are), and either corn or flour tortillas.

Makes about 6 servings.

Arturo Venegas Jr.
Chief of Police
Sacramento, California

Mr. Wolfe's Salmon Pâté

2 envelopes plain gelatin
1 cup hot chicken broth
1 16-ounce can salmon, drained
½ cup mayonnaise
2 heaping teaspoons chopped parsley
1 heaping teaspoon dill weed
⅓ medium onion
1 cup whipping cream
  Salt and pepper
  Crackers, plain

In a blender, dissolve the gelatin in the chicken broth. Add the remaining ingredients, except crackers, and blend for approximately 2 minutes. Pour into a mold and refrigerate for at least 2 hours. Serve with plain crackers. Enjoy!

Makes about 5 cups.

William Conrad
Submitted by Tippy (Mrs. William) Conrad

Although he gained fame as Cannon in 1971, William Conrad also starred in 1981 as Nero Wolfe, a New York City crime-solving genius who was a lover of gourmet food. Conrad also supplied the voice of the narrator for producer Quinn Martin's *The Fugitive* and was the cop turned district attorney Jason McCabe in *Jake and the Fatman*.

Jack Webb's Joe Friday and Harry Morgan's Bill Gannon went by the book when they starred in *Dragnet*. The big police show hit of the 1950s was revived for three additional seasons in 1967.

Officer Bill Gannon's Purée of Tomato with Tapioca

1½ pints tapioca, lightly prepared in a chicken consommé
     Additional chicken consommé
3 medium, very red tomatoes
2 ounces grated cheese

Prepare the tapioca according to its package instructions, but use chicken consommé as the liquid and make the tapioca a little less thick than usual. Peel and press the tomatoes, and then dice the pulp. Poach the tomatoes in enough chicken consommé to cover them. Add the tomato mixture to the tapioca and mix well. Serve with grated cheese.

Makes about 1 quart.

Harry Morgan

Sandwich Crab Delite Hors d'Oeuvre

13 ounces cream cheese, softened
¼ cup mayonnaise
⅛ teaspoon onion salt
     Dash Worcestershire sauce
1 6-ounce can crabmeat, drained
     Ritz crackers or saltines
     Paprika

In a mixing bowl, blend thoroughly the cream cheese, mayonnaise, onion salt, and Worcestershire sauce. Fold in the crabmeat. Refrigerate until ready to serve. Preheat the oven to 350°. Spread a small amount of crab mixture on crackers. Place on a cookie sheet and sprinkle with paprika. Bake until heated through.

Variation: You can also put the crab-meat mixture in an ovenproof dish and heat until bubbly and serve with crackers.

Makes about 2 cups.

Robert D. Whearty
Chief of Police
Sandwich, Massachusetts

Northern California Nachos Mexicanos

■ I was introduced to this recipe by Mary, owner of Al's Restaurant in Fresno, California, and mother of a Fresno police detective. Al's is a small place but a great diner that's always full of cops, probation officers, and friends.

Plain or salted tortilla chips
Refried beans
Chile Verde Sacramento (p. 16)
Monterey Jack or cheddar cheese, grated

Preheat the oven to 350°. In the bottom of an ovenproof dish, arrange a layer of tortilla chips. Top with some beans, then with either the Steak or Chile Verde. Cover with some of the cheese. Repeat layers until you have a heap. Place in the oven and bake until the cheese has melted. This dish can also be heated in the microwave.

Makes enough for a full meal or to be shared as an appetizer.

Arturo Venegas Jr.
Chief of Police
Sacramento, California

Decoy Bean Dip

Alias Delicious!

■ My grandson is a policeman in San Francisco. He loves the streets. I'm very proud of him!

2   10½-ounce cans Frito's bean dip
1   cup sour cream
1   8-ounce package cream cheese, softened
1   1¼-ounce package taco seasoning mix

20   drops (yes, exactly) Tabasco sauce
1   bunch green onions, chopped
½   pound sharp cheddar cheese, grated
½   pound Monterey Jack cheese, grated
    Tortilla chips

With an electric mixer, combine all the ingredients except the cheeses and chips. Spoon the mixture into a shallow, greased 2-quart casserole dish. Top with the grated cheeses. At this point, the dish may be refrigerated until party time.

Preheat the oven to 350°. Bake, uncovered, for 15 minutes or until the cheeses are melted. Wrap the casserole in gaily colored napkins and serve with a basket of crisp tortilla chips.

Makes 8 or 9 servings.

Beverly Garland

Perhaps television's first female policewoman to work solo was Beverly Garland. She starred as New York City cop Casey Jones in 1957's *Decoy* and the 1958 retitled show, *Police Woman Decoy*. Garland also appeared in the films *DOA* and *The Glass Web*.

"Where's the Fire?" Salsa

The jalapeño hotline!

8 fresh jalapeño peppers
2 28-ounce cans peeled whole tomatoes
1 large white onion
2 cloves fresh garlic
   Fresh cilantro
   Tortilla chips, regular or baked

Bring a small pot of water to a boil and cook the jalapeño peppers for about 5 minutes. Drain and set aside. Drain about 1 cup of the juice from the canned tomatoes and pour into a blender. Chop the tomatoes to a medium size and set aside. Finely chop the onion and set aside. Remove the stems from the jalapeños and add the peppers to the juice in the blender. Add the garlic and some of the cilantro to the blender. Blend all of the blender contents until smooth. In a large mixing bowl, combine the chopped tomatoes, chopped onion, some of the chopped cilantro, and the blended mixture. Let the salsa sit for a few hours to allow the flavors to blend. Serve with tortilla chips. If served with baked tortilla chips, this is a low-fat snack.
   Makes about 3 cups.

Dennis E. Nowicki
Chief of Police
Charlotte-Mecklenburg, North Carolina

Hot Pursuit Hot Dogs

1 cup catsup
1 cup firmly packed brown sugar
½ cup bourbon
1 pound hot dogs, cut up (or little smokies)

Preheat the oven to 350°. Stir the catsup, sugar, and bourbon together in a baking pan until the sugar is dissolved. Add the hot dogs and stir. Bake, uncovered, for 1 hour, stirring every 20 minutes. Serve with toothpicks.
   Makes 3 to 4 dozen.

David D. Whipple
Executive Director
Association of Former Intelligence Officers

Actor Tom Williams, famous for his voice-overs as crying babies and talking birds, was the traffic cop in the famous Di-Gel commercial in which he says, "I like hot dogs. But they don't like me."

Wanted Dead or Olive-Cheese Balls

Just about the best cheese balls you'll find almost anytime, anywhere!

■ I have lots of good recipes, but this old favorite has served me well for holiday festivities and other times when I entertain.

> 2 cups shredded sharp natural cheddar cheese
> 1¼ cups all-purpose flour
> 1 stick butter, melted
> 36 pimiento-stuffed, small olives, drained

In a large bowl, mix the cheese and flour together. Add the butter and mix thoroughly by working the dough with your hands. Mold 1 teaspoon of dough around each olive and shape into a ball. Place 2 inches apart on an ungreased baking sheet. Cover and chill for at least 1 hour. Preheat the oven to 400°. Bake for 15 to 20 minutes.

Norma Tillman, P.I.

Norma Tillman is a nationally recognized private investigator who specializes in finding missing persons. She is the author of *How to Find Almost Anyone, Anywhere* and *The Man with the Turquoise Eyes*, a book she wrote with cop turned author David Hunter.

Chief's 10-4 Salsa by the Gallon

That's OK by us.

> 1 medium onion
> 5 to 6 jalapeño peppers
> 1 bunch cilantro
> 1 bunch parsley
> 4 28-ounce cans diced tomatoes, drained
> 1 teaspoon vegetable oil
> 1 10-ounce can Ro-Tel
> Juice of 1 lemon

Coarsely chop the onion, peppers, cilantro, and parsley, and combine in a large mixing bowl. Stir in the tomatoes, oil, and Ro-Tel. Add the lemon juice. Serve.

Makes about 1 gallon.

*Phil Cotten
Chief of Police
Norman, Oklahoma*

Detective Sinclair's Guacamole

It'll carry your taste buds to another world!

> 3 medium, ripe avocados
> 3 tablespoons finely chopped onion
> 2 cloves garlic, minced
> 1 tablespoon minced cilantro
> 1 diced tomatillo
> 1 tablespoon chopped jalapeño
> Dash salt
> Dash freshly ground pepper
> Splash olive oil
> Juice of 1 or 2 small limes

Peel and seed the avocados, and put the flesh into a mixing bowl. Blend with a fork while slowly adding each ingredient until mixture is very smooth. Cover and chill until serving time. Give it a little stir before presenting to freshen up the color.

Makes about 3 cups.

Tim Gibbs

Lieutenant Columbo's Pumpkin Ravioli

4   quarts water
2   teaspoons salt
12 ounces jumbo shell pasta
2½ cups pumpkin purée, preferably fresh
⅔   cups slivered almonds, toasted and chopped
⅛   teaspoon ground nutmeg
     Salt and pepper to taste
     Olive oil
     Topping (recipe follows)

Bring the 4 quarts of water and 2 teaspoons of salt to boil in a large (at least 6-quart) pot. Add about 20 of the best pasta shells, one at a time, to the water while stirring to keep the shells from sticking to the bottom of the pan. After the water comes back to a boil, cook the pasta for about 10 more minutes, continuing to stir occasionally to prevent the pasta from sticking to the pan. Move the pot of pasta to a sink where you can run cold water into the pot to cool the pasta. Remove the pasta with your hand and set it aside to drain in a colander.

Preheat the oven to 350°. In a large bowl, combine the pumpkin, almonds, nutmeg, salt, and pepper. Put about 2 tablespoons of the mixture into each pasta shell. Arrange the shells open-side up and about ½ inch apart in a lightly greased (with olive oil) 9x13-inch baking dish. Cover with aluminum foil that has been oiled very lightly on the bottom. Bake for about 30 minutes or until the pumpkin is heated through.

Topping:

1   stick butter or margarine
½   clove garlic, minced
½   cup soft bread crumbs
1   teaspoon minced fresh sage
     Fresh parsley
     Freshly grated Parmesan cheese (optional)

While the pasta shells are baking, brown the butter in a skillet over medium heat and stir constantly, being careful not to let it burn. Add the garlic and sauté until it becomes translucent. Remove from heat. In a separate skillet (with no oil), lightly toast the bread crumbs. Add the bread crumbs and sage to the garlic-butter mixture and mix thoroughly using a fork.

To serve, place the shells (3 per serving) on heated plates. Top with 1 teaspoon of the breadcrumb mixture and garnish with parsley. Oh, and just one more thing: Pass the Parmesan cheese at the table.

Makes 3 servings, with 2 shells left over for the cook to nibble on.

Peter Falk

As Lt. Philip Columbo, one of the most resourceful detectives on the Los Angeles police force, Peter Falk became as comfortable as an old raincoat to television viewers around the world. The series, which featured Falk as a cigar-smoking detective who drove a beat-up old Peugeot and had a pet basset hound, began in 1971 and ran through 1977. Originally an *NBC Sunday Night Mystery Movie*, the show was revived in 1989 for a series on *The ABC Mystery Movie*.

Baked Goat Cheese with Pesto Arresto

Really, kids, it's not baaad!

1 pound goat cheese
¼ cup extra virgin olive oil
½ cup pesto
1 to 2 heads mixed salad greens
  (romaine, butter, Bibb, etc.)
1 cup bread crumbs
½ cup vinaigrette dressing
12 to 16 Calamata olives, pitted
12 to 16 sun-dried tomatoes
½ cup yellow onion, finely minced
  Croutons (recipe follows)

Ann Rule is one of the nation's leading true-crime writers. Her titles include *The Stranger Beside Me* (the Ted Bundy story), *You Belong to Me*, and *A Rose for Her Grave*. Her works frequently become the basis for movies and miniseries, including *Everything She Ever Wanted* and *Fever in the Heart* in 1997.

Cut or form the goat cheese into wheels that are ¾-inch thick and 2½ inches in diameter. (If you cut the cheese, use a stainless steel knife and dip it in hot water after each cut.) Spread some of the olive oil on a baking sheet and place the cheese wheels about 1 inch apart on the sheet. Drizzle the remaining olive oil over the cheese. Cover the top of each cheese wheel with a thin layer of the pesto. Marinate the cheese overnight in the refrigerator or for 2 or 3 hours at room temperature.

Preheat the oven to 400°. Wash and dry the greens and make the Croutons. Dip the goat cheese wheels in the bread crumbs and return them to the baking sheet. Bake for 4 or 5 minutes or until the goat cheese begins to slide when you shake the pan. Toss the salad greens with the vinaigrette dressing and place on salad plates. Add the cheese and garnish with the olives, sun-dried tomatoes, onion, and Croutons.

Croutons:

1 baguette
½ stick butter
¼ cup extra virgin olive oil
1 tablespoon minced garlic

Preheat the oven to 400°. To make croutons, cut the baguette into thin slices. In a skillet, heat the butter, olive oil, and garlic, being careful not to burn. Using a basting or pastry brush, paint the croutons with the skillet mixture and place on a baking sheet. Bake until golden brown (just a few minutes). You might want to make more than this recipe calls for, because they have a way of disappearing.

Makes 6-8 servings.

Ann Rule

In 1972 Robert Forster starred as Miles Banyon, a 1930s Los Angeles private eye, on *Banyon*. Forster also played a cop when he guest-starred on *Police Story*. Returning to television in 1974, he played a Navajo deputy named Nakia Parker on *Nakia*.

Nakia's Never-Fail Chicken Strips

4 skinned chicken breast halves, sliced into 3 strips per breast half
1 cup lemon juice
2 eggs, beaten
1 cup seasoned bread crumbs
1 clove garlic
1 tablespoon olive oil
1 to 2 tablespoons butter
½ lemon

Marinate the chicken strips in lemon juice for 10 minutes. Combine the eggs and bread crumbs in a mixing bowl. Dip the chicken strips into the mixture and cover thoroughly. In a skillet, brown the garlic in the olive oil and add butter until frothy. Add the chicken and brown over medium heat. Remove the chicken from the pan and place on paper towels to absorb the excess oil. Serve as a finger food or with pasta.

Makes about 4 servings.

Robert Forster

Rochester Roll Call Spinach Dip

1   **10-ounce package frozen chopped spinach**
8   **ounces sour cream**
1   **cup Miracle Whip**
    (mayonnaise is not as good)
1   **red onion, finely minced**

Thaw and cook the spinach then squeeze out the liquid. Mix the spinach with all the remaining ingredients and refrigerate. Serve cold with crackers. Triscuits are particularly good with this dip.

   Makes about 3½ cups.

Robert Warshaw
Chief of Police
Rochester, New York

Dragnet's explosive popularity led to an NBC feature film in 1954 starring Jack Webb as Sgt. Joe Friday.

Judge Wapner's Eggplant Hors d'Oeuvre

1   eggplant
¼   onion
1   clove garlic
1   14-ounce jar Cara Mia artichokes
1   4½-ounce jar sliced mushrooms or 6 fresh mushrooms, sliced
2   ribs celery
1   tomato
12 cocktail onions

12 green olives with pimiento centers
2   tablespoons olive oil
6   pinches oregano
4   tablespoons wine vinegar
    Salt and pepper to taste
⅓   5-ounce jar capers

Preheat the oven to 350°. Bake the eggplant for 1 hour. Peel it then chop it in a food processor. Dice the onion. Mash the garlic. Cut up the artichokes and reserve the juice. If the mushrooms are fresh, slice them. Dice the celery. Mince the tomato.

Since 1981, retired Superior Court Judge Joseph Wapner has arbitrated the grievances of people in the Los Angeles area on *The People's Court*. Bailiff Rusty Burrell attests to the fact that Judge Wapner loves to cook.

Cut the cocktail onions and olives in half. Pulse together. Add the artichoke juice, olive oil, oregano, wine vinegar, salt, pepper, and capers to the eggplant mixture. Blend all the ingredients to the consistency of a spread. Chill and allow to sit for 6 to 24 hours. Serve with crackers.

Makes about 1½ cups.

Judge Joseph A. Wapner (retired)

Lieutenant Goldblume's Fresh Ricotta Cheese

■ Here's a recipe I originally found in *Sunset Magazine*. I've changed it very little. It may not be completely authentic, but it tastes great. I am sharing it because I watched my aunt and uncle make a very authentic ricotta in a smoky goat shed in San Nicola di Ardore, Calabria, Italy. Being Italian, I was thrilled to find I could cook a recipe that awakened my childhood memories.

2 quarts whole milk
2 cups buttermilk
Salt and pepper
Extra virgin olive oil

Joe Spano was sensitive Community Affairs Officer Henry Goldblume (left) on *Hill Street Blues*. Also pictured is Taurean Blacque as Det. Neal Washington. Spano won an Emmy in 1989 for a guest-star role on the police-related drama *Midnight Caller*.

In a 3- to 4-quart heavy pan, mix the milk and buttermilk to blend. Warm the milk mixture (do not stir) over medium heat until the temperature reaches 180° in the center of the pan (about 25 to 30 minutes). Reduce the heat to low and keep the milk temperature between 185° and 200° until at least half of the milk clot that forms on top feels like baked custard when gently pressed (about 10 to 15 minutes).

Line a large colander with 4 layers of damp cheesecloth (or use a clean, damp, tightly woven, bowl-shaped basket). Set the colander in a sink and pour the milk clot into the colander; do not scrape the bottom of the pot if the milk there is scorched. Let drain until the cheese is firm (at least 45 minutes). Serve inverted on a plate, or cool, cover, and chill for up to 2 days. Sprinkle with salt, pepper, and olive oil. You might also want to sprinkle with fresh herbs (chives or what have you).

Makes about 3 quarts.

Joe Spano

Edd Byrnes (right), better known as Gerald Lloyd Kookson III, or Kookie, was one of television's hottest hunks of the early 1960s. Originally a parking lot attendant with a fast comb, Kookie eventually became a detective at *77 Sunset Strip*. He's chatting here with Efrem Zimbalist Jr., who portrayed Det. Stuart Bailey.

Arizona Chief's Chalupa

3 **pounds boneless pork roast, trimmed of fat**
1 **pound dry pinto beans**
1 **4-ounce can diced green chile peppers**
1 **teaspoon cumin**
2 **tablespoons chili powder**
1 **tablespoon salt**
1 **teaspoon oregano**
  Corn chips
  Grated cheese
  Chopped tomatoes
  Chopped green onions
  Chopped lettuce
  Black olives
  Sour cream
  Guacamole
  Salsa

Combine first 7 ingredients in a Crock-Pot and cover with water. Cook on high for 1 hour. Turn to low and cook for 6 to 7 hours. Stir to flake the meat and mix it with the beans. Serve over corn chips. Garnish with grated cheese, chopped tomatoes, green onions, lettuce, black olives, sour cream, guacamole, and lots of salsa.

Makes 8 to 10 servings.

Dennis Garrett
Chief of Police
Phoenix, Arizona

Kookie's Sunset Strip Soda

Come and get it!

¾ **glass cranberry juice cocktail**
¼ **glass club soda**
1 **packet E-Mergen-C (available at your local health food store)**

Just mix all the ingredients together. It's a great pick-me-up!

Makes 1 serving.

Edd Byrnes

Boris's Super Sonic Mustard

■ My father cooked often. The following two recipes demonstrate his marvelous sense of humor.

Dry Coleman's mustard
Very dry gin

Take dry Coleman's mustard and NEVER, NEVER mix it with water. Instead, mix it with very dry gin until it is the desired consistency. It not only enhances most everything, but it clears your sinuses, scalds your palate, and is a must in every self-respecting English kitchen.

Boris Karloff
Submitted by daughter Sara Karloff

Mr. Wong's Foolproof Cure for a Hangover

■ I think the theory behind this was that if the concoction didn't kill you, the hangover wouldn't either, so you could get up and get on with your day.

1 egg
2 tablespoons Worcestershire sauce
6 to 8 ounces orange juice

In a tall drinking glass, put egg (unbeaten), Worcestershire sauce, and orange juice. Close your eyes and pour the mixture down the hatch.
   Makes 1 remedy.

Boris Karloff
Submitted by daughter Sara Karloff

(clockwise):

With a patch over one eye, Boris Karloff was the intrepid *Colonel March of Scotland Yard* in 1959.

Once the makeup comes off, there's nothing like a good cup of hot coffee—or is that Boris Karloff's cure for a hangover?

British film star Boris Karloff was an actor of many talents and a man of many faces. In 1938 and 1939 he portrayed Mr. Wong, a gentlemanly Asian detective in *Mr. Wong, Detective* and *Mr. Wong of Chinatown*.

David Janssen in *Richard Diamond, Private Detective.*

Reinforcements

SALADS

Cool Hand Cucumber Salad

Luke's cukes.

■ The amount of each vegetable used really isn't important here, though the cucumbers should dominate the other flavors. I've found that all salads taste better if the salad leaves are washed and put in the refrigerator in a damp towel about an hour before serving to allow them to get crisp and cold. The salad plates should also be put in the refrigerator.

Cucumbers, sliced wafer thin and peeled if waxed
Ripe tomatoes, diced
Romaine lettuce, chopped
Red bell peppers, cubed
Green bell peppers, cubed
Newman's Own salad dressing (or other vinaigrette dressing)

Toss the vegetables in a bowl with the salad dressing to taste. Serve on chilled plates.

Paul Newman

Paul Newman starred as Lew Harper, Ross MacDonald's tough, footloose private eye, in a pair of films, *Harper* (1966) and *The Drowning Pool* (1976).

Dennis Becker's One Hot Italian Night

■ This is my own concoction, and it is fantastic! It must be done with blind faith and with good taste.

6 spears asparagus with the ends cut off and discarded
4 red-ripe Italian tomatoes, sliced into quarters
  Ground oregano
  Ground black pepper
1 whole ripe avocado, peeled, cored, and cut into chunks
1 jalapeño pepper, cut in half, seeded (including removing the white coating), and then cut in half again
1 heart of celery, cut into 1-inch bites
1 roasted red pepper, preferably canned
6 fresh basil leaves
  Good amount of olive oil
  Good amount of balsamic vinegar
1 teaspoon olive oil
2 teaspoons chicken broth
4 hot Italian sausages
2 cloves garlic, left whole
  Additional oregano to taste
8 quarts water
1 pound ziti or penne pasta
  Pinch salt
  Italian cheese, grated
  Crushed red pepper
  Cilantro
1 large glass cold red Italian wine
1 slice thick Italian bread

Steam the asparagus until tender. Cut into bite-sized pieces. Season the tomatoes with oregano and black pepper to taste. In a large salad bowl, combine the asparagus, avocado, tomatoes, jalapeño pepper, celery, roasted red pepper, and basil leaves. Next, pour in good amounts of olive oil and balsamic vinegar. Season and toss with your hands. Cover the bowl and refrigerate for 1 hour.

In an aluminum baking dish, combine the 1 teaspoon of olive oil, chicken broth, Italian sausages, garlic, and oregano to taste. Broil the sausages until they scream or are nice and dark. Remove from oven and set aside.

Next, boil the water and add the pasta and a pinch of salt. Cook the pasta according to package directions. Drain and rinse.

Immediately remove the salad from the refrigerator (it should be nice and cold). Pour the hot pasta over the cold salad and toss with spoons. Sprinkle the Italian cheese and crushed red pepper on top. Place the pasta salad on two plates and garnish with a few leaves of cilantro. Add the sausages and garlic on the side. Serve with a large glass of cold red Italian wine and a slice of thick Italian bread. Eat fast and don't think. Don't worry about calories. It's for one hot Italian night!

Makes 2 servings.

Joe Santos

On *The Rockford Files*, Joe Santos was Det. Dennis Becker, Jim Rockford's go-to man at the LAPD. Dennis had to run more than his share of license plates for his P.I. pal, but he frequently benefited from Rockford's help in catching bad guys.

Frank Sinatra tackled the role of tough private eye Tony Rome in the 1967 film and reprised the part a year later in *Lady in Cement.*

Tony Rome's Pesto Pasta Tortellini Salad

18 ounces cheese tortellini (dry, frozen, or refrigerated)
½ cup pitted black olives, drained and cut in half
1 8½-ounce jar artichoke hearts, drained and cut into quarters
1 4½-ounce jar whole mushrooms, drained
10 cherry tomatoes, cut in half
1 15-ounce jar Frank Sinatra's Pesto Sauce

Cook the tortellini according to the package instructions. Combine the pasta, olives, artichoke hearts, mushrooms, and tomatoes. Add the pesto sauce and stir gently until combined. Cover and chill overnight to blend the flavors.

Variation: Substitute 1 pound of your favorite dry pasta for the tortellini. Cook according to the package directions. For additional variety, stir in any of the following: sun-dried tomatoes, pepperoni, provolone cheese, diced red or green peppers, roasted red peppers, or chopped green onions.

Makes 8 servings.

Frank Sinatra

Tom Atkins starred on *Serpico* in 1976 as undercover agent Tom Sullivan (pictured here) and for two seasons co-starred on *The Rockford Files* as Lt. Alex Diehl.

Caesar Salad Sullivan

1 head romaine lettuce
1 clove garlic
¼ teaspoon salt
½ teaspoon pepper
1 teaspoon anchovy paste
1 teaspoon lemon juice
1 egg, coddled
¼ teaspoon Worcestershire sauce
⅓ cup olive oil
½ cup grated fresh Parmesan cheese,
    divided
1 cup Pepperidge Farm onion and garlic
    croutons

Remove each leaf of romaine from its head; wash and dry. Smash the garlic into a paste. In a small bowl, combine the garlic, salt, pepper, anchovy paste, lemon juice, egg, and Worcestershire sauce. Mix together well and then mix in the olive oil. Tear the romaine into bite-sized pieces and put into a large salad bowl. Sprinkle ¼ cup of the Parmesan cheese over the romaine. Pour the dressing over the romaine and toss well. Add the croutons and toss again. Serve the salad and put the remaining ¼ cup Parmesan in a small bowl to pass for topping the individual salads.

Makes 6 servings.

Tom Atkins

Policeman's Picnic Coleslaw

1 large head cabbage
1 large carrot
1 bell pepper
1 white or purple onion
1 tablespoon salt
1 cup vinegar
1¼ cups water
2 cups sugar
1 teaspoon celery seed
1 tablespoon mustard seed

Grate the cabbage, carrot, pepper, and onion. Sprinkle with salt and set aside for 1 hour to drain. Boil the vinegar, water, sugar, celery seed, and mustard seed for 1 minute. Cool until lukewarm, pour over the cabbage, and stir together. The slaw may be refrigerated for up to 2 weeks.

Makes 10 servings.

Charles Smith
Assistant Chief of Police
Nashville, Tennessee

Pete Cochran's "I Hate Cole Slaw" Cole Slaw

■ This recipe may sound strange, but I promise you it is great—and easy!

1 package pre-shredded slaw
1 package beef-flavored ramen dry
  noodle soup mix
3 green onions, chopped
1 4- to 6-ounce package slivered almonds
1 tablespoon butter
1 4- to 6-ounce package salted
  sunflower seeds
½ cup sugar
½ cup apple cider vinegar
⅓ cup vegetable oil

Place the shredded cole slaw in a large bowl. Crumble the ramen noodles and add to the cole slaw, reserving the seasoning packet from the soup mix. Add the green onions. In a skillet, sauté the sliv-

Michael Cole starred as Pete Cochran, one of three hippie cops on *The Mod Squad* from 1968 to 1973. Here Cole cooks up supper in 1969.

ered almonds in the butter until brown. Drain the almonds on a paper towel to remove the excess butter and to cool. Add the almonds and sunflower seeds to the cole slaw. Make a dressing by combining the sugar, vinegar, oil, and the seasoning package from the soup. Pour the dressing over the salad and toss thoroughly.

Note: It's good fresh, and it's even good when served as a leftover after it's soggy.

Makes about 4 servings.

Michael Cole

Private Eye's Chicory and Kidney Bean Salad

2 heads chicory
1 16-ounce can red kidney beans
1 medium onion, sliced into small pieces
3 tablespoons olive oil
2 tablespoons red wine vinegar
   Salt and pepper to taste

Wash the chicory. Discard the tougher outer leaves (unless you're an antelope). If you have a lettuce dryer, give the chicory a few spins in it. Pour the kidney beans and liquid into a bowl and mash lovingly with a potato masher. Put the chicory into a bowl and pour the kidney beans on top. Add the onion, olive oil, vinegar, and salt and pepper. Toss until it looks suitable for serving.

I like this salad best with pita, Italian, or French bread. It's yummy. Once you get the hang of it, you can adjust the amount of onion, oil, and vinegar to suit your own taste buds. Enjoy!

Makes 4 to 6 servings.

Tim Conway

A tip of the hat and Tim Conway's private eye Ace Crawford is off to solve another mystery.

Spike's Sweetheart Salad

2   cups crushed, fresh, or canned-in-its-
    own-juice pineapple, undrained
½   cup sugar
1½ teaspoons gelatin
¼   cup cold water
2   tablespoons lemon juice
3   tablespoons cherry juice
6   ounces cream cheese, softened
½   pint whipping cream
12 cherries, chopped

In a saucepan, heat the pineapple with sugar. Soak the gelatin in water and then add to the pineapple. Stir until melted. Add the lemon juice and cherry juice and let cool. In a mixing bowl, mash the cream cheese and add the cherries. Add the pineapple mixture, a small amount at a time, to the cream cheese. Chill until slightly thickened. Whip the cream and blend into the pineapple/cream cheese mixture. Pour the mixture into an oiled gelatin mold. Refrigerate until firm.

Makes 4 to 6 servings.

Dwight "Spike" Helmick
Commissioner
California Highway Patrol

EATS AND DRINKS

Match the television series with the cop's hangout.

1. *Crime Photographer*   A. The Blue Note Cafe
2. *Harbourmaster*   B. Bluebird Diner
3. *Magnum, P.I.*   C. The Calico Cat
4. *Mr. Lucky*   D. The Waterfront
5. *Peter Gunn*   E. The Dolphin
6. *The Rockford Files*   Restaurant
7. *77 Sunset Strip*   F. Mother's
8. *Staccato*   G. A taco stand
9. *Homicide*   H. Waldo's
10. *The Andy Griffith Show* I. Dino's
                             J. Cafe American

SOLUTION
1. A, 2. E, 3. J, 4. C, 5. F, 6. G, 7. I, 8. H, 9. D, 10. B

Richard Diamond's Caesar Salad

You'll come back for this!

■ When people asked David why he married me, he replied, "Because she makes the best Caesar salad I've ever tasted."

2 cloves garlic
6 anchovy strips
¼ cup olive oil
2 tablespoons freshly ground pepper
2 tablespoons wine vinegar
2 tablespoons Worcestershire sauce
¼ cup fresh coarsely grated Romano cheese
Romaine lettuce
1 warm egg, slightly coddled
Juice of ½ lemon
Garlic Croutons (recipe follows)
2 tablespoons Parmesan cheese

David Janssen gained fame running from the law as Dr. Richard Kimble on *The Fugitive* from 1963 to 1967. He also starred in three other television series as a crime solver: He starred in *Richard Diamond, Private Detective* from 1957 to 1960, *O'Hara U.S. Treasury* as Jim O'Hara in 1971, and in *Harry-O* (above) as bus-riding Det. Harry Orwell from 1974 to 1976.

In a wooden bowl, combine and mash the garlic and anchovies. Add the oil and pepper and mix well. Add the wine vinegar and the Worcestershire sauce and mix well. Add the Romano cheese and lettuce and toss. Push the lettuce mixture to one side, drop the egg and lemon juice into the empty side of the bowl, and beat together. (The lemon juice will sort of cook the egg.) Mix with the rest of the salad. Serve in chilled bowls and top with warm Garlic Croutons and Parmesan cheese.

Garlic Croutons:

1 clove garlic, minced
¼ cup olive oil
⅓ teaspoon salt
5 to 6 cups sourdough bread cubes, about ½ inch square

Place the garlic and oil in a small frying pan over medium heat for about 4 minutes. With a large spoon, press on the minced garlic to release the flavor into the oil. Pour the mixture through a sieve and keep only the oil. Add the salt. Preheat the oven to 375°.

Toss the sourdough bread with the garlic oil until all the bread pieces are covered. Spread the bread cubes onto a jelly roll pan. Bake for approximately 10 minutes or until the bread cubes are slightly browned.

Makes 6 servings.

David Janssen
Submitted by Dani (Mrs. David) Janssen

David Soul (right) and Paul Michael Glaser were Ken Hutchinson and Dave Starsky respectively a top-notch police unit that spelled trouble for criminals, on *Starsky and Hutch* from 1975 to 1979.

Torino Salad Dressing and Fixings

Soul food.

1   **cup light virgin olive oil**
½   **cup balsamic vinegar**
¼   **cup orange juice, preferably fresh
    squeezed**
1   **tablespoon sugar
    Fresh (or approximately 2 tablespoons
    dried) herbs and spices of your choice
    from your hutch**

Combine all the above ingredients in a large jar or bottle and shake together vigorously. Store in the refrigerator. The longer the dressing sits, the smoother and more tasty it becomes.

Serving Suggestion: David's favorite salad is simply endive that is pulled apart or chopped into little rings. Rinse the leaves in cool water and air dry, or put the leaves in the refrigerator to dry—this creates a firmer leaf. Once the endive is separated or chopped, dried, and chilled, arrange the leaves on salad plates.

Another way to have endive as a starter is to use the whole leaves that have been separated, rinsed, and chilled. Thinly spread the leaves with a mixture of cream cheese and finely chopped green olives and pimiento pieces. Or sprinkle the chilled leaves with fresh-squeezed lemon juice and crumble on bleu cheese and finely chopped walnuts.

For toppings, my favorite combination is a simple one of chopped walnuts and a few raisins or sultanas and 1 or 2 splashes of the dressing. However, quite often I dress it up with chopped orange sections or whole mandarin orange sections and bleu or goat cheese crumbles. Also tasty (when in season) are chopped seedless grapes, chopped cranberries, or chopped apples—or whatever tart ingredients are around!

In any combination, this dressing makes a tasty, refreshing, and light starter that's suitable for party platters. Enjoy!

David Soul

FEMMES FATALE

Match the actress to her role.

1.	Nell Carter	A.	Pepper Anderson
2.	Tyne Daly	B.	Lucille Bates
3.	Angie Dickinson	C.	Chris Cagney
4.	Farrah Fawcett-Majors	D.	Nora Charles
5.	Anne Francis	E.	Kate Columbo
6.	Sharon Gless	F.	Jessica Fletcher
7.	Teresa Graves	G.	Hildy Granger
8.	Phyllis Kirk	H.	Maddie Hayes
9.	Angela Lansbury	I.	Laura Holt
10.	Kate Mulgrew	J.	Hildy Jones
11.	Cybill Shepherd	K.	Mary Beth Lacey
12.	Suzanne Somers	L.	Christie Love
13.	Susan St. James	M.	Sally McMillan
14.	Betty Thomas	N.	Jill Munroe
15.	Jessica Walter	O.	Amy Prentiss
16.	Stephanie Zimbalist	P.	Honey West

SOLUTION

1. J, 2. K, 3. A, 4. N, 5. P, 6. C, 7. L, 8. D, 9. F, 10. E, 11. H, 12. G, 13. M, 14. B, 15. O, 16. I

Two cops who mean business.

Morgan Freeman tracked down a serial killer as homicide detective William Somerset in *Seven*. As forensic psychologist Alex Cross, Freeman followed the trail of another serial killer in 1997's *Kiss the Girls*.

Seventh Heaven Tropical Fruit Salad

1   cup sliced bananas
1   tablespoon orange or pineapple juice
2   tangerines, peeled and sectioned
1   Golden Delicious apple, cored and
   cubed
1   cup red, seedless grapes
2   tablespoons unsweetened, shredded
   coconut
½   teaspoon finely shredded lemon rind
⅛   teaspoon ground cinnamon
⅛   teaspoon ground nutmeg

Place the bananas in a medium bowl. Add the orange or pineapple juice and gently toss to coat. Cut the tangerine sections in half crosswise, removing and discarding the seeds. Add these sections to the bowl.

Add the apple, grapes, coconut, lemon rind, cinnamon, and nutmeg. Gently toss to mix. Cover and refrigerate for at least 20 minutes to allow the flavors to blend.
Makes 4 servings.

Morgan Freeman
Submitted by wife Myrna Colley-Lee

Sheriff Metzger's Taco Salad Olé!

1   tablespoon light vegetable oil
2   pounds lean ground beef
1   small onion, chopped
2   heads lettuce, chopped
1   16-ounce bag tortilla chips
1   1½-ounce package taco seasoning with
   water added to keep moist
5   large tomatoes, chopped
1   quart sour cream
1   12-ounce jar salsa
1   4-ounce can chopped black olives
2   pounds cheddar cheese, grated

Put the oil in the bottom of the skillet and brown the beef and onions. Drain off excess grease. Put the lettuce in a large bowl, the beef in another, and the chips in another large bowl or basket. Place each of the other ingredients individually in smaller bowls. Serve buffet style in order for your guests to make their own salad. Use the chips as scoops.
Makes 6 to 8 servings.

Ron Masak

Lieutenant Trench's Fresh Raw Vegetable Salad

1 uncooked ear of corn
1 carrot
A generous portion of marinated/ sautéed or packaged/smoked tofu
1 ripe avocado
Several scallions
½ cucumber
½ zucchini
Tomatoes
Spinach
Celery
Black olives
Romaine lettuce
Other selected greens of your choice
Garlic olive oil
Garlic wine vinegar
1 handful pine nuts

Slice the corn from the cob, shred the carrot, and dice the tofu and remaining vegetables, including the spinach, lettuce, and greens. Douse with a generous quantity of oil and vinegar and mix well. Toss in pine nuts. Complement with a dry Italian red table wine.

Serves 2 on a summer evening.

Anthony Zerbe

Anthony Zerbe was Lt. K. C. Trench of the LAPD as he worked opposite David Janssen and maintained a delicate détente in *Harry-O* from 1975 to 1976. Among Zerbe's film credits are *The Laughing Policeman* and, with Robert Mitchum, *Farewell, My Lovely.*

Kojak's Horiatiki Salata (Greek Village Salad)

You'll love this, baby!

Salad:

1 head romaine lettuce, chopped
1 red bell pepper, chopped
1 large red onion, chopped
1 cucumber, chopped
2 large tomatoes, chopped
8 ounces feta cheese, crumbled

Dressing:

Olive oil
Balsamic vinegar
Fresh oregano
Salt and pepper to taste

In a large salad bowl, combine salad ingredients (lettuce, vegetables, and feta). Then, in a separate bowl, combine the dressing ingredients to taste, keeping 2 parts oil to 1 part vinegar. Combine the salad and dressing, toss, and serve.

Makes 8 to 10 servings.

Telly Savalas
Submitted by Julie (Mrs. Telly) Savalas

"Who loves ya, baby?" asked Telly Savalas's Lt. Theo Kojak of the New York Police Department. The lollipop-loving cop eventually became chief of detectives for the Manhattan South District's Thirteenth Precinct. The popular series ran from 1973 to 1978.

EMMY WINNERS

BEST MYSTERY, ACTION OR ADVENTURE PROGRAM
Dragnet (1952, 1953, 1954)

OUTSTANDING DRAMA SERIES
Police Story (1975)
The Rockford Files (1977)
Hill Street Blues (1980, 1981, 1982, 1983)
Cagney & Lacey (1984, 1985)
NYPD Blue (1995)

OUTSTANDING COMEDY SERIES
Barney Miller (1981)

OUTSTANDING LIMITED SERIES
Columbo (1973)

OUTSTANDING PERFORMANCE BY AN ACTOR IN A DRAMA SERIES
Raymond Burr (*Perry Mason*, 1958, 1960)
Robert Stack (*The Untouchables*, 1959)
Peter Falk (*Columbo*, 1971, 1975, 1989)
Telly Savalas (*Kojak*, 1973)
Robert Blake (*Baretta*, 1974)
James Garner (*The Rockford Files*, 1976)
Daniel J. Travanti (*Hill Street Blues*, 1980, 1981)
Tom Selleck (*Magnum, P.I.*, 1983)
Bruce Willis (*Moonlighting*, 1986)
James Earl Jones (*Gabriel's Fire*, 1990)
Tom Skerritt (*Picket Fences*, 1992)
Dennis Franz (*NYPD Blue*, 1993, 1996)

OUTSTANDING PERFORMANCE BY AN ACTRESS IN A DRAMA SERIES
Barbara Babcock (*Hill Street Blues*, 1980)
Tyne Daly (*Cagney & Lacey*, 1982, 1983, 1984, 1987)
Sharon Gless (*Cagney & Lacey*, 1985, 1986)

OUTSTANDING PERFORMANCE BY AN ACTOR IN A SUPPORTING ROLE
Don Knotts (*The Andy Griffith Show*, 1961, 1962, 1963, 1966, 1967)

OUTSTANDING PERFORMANCE BY AN ACTRESS IN A SUPPORTING ROLE IN A DRAMA SERIES
Barbara Hale (*Perry Mason*, 1958)
Barbara Anderson (*Ironside*, 1967)
Gail Fisher (*Mannix*, 1969)
Betty Thomas (*Hill Street Blues*, 1984)

OUTSTANDING PERFORMANCE BY A SUPPORTING ACTOR IN A DRAMA SERIES
Anthony Zerbe (*Harry-O*, 1975)
Stuart Margolin (*The Rockford Files*, 1978, 1979)
Michael Conrad (*Hill Street Blues*, 1980, 1981)
Bruce Weitz (*Hill Street Blues*, 1983)
Edward James Olmos (*Miami Vice*, 1984)
John Hillerman (*Magnum, P.I.*, 1986)

OUTSTANDING LEAD ACTOR IN A LIMITED SERIES
William Holden (*The Blue Knight*, 1973)
Peter Falk (*Columbo*, 1974)

OUTSTANDING LEAD ACTRESS IN A LIMITED SERIES
Mildred Natwick (*The Snoop Sisters*, 1973)
Jessica Walter (*Amy Prentiss*, 1974)
Helen Mirren (*Prime Suspect*, 1996)

Things really heat up when landlady Mrs. Mendelbright (Enid Markey) catches Barney Fife (Don Knotts) cooking chili in his boarding house room.

In Stir

SOUPS, CHILIES, AND STEWS

J. C.'s Rhythm and Beans and Squash Stew

■ Nutrition is the source to heal the body, mind, and spirit—so believes my personal chef, DeBorah Gittens. DeBorah, who has trained at the Natural Gourmet Institute for Food and Healing in New York City, also specializes in healthful recipes for those living with chronic illness. Cooking without preservatives is the first step to eating right. Her dishes are not only delicious, but add nutritional value. Concentrating on grains, fruit, and vegetable dishes seasoned with fresh herbs and spices, DeBorah creates healthful international dishes that even meat eaters yearn for. This is one of my favorite recipes.

1 cup diced onions
2 cloves garlic
1 cup adzuki beans
1 7-inch piece kombu (kelp)
   Water
1 medium butternut squash, chopped
1 small yam, chopped
½ cup fresh basil leaves
1 tablespoon Spike seasoning
2 tablespoons minced parsley
1½ tablespoons shoyu (soy sauce)
1 tablespoon canola oil

Sauté the onion and garlic in a saucepan until the onions are translucent and set aside. Wash the beans and drain well. Place in a 2- to 3-quart pot with the kombu and water, bring to a boil, and then reduce heat and simmer for 30 minutes. Add the sautéed onion mixture, the chopped squash and yams, and the remaining ingredients. Simmer for 1 hour or until cooked down to the desired consistency. Serve with jasmine rice and salad. Enjoy!

Makes about 4 servings.

Malik Yoba

As Det. J. C. Williams on *New York Undercover*, Malik Yoba has created one of the coolest cops in one of the hippest dramas of the 1990s. Yoba also played a cop in the 1997 feature film *Cop Land* with Robert DeNiro and Sylvester Stallone. Yoba is a co-owner of a Manhattan restaurant specializing in soul food, including American-southern, Caribbean, and African cuisine.

Cannon's Gazpacho Valenciana

2 cloves garlic, crushed
1 teaspoon salt
¼ teaspoon ground cumin
¼ cup Spanish olive oil
2 cups canned tomato purée or 8 large,
    sun-ripened tomatoes, peeled, seeded,
    and diced
1 tablespoon vinegar
1 cup bread cubes (for croutons)
    Additional olive oil
1 bottle club soda
½ large cucumber, peeled and coarsely
    chopped
1 dozen small radishes, thinly sliced
1 sweet red or green pepper, coarsely
    chopped
2 scallions, diced

Mix the garlic with the salt and cumin; in a blender, mix garlic and spices with the ¼ cup olive oil and then combine with the tomato purée and vinegar. Beat briefly so that the mixture does not become completely smooth. Cover and chill thoroughly for 3 to 4 hours.

Prepare croutons by browning bread cubes in more olive oil until golden and crisp. Drain the croutons on a paper towel. Pour the chilled tomato mixture into 6 soup dishes. Add a small amount of club soda to each bowl. Add the croutons; pass the vegetables in separate bowls for garnish.

Makes 6 servings.

William Conrad
Submitted by Tippy (Mrs. William) Conrad

APB Baked Potato Soup

4 large baking potatoes
1 stick plus 6 tablespoons butter or
    margarine
⅓ cup all-purpose flour
6 cups milk
¾ teaspoons salt
½ teaspoon pepper
4 green onions, chopped (reserve some
    for topping)
12 slices bacon, cooked until crisp and
    crumbled (reserve some)
1¼ cups cheddar cheese, divided
8 ounces sour cream

William Conrad enjoyed fine cuisine as Frank Cannon, one of television's biggest guns, on *Cannon* from 1971 to 1976. The actor collected model and antique cannons and at one time owned the actual statuette used as the black bird in the 1941 film *The Maltese Falcon*.

Preheat the oven to 400°. Wash the potatoes and prick them several times with a fork. Bake for 1 hour or until the potatoes are done. Let cool. Cut the potatoes in half lengthwise and scoop out the pulp.

Melt the butter in a heavy saucepan over low heat. Add the flour and stir until smooth. Cook for 1 minute, stirring constantly. Gradually add the milk. Cook over medium heat, stirring constantly, until the mixture is thickened and bubbly. Add the potato pulp, salt, pepper, 2 tablespoons green onions, ½ cup bacon, and 1 cup cheese. Cook until thoroughly heated. Stir in the sour cream. (Add extra milk, if needed, for the desired thickness.) Serve garnished with the remaining onion, bacon, and cheese.

Makes 4 to 6 servings.

Floyd O. Bartch
Chief of Police
Kansas City, Missouri

Shaggy's Vegetarian Soup

It's so good, it's spooky!

■ Become a vegetarian. Your body will respect you for your wisdom, and the animals will love you for your compassion.

1 **10-ounce box frozen green beans or ¾ pound fresh green beans**
1 **green pepper, sliced or chopped**
½ **large (or 1 small whole) cauliflower, cut into florets**
6 **ribs celery, sliced or chopped**
¼ **cup yellow onion, chopped**
1 **16-ounce can peeled tomatoes**
1 **16-ounce can V-8 juice**
2 **teaspoons thyme**
1 **10-ounce package frozen whole baby okra (optional)**
　 Salt
　 Pepper

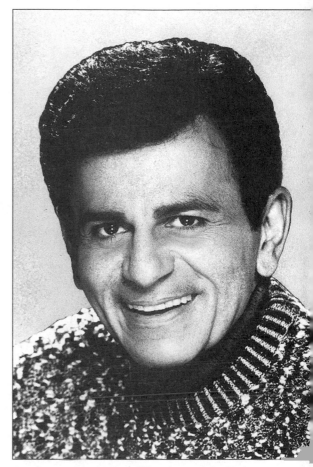

Casey Kasem's voice is well known to radio listeners as the host of "America's Top-40 Countdown," but he also did the talking for that ever-hungry cartoon mystery solver Shaggy on *Scooby Doo*.

Mix all the ingredients together, except salt and pepper, in a large pot and simmer over medium heat for 15 minutes. Add water as needed. Add salt and pepper to taste. This soup will keep for a week under cover in the refrigerator.

Makes about 8 servings

Casey Kasem

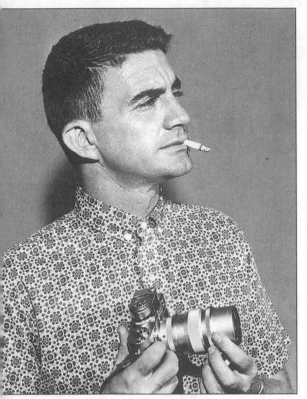

Producer, writer, and director Blake Edwards brought two great detectives to the public—Peter Gunn in 1958's *Peter Gunn* and Inspector Jacques Clouseau in *The Pink Panther* in 1964.

Pink Panther's Soup Francine

1   generous tablespoon clarified butter, margarine, or corn oil
1   medium onion, diced
1   medium potato, diced
    Vegetables of your choice (to taste and according to the number of servings needed), cut into small pieces, including stalks
    Ground pepper to taste
    Seasonings of your choice
    Parsley patch (a bunch)
    A little curry (optional)
    Chicken or vegetable stock

Heat the butter in a large, heavy saucepan. Add the remaining ingredients, except the stock. Allow to simmer over low heat until the onions are soft and a light, golden color. Stir frequently for about 15 minutes.

Add the stock (a chicken bouillon cube in boiling water, for example). Bring to a boil and then allow to simmer for another 15 minutes. Let cool. Blend in a blender. If it's too thick, add a little more stock. If the soup needs a little more zest, add some V-8 juice. Since the soup is stored in the refrigerator, it may thicken; so add the V-8 juice as the week goes by.

Note: The amount of stock used is optional. My wife, Julie, cooks for a large family, so she uses about a quart. But for single people or a couple, a pint should do. Also, if cooking for more people, use 2 potatoes and more vegetables.

Carrot soup and broccoli soup turn out just marvelously with this method, and cauliflower, peas, tomatoes, celery, watercress, etc., can be used equally well. And a leftover vegetable soup is good too.

Servings depend on the quantities of stock and vegetables.

Blake Edwards

Warm-Up-the-Night-Shift Potato Soup

2   quarts water
6   cubes chicken bouillon
6   medium white potatoes, cut into 1-inch chunks
1   medium onion, thinly sliced
1   pound slab fat-free smoked ham, cut into 1-inch chunks
1½ cups chopped celery
1   16-ounce package frozen corn
    Salt and pepper to taste
1   16-ounce package light Velveeta cheese

In a large pot, bring the water and chicken bouillon to a boil. Add the potatoes and boil until the potatoes are just tender. Add the onion, ham, celery, corn, and salt and pepper. Simmer for 30 to 40 minutes until the potatoes are good and tender. Reduce heat to very low and add the cheese. Stir occasionally until the cheese melts. (Do not boil.)

Serves the entire shift.

Phil Cotten
Chief of Police
Norman, Oklahoma

Sergeant Hudson's Veggie Soup

1 pound fresh, just-ripe tomatoes, peeled and seeded
2 tablespoons unsalted butter or canola oil (or none)
1 yellow onion, finely chopped
6 cups chicken broth with no salt or fat, or 6 cups water
1 bay leaf
3 sprigs fresh oregano
2 sprigs fresh parsley
   Fresh lemon zest
1 cup carrots, thinly sliced
½ cup carrots, finely chopped
1 pound new potatoes, cut up
½ teaspoon salt
   Ground black pepper
1 cup canned or fresh corn
¼ pound green beans, French cut
½ cup zucchini, cut into small pieces

Brenda Vaccaro starred as Det. Kate Hudson in the 1979 television series *Dear Detective*.

Cut the tomatoes into small pieces and set aside. In a large pot, melt the butter and sauté the onion until golden brown. Add the chicken broth or water. Add all the herbs and vegetables and any other vegetables that you like. Cook for a few minutes over medium heat and then reduce heat and simmer for 35 minutes or more. Adjust the seasoning to taste while cooking. Serve right away with white wine and bread—either Parmesan cheese bread or garlic bread would be good.

Makes about 8 servings.

Brenda Vaccaro

Smith and Wesson Wild Rice Soup

1 large onion, chopped
1 cup chopped celery
1 8-ounce can chopped mushrooms, drained
1½ sticks margarine or butter
1 cup all-purpose flour
2 cups cooked wild rice (directions follow)
8 cups water
9 chicken bouillon cubes
1 cup whipping cream

In a skillet, sauté the onions, celery, and mushrooms in the margarine or butter until tender. Sprinkle the flour over the vegetables until well coated (the mixture will be pasty). In a large saucepan, combine the wild rice, water, and bouillon cubes. Add the coated vegetables and whipping cream. Heat and stir to make sure the vegetables blend into the soup. Cook for 30 minutes. Do not boil.

Wild Rice:

Thoroughly wash 1 cup of wild rice. Bring to a boil in 4 cups of salted water in a heavy saucepan. Simmer, covered, for about 45 minutes. Uncover. Fluff with a fork. Simmer for 5 more minutes. Drain the excess liquid, if any.

Makes 6 to 8 servings.

William K. Finney
Chief of Police
Saint Paul, Minnesota

Paul Michael Glaser was the cool, streetwise Dave Starsky, half of the plainclothes detective team *Starsky and Hutch* (1975–79).

Starsky's Curried Squash Soup

2 cups chopped onions
3 tablespoons sweet butter
4 to 5 tablespoons best quality curry powder
3 pounds butternut squash, peeled and cubed
1 pound apples, cored and chopped
3 cups homemade chicken stock
1 cup unfiltered apple juice
Fresh cilantro for garnish

In a large saucepan, sauté the onions in the butter until translucent, about 15 minutes. Add the curry powder, stir to coat evenly, and cook for another 5 minutes. Add the squash and chopped apple. Add the stock and bring to a boil. Reduce heat and simmer, partially covered, for 45 minutes. Remove from heat and purée with an immersion blender or food processor. Add the apple juice to taste and heat as needed. Serve in heated bowls. Snip the fresh cilantro with kitchen scissors and use as garnish.

Makes about 4 servings.

Paul Michael Glaser

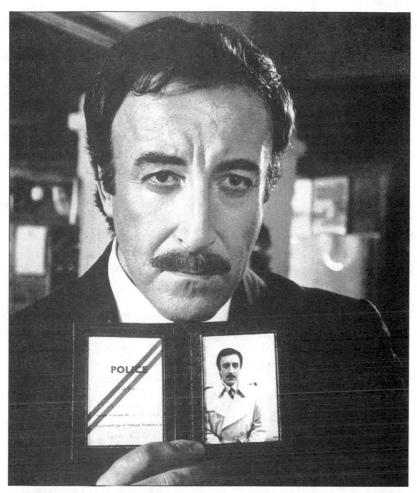

In more than a half-dozen feature films, beginning with *The Pink Panther* in 1964, Peter Sellers portrayed the incomparable, accident-prone, and bumbling sleuth, Inspector Jacques Clouseau.

Clouseau's Cucumber Soup

1 onion
1 medium cucumber
¼ to ½ butter or margarine
2 tablespoons all-purpose flour
1 pint chicken stock
  Salt and pepper to taste
4 ounces cream
4 ounces milk
½ teaspoon green food coloring

Peel and finely chop the onion. Cut the cucumber (with skin on) into cubes with the skin on. Melt the butter in a pan and add the onion and cucumbers. Cover and cook over medium heat for 10 minutes, stirring from time to time. Stir in the flour and continue to cook and stir for 1 or 2 minutes. Remove from heat. Stir in the stock and season with salt and pepper to taste. Return to heat, bring to a boil, and then simmer for 5 minutes. Cover and refrigerate overnight. The next day stir in the cream, milk, and food coloring. Gently reheat and serve.

Makes 2 or 3 servings.

Peter Sellers
Submitted by mother-in-law Iris Frederick

Hannigan Goulash Soup

3 medium onions, sliced
1 clove garlic, finely chopped
3 tablespoons olive oil
2 teaspoons paprika
½ pound ground lean veal
½ pound ground lean pork
3 cups beef stock or bouillon
½ teaspoon salt
⅛ teaspoon pepper
3 cups Merlot wine
3 medium potatoes, sliced
4 small tomatoes, chopped

Using a 4-quart Dutch oven or soup kettle, sauté the onion and garlic in hot olive oil until lightly browned. Add the paprika; cook for 1 minute. Stir in the ground meats and sauté until lightly browned. Gradually add the stock, seasonings, and Merlot; cover. Simmer for 20 minutes. Add the potatoes and tomatoes; cover. Simmer for 25 minutes or until the potatoes are soft.

Serving Suggestion: The ideal combination with this dish is a loaf of French bread, a glass of red wine, and Monday night football.

Makes 6 servings.

M. J. Hannigan
Commissioner Emeritus, California Highway
Patrol, as well as host and technical director of
Real Stories of the Highway Patrol.

---

*"Never get your hair cut
by a bald barber."*

—Det. Mary Beth Lacey
(Cagney & Lacey)

The Big Easy Traffic Jambalaya

1 pound smoked sausage, thinly sliced
3 tablespoons olive oil
2 cloves garlic, minced
¾ cup chopped green pepper
¾ cup chopped parsley
¾ cup chopped celery
2 16-ounce cans whole tomatoes
3 cups chicken broth
1 cup chopped green onions
2 tablespoons Worcestershire sauce
3 bay leaves
1½ teaspoons thyme
2 teaspoons oregano
1 tablespoon Creole seasoning
½ teaspoon salt
½ teaspoon black pepper
2 cups converted long-grain rice, rinsed
2½ pounds raw shrimp, peeled and deveined

Sauté the sausage in a large, heavy pot. Remove the sausage. Add the olive oil to the drippings and sauté the garlic, green pepper, parsley, and celery for 5 minutes. Chop the tomatoes and reserve the liquid. Add the tomatoes with liquid, broth, and onions. Stir in the spices. Add the rice and sausage and cook covered for 30 minutes over low heat, stirring occasionally. After most of the liquid has been absorbed by the rice, add the shrimp and cook until pink. Preheat the oven to 275°. Transfer the mixture to a baking dish. Bake for 20 to 25 minutes.

Makes 8 to 10 servings.

Richard Pennington
Chief of Police
New Orleans, Louisiana

Ace Crawford's Tomato Soup

■ This is my favorite recipe. It is from the army—when I was a cook—so I can prepare it only for fifty people or more. It's nice if we have a crowd over for dinner; but if it's just me, I'm up all night eating this stuff.

2 cups chopped shallots
4 sticks butter
3 cups gin
3 #10 cans* diced tomatoes
2 tablespoons chopped
   parsley
2 tablespoons basil
6 bay leaves
½ cup sugar
2 tablespoons black pepper
2 tablespoons seasoned salt
1 tablespoon salt
½ gallon cream
½ gallon half & half

A #10 can is approximately 7 pounds or 12 to 13 cups.

Sauté the shallots in butter until lightly browned. Add the gin and reduce to ¼ volume. Add the rest of the ingredients, except the cream and half & half, and simmer for 30 minutes. Stir in the cream and half & half and heat through.

Makes enough to feed an army.

Tim Conway

He was a hard-nosed private eye in a trench coat, and he could get tough with the best of them—when it came to laughs. He was Tim Conway as *Ace Crawford, Private Eye* in 1983. Conway also paired with pal Don Knotts as a couple of Scotland Yard sleuths in the 1980 flick *The Private Eyes.*

Ronny Cox has created several memorable cops. He was Capt. Bogomill in the two *Beverly Hills Cop* flicks, he starred in *Robocop*, and he was Chief Roger Kendrick on television's police musical series *Cop Rock*.

Beverly Hills Cop Corn and Chicken Soup

■ Ronny enjoys eating a great deal but doesn't do much cooking. I am happy to share this recipe for what is possibly his favorite dish in the whole world. This is actually a variation of Chinese corn soup, but over the years I have adapted it to his tastes. Since it is my own adaptation, I can't really give the quantities precisely. I am one of those "some of this and a little of that" type of cooks, but here are my best estimates.   —*Mary (Mrs. Ronny) Cox*

1 chicken
6 cups water
1 teaspoon salt
10 peppercorns
½ cup diced ham
2 16-ounce cans cream-style corn, puréed
½ cup diced water chestnuts
1 tablespoon cornstarch dissolved in 2 tablespoons water
   Salt and pepper

Boil the chicken in water with the salt and peppercorns for 2 to 3 hours. Remove to a plate. Adjust the chicken stock to 6 cups and skim off any fat. Remove the meat from half of the chicken and dice. Reserve the other half of the chicken for use later. Add the diced chicken, ham, corn, and water chestnuts to the stock and bring to a boil. Add the cornstarch mixture and cook for 5 minutes. Add salt and pepper to taste.

Makes about 8 servings.

Ronny Cox

Rocky's Bouillabaisse

Stock:

1 pound fish bones, skins, and heads
7 cups water
1 small onion, thinly sliced
1 small carrot, thinly sliced
1 bay leaf
6 black peppercorns
1 blade mace
1 sprig thyme
1 lemon slice

Bouillabaisse:

6 tablespoons butter or margarine
1 carrot, sliced
3 leeks, well washed and thinly sliced
1 clove garlic
   Pinch saffron
⅓ to ½ cup dry white wine
8 ounces canned tomatoes
1 lobster
1 pound cod or halibut fillets
1 pound mussels, well scrubbed
1 pound small clams, well scrubbed
1 pound scallops
   Chopped parsley
8 ounces large shrimp, peeled and deveined

First prepare the stock. Place all the stock ingredients in a large stock pot and bring to a boil over high heat. Lower the heat and allow to simmer for 20 minutes. Strain and reserve the stock. Discard the fish bones and vegetables.

Melt the butter in a medium-sized saucepan and add the carrots, leeks, and garlic. Cook for about 5 minutes until slightly softened. Add the saffron and wine and allow to simmer for about 5 minutes.

Add the fish stock along with all the remaining bouillabaisse ingredients, except the shrimp. Bring the mixture to a boil and cook until the lobster turns red and the mussels and clam shells open. Turn off the heat and add the shrimp. Cover the pan and let the shrimp cook in the residual heat. Divide the ingredients among 4 soup bowls. Remove the lobster and section to divide evenly.

Makes 4 servings.

Sand Castle Restaurant
Paradise Cove
Malibu, California

Sand Castle Corn Chowder

4 slices bacon, diced
1 white onion, minced
2 potatoes, diced
2 ribs celery, diced
1 green pepper, minced
1 cup chicken stock
¼ cup sherry
1 bay leaf
1 teaspoon nutmeg
1 teaspoon dried thyme
1 teaspoon sugar
3 cups heavy cream, divided
1 tablespoon cornstarch
2 cups corn kernels
1 pimiento, minced
   Salt and white pepper

In a 3-quart saucepan, sauté the bacon until crisp. Remove the bacon and drain. Use about 2 tablespoons of bacon fat to sauté the onions. Add the potatoes, celery, and pepper. Cook for 3 minutes. Add the chicken stock, sherry, bay leaf, nutmeg, thyme, and sugar. Simmer until the potatoes are tender.

In a bowl, combine 2 tablespoons of the cream with the cornstarch. Add the remaining cream to the saucepan. Slowly stir in the cornstarch mixture and simmer for 3 minutes. Add the corn, pimiento, and bacon, and simmer for 5 minutes. Add salt and pepper to taste.

Makes 6 to 8 servings.

Sand Castle Restaurant
Paradise Cove
Malibu, California

They say a man's home is his castle, but for Jim Rockford, whose home is a trailer, the castle is across the parking lot. Many of *The Rockford Files* scenes were shot in and around the Sand Castle restaurant (seen here during the 1970s). The popular Malibu eatery is still pleasing Paradise Cove diners with breakfast, lunch, dinner, and a spectacular ocean view.

In 1989 Ron Masak became Sheriff Mort Metzger, top lawman in Cabot Cove, Maine, on *Murder, She Wrote.*

Cabot Cove Albondigas Soup

4   10½-ounce cans beef bouillon
    Enough water to fill large soup pot
    half way
2   cups chopped celery
2   cups sliced carrots
1   medium onion, chopped
½   cup chopped cilantro
½   tablespoon dried chili pepper
1   20-ounce can chopped tomatoes
1   16-ounce package frozen meatballs

Starting with the bouillon and water first, combine all the ingredients except the meatballs in a large soup pot. Cook over medium heat for 30 minutes. Add the meatballs, cover with a lid, and cook for 30 minutes longer.

Makes about 8 servings.

Ron Masak

> *"When you're a lawman and you're dealing with people, you do a whole lot better if you go not so much by the book, but by the heart."*
>
> —Sheriff Andy Taylor
> (*The Andy Griffith Show*)

Hardcastle's Fish Chowder

¼ **pound salt pork or bacon (the best is Italian pancetta), chopped**
2 **or 3 onions, chopped**
2 **large potatoes, cut into 1-inch squares**
1 **cup fresh corn or canned corn niblets**
1 **cup water**
1 **cup milk or cream**
  Garlic salt and ground black pepper
1 **pound cod fish, sea bass, striped bass, or orange roughy, cut into 1-inch squares**

In a large pot, fry the salt pork and set aside. Fry the onions and potatoes, stirring until half cooked. Add the pork, corn, water, milk or cream, and salt and pepper to the pan drippings. When the potatoes are soft, add the fish. Stir the fish in and then turn the heat off. Put the lid on and remove the pot from the stove. Wait 5 minutes and serve. Be careful not to let the fish cook too long on the stove or it will be tough. It needs only to heat through.

Serving suggestion: Garlic bread or toasted French bread goes well with this. Put a chunk in the bowl and ladle chowder over it.

Makes about 8 servings.

Brian Keith

Brian Keith starred as Ross MacDonald's popular detective Lew Archer on *Archer* in 1975. He also played Milton G. Hardcastle, a crusty judge and wily detective, on *Hardcastle & McCormick* from 1983 to 1986.

Kristian Alfonso helps put criminals behind bars as Officer Hope Brady on the popular daytime drama *Days of Our Lives.*

Hope for More Low-Fat Clam Chowder

⅔ cup chopped onion
   Pinch thyme
   Pinch basil
¼ teaspoon salt
¼ teaspoon pepper
8 ounces clam juice
2 cups skim milk
1 package Goya ham concentrate
2 cups instant potato buds
½ pound chopped clams
   Cracked pepper

In a 1-quart saucepan coated with cooking spray, sauté the onion until soft but not brown. Stir in the thyme, basil, salt, and pepper. Add the clam juice and milk. Stir in the ham concentrate and potato buds. Add the clams and stir until the desired thickness is reached. Sprinkle each serving with cracked pepper and serve.

Note: When making corn chowder, substitute 1 10-ounce can of kernel corn for the clams. Drain the juice from the can in a separate bowl and add enough milk to make 3 cups. Also increase the thyme to ¼ teaspoon.

Makes 4 to 6 servings.

Kristian Alfonso

Pete Malloy's Clam Chowder

¾ cup virgin olive oil
1 cup all-purpose flour
1 cup diced onion
¾ cup chopped celery
1 tablespoon sweet butter
¼ cup white wine
2 ounces fish bouillon
6½ cups clam juice
1½ pounds chopped clams
1 pound diced red potatoes
4 slices bacon, cooked
1 bay leaf
½ tablespoon dried tarragon
½ teaspoon dried thyme
1½ teaspoons Old Bay seasoning
Fresh ground pepper to taste
2 cups half & half

Heat the oil in a saucepan while slowly adding the flour. Set on low heat and stir until a white roux forms. In a large pot, cook the onion and celery in the butter for 10 minutes. Add the remaining ingredients, except the half & half, and simmer until the potatoes are done. Stir in the roux and simmer for 10 minutes. Stir in the half & half.

Makes 10 to 12 servings.

Martin Milner

Martin Milner, left, and Kent McCord patrolled the streets of Los Angeles as Officers Pete Malloy and Jim Reed respectively in the Jack Webb-produced *Adam 12*. The popular police show ran from 1968 to 1975.

Anticrime crusader John Walsh is host of *America's Most Wanted,* a television show that has been praised by law enforcement officials for helping to apprehend several of the nation's most dangerous fugitives.

America's Most Wanted Chili

1 **pound beef top sirloin steak**
¼ **cup dry sherry, divided**
2 **tablespoons soy sauce**
2 **tablespoons vegetable oil, divided**
1 **tablespoon cornstarch, divided**
1 **medium onion, cut into slices**
2 **large cloves garlic, crushed**
1 **to 2 large jalapeño peppers, seeded and chopped**
1 **tablespoon minced fresh ginger**
1 **tablespoon chili powder**
1 **28-ounce can peeled whole tomatoes, broken up**
1 **tablespoon water**

Trim the excess fat from the sirloin steak. Cut the steak into ¼-inch-thick slices; cut the slices into 1-inch long pieces. To make a marinade, combine 2 tablespoons of the sherry with the soy sauce, 1 tablespoon of the vegetable oil, and 1 teaspoon of the cornstarch. Place the steak pieces in a plastic bag; add the marinade, turning to coat. Close the bag securely and marinate in the refrigerator while preparing the chili. Cut the onion slices in half and separate. Heat the remaining tablespoon of oil in a Dutch oven over medium heat. Stir-fry the onion, garlic, jalapeño peppers, and ginger for 2 minutes. Stir in the chili powder and tomatoes. Bring to a boil; reduce heat. Cover and simmer for 30 minutes, stirring occasionally.

Remove the beef from the marinade about 5 minutes before the end of the cooking time; reserve the marinade. Combine the marinade, the water, and the remaining 2 teaspoons of cornstarch; stir into the chili. Bring to a boil and cook until thickened, stirring constantly. Heat a nonstick skillet over medium-high heat until hot. Stir-fry the marinated beef, half at a time, for 1 or 2 minutes and remove. Deglaze the pan with the remaining 2 tablespoons of sherry, stirring to dissolve the browned meat juices. Stir the mixture into the chili; add the beef pieces. Serve immediately.

Serving suggestion: Top the chili with cilantro leaves, sliced green onion, chopped water chestnuts, and toasted slivered almonds. Serve with steamed flour tortillas.

Makes 4 servings.

John Walsh

Willie's Smoking Chili

2 **pounds lean ground beef (or substitute ground turkey)**
   Dash sage
   Garlic pepper, coarsely ground
   Crushed red pepper, divided
   Salt
   Light vegetable oil

1 **medium red onion, chopped**
1 **medium green or red bell pepper, diced**
2 **to 3 fresh tomatoes, diced, and fresh green chili peppers, diced (or substitute 1 10-ounce can Ro-Tel**
2 **16-ounce cans red kidney beans, drained**
1 **16-ounce can Manwich sauce**
⅓ **cup water**
  Louisiana Hot Sauce

In a large skillet, sauté the ground beef until lightly browned, approximately 15 to 20 minutes. (If using turkey, sauté until the pink is completely gone.) Halfway through sautéing the meat, sprinkle on the sage, garlic pepper, crushed red pepper, and salt. Continue cooking until done; drain off excess fat.

In a separate skillet, heat a little vegetable oil and sauté the onion and bell pepper until they start to become soft. Add the diced tomato and green chilies to the mixture. Sauté over medium heat until the mixture is just soft and then blend with a fork. (Don't mix or mash.)

In at least a 3-quart pot, combine the drained meat mixture and drained kidney beans; blend with a spoon or spatula, slowly, so as not to mash the mixture. Add the onion-tomato-chili mixture and blend lightly. Add the Manwich sauce, 3 dashes crushed red pepper, and ⅓ cup of water. Cover and cook over medium-low heat for 25 minutes. Stir occasionally to prevent sticking. Then add 2 dashes crushed red pepper and liberal dashes of Louisiana Hot Sauce (let your taste or stomach be your guide).

Cover and continue cooking over medium-low heat for 15 minutes, stirring occasionally. Remove from heat and let stand for at least 30 minutes before serving. If you're not serving it within 1 hour, the chili can be refrigerated and later warmed over medium heat.

For the brave and adventurous: Cook the chili, refrigerate overnight, and heat and serve the next day. This will allow time for all the seasonings to "blend, mellow, and come alive." This is a great meal to warm you on a cold winter evening or bring life to you at a summer barbecue or cookout.

Makes about 8 servings.

Willie L. Williams
Chief of Police
Los Angeles, California

Obey All Rules Chili Soup

2 **tablespoons vegetable oil**
2 **onions, chopped (preferably Walla Walla Sweet or Vidalia)**
2 **pounds ground hamburger or turkey**
1 **26-ounce can Campbell's tomato soup**
2 **10-ounce cans diced tomatoes**
2 **16-ounce cans garbanzo beans**
2 **16-ounce cans red kidney beans**
2 **16-ounce cans whole-kernel corn**
2 **4-ounce cans mushrooms with stems and pieces**
  Minced garlic or garlic powder
  Chili powder
  Salt and pepper
  Cheddar or Parmesan cheese, grated

In a skillet, heat the oil and cook the onions until they soften. Add the meat and brown completely. Drain off excess grease. Pour in the soup, tomatoes, beans, corn, and mushrooms. Add more of anything that pleases you the most, cook, while stirring, until hot and all mushed together. Season to taste with the garlic powder, chili powder, and salt and pepper. Pour into bowls and top with cheese. This is better the second day.

Serving Suggestion: After a football or basketball game—or a late-night raid—it's great with French bread and fruit. Cornbread is good too.

Makes 10 to 12 servings.

Ann Rule

Dark and Stormy Night Chili

■ This takes away the chill on those cold, winter South Dakota nights.

1 cup sliced carrots
2 cups diced potatoes
1 12-ounce can green beans
1 or 2 pounds ground beef
1 teaspoon onion powder
½ teaspoon garlic powder
2 tablespoons chili powder
1 10¾-ounce can tomato soup
1 16-ounce can stewed tomatoes
1 16-ounce cans kidney beans, drained
3 to 4 soup cans water

In a large saucepan, boil the carrots and potatoes. Remove from heat; drain and reserve the water. Add the green beans to the carrots and potatoes.

In a large heavy-bottom skillet, brown the ground beef. Drain and rinse. Add the onion powder, garlic powder, and chili powder and blend well. Add the soup, tomatoes, and kidney beans. Add 3 to 4 cups of the reserved water used to cook the vegetables, making up the balance with plain water. Add the carrots, potatoes, and green beans. Bring to a boil for 5 minutes and then simmer for 45 minutes.

Serving Suggestion: Serve with biscuits for a hearty, nutritious meal.

Makes 10 to 12 servings.

Terry Satterlee
Chief of Police
Sioux Falls, South Dakota

Calling All Cards Chocolate Chili

Especially good with chips.

3 pounds ground meat
2 onions, chopped
3 cloves garlic, minced
2 tablespoons chili powder
1 tablespoon all-purpose flour
1 28-ounce can whole tomatoes

2 teaspoons cumin seed
1 teaspoon oregano
1 teaspoon salt
2 bay leaves
½ teaspoon coriander
1 square (1 ounce) unsweetened chocolate
   Salt and pepper
   Grated cheddar cheese

Brown the meat, onions, and garlic in a large Dutch oven or heavy skillet. Drain off excess grease. Combine the chili powder and flour and add to the meat mixture. Purée the tomatoes, combine with the spices, and add to the meat mixture. Cover and simmer slowly for 2 hours. Add the chocolate during the last ½ hour. Add salt and pepper to taste. Pour into bowls. Top with grated cheddar cheese.

Serving Suggestion: Serve with corn chips, cornbread, or crackers.

Makes 1½ quarts.

Jerry Keller
Sheriff
Las Vegas, Nevada

Mock Trial White Chili

4 boneless chicken breasts
2 chicken bouillon cubes, dissolved in
   5 cups water
3 15-ounce can Great Northern beans
1 tablespoon vegetable oil
1½ medium onions or 1 large onion, finely chopped
3 large or 5 small jalapeño peppers, finely chopped
½ teaspoon garlic powder
1 teaspoon salt
½ teaspoon curry powder
1 teaspoon dried oregano
   Pinch ground cloves
   Pinch ground white pepper
   Several small green onions, chopped
½ cup grated Monterey Jack or other cheese, or sour cream

In a large saucepan, boil the chicken breasts in the bouillon water until the meat is tender enough to be easily pulled apart. Remove the chicken from the pan, reserving the broth. Chop the chicken into 1-inch lengths. Add the chicken back to the broth. Add the beans and simmer on medium heat.

As the chicken and beans simmer, place the vegetable oil in a large skillet and sauté the onion and peppers until the onions are translucent. Add the onion, peppers, and all remaining ingredients, except the green onions and cheese, to the chicken and beans. Continue to simmer until the broth begins to thicken and serve. Garnish the finished chili with green onions and cheese or sour cream if preferred.

Makes 8 to 10 servings.

David Hunter

Cheyenne Spicy Hot Elk Chili

1 pound ground elk or cubed elk steak
1 medium onion, chopped
2 cloves garlic, minced
½ cup chopped green pepper
1 28-ounce can tomatoes, cut up and juice reserved
1 16-ounce can red kidney beans, drained
2 16-ounce cans hot chili beans
1 6-ounce can tomato paste
¾ cup tomato juice
1 4-ounce can green chili peppers, chopped
1 pickled jalapeño pepper, rinsed, seeded, and chopped
2 cups water
1 tablespoon chili powder
A few drops bottled hot pepper sauce
1 teaspoon salt
½ teaspoon pepper

In a large saucepan, cook the ground elk, onion, garlic, and green pepper until the meat is browned. Drain off excess fat. Stir in the tomatoes, juice, kidney beans, chili beans, tomato paste, tomato juice, green

Knoxville, Tennessee, author and former bounty hunter David Hunter has penned nine novels, including *Black Friday Coming Down*, *Jigsaw Man*, and *Homicide Game*, and was a detective with the Knox County Sheriff's Department until his retirement in 1993.

chili peppers, jalapeño pepper, water, chili powder, hot pepper sauce, salt, and pepper. Cover and simmer for 1 hour.

Makes 6 to 8 servings.

John R. Powell
Chief of Police
Cheyenne, Wyoming

Fraternal Order Posole

■ Posole is a traditional dish served in New Mexico during the holiday season.

1 32-ounce package fresh posole (hominy)
7 red chile pods with stems and seeds removed and pods rinsed
6 quarts water, divided
2 pounds lean beef stew meat or pork
6 small pigs feet
1 large onions diced
6 cloves garlic, minced
4 teaspoons granulated garlic (or less, according to taste)
1½ tablespoons ground oregano
Red Chile Sauce (recipe follows)

Soak the posole overnight in cool water. Rinse the posole thoroughly. Place the posole, chile pods, and 3 quarts of the water in a 12-quart pot. Boil over medium heat for 1 hour.

In a separate pot, boil the meat and then simmer for ½ hour. Drain the meat.

Place the meat, pigs feet, and remaining ingredients, except Red Chile Sauce, into the pot with the posole, and bring to a boil; then reduce heat and simmer until the posole pops open (1 to 2 hours). Posole is generally ready whenever the pigs feet fall apart. Top with Red Chile Sauce, which can be added to each serving of posole according to individual taste.

Red Chile Sauce:

1 tablespoon vegetable oil
1 heaping tablespoon all-purpose flour
2 cups water
14 ounces red chile purée (hot)
1 teaspoon salt
¼ teaspoon ground oregano
1 clove garlic, crushed

Melt the shortening in a hot skillet. Add the flour and brown. Add the water, chile purée, and spices. Boil, reduce heat, cover, and simmer for 20 minutes.

Makes 12 16-ounce servings.

Gilbert G. Gallegos
National President
Fraternal Order of Police

Border Patrol Stew

2 pounds lean meat
2 16-ounce cans pinto beans
2 16-ounce cans kidney beans
2 10-ounce cans corn
2 16-ounce cans tomato sauce
2 1½-ounce packages taco seasoning mix
1 1-ounce envelope ranch dressing mix

In a large heavy pot or Dutch oven, brown the meat; drain off the fat. Add the rest of the ingredients and mix together. Simmer very slowly for 45 minutes to 1 hour, stirring occasionally.

Makes 12 to 16 servings.

Frank Latham
Chief of Police
Hewitt, Texas

WHO SAID IT?

Match the character to the quotation.

1. Harry Callahan	A. "Book 'em, Danno."
2. Columbo	B. "The thing of it is, is..."
3. Joe Friday	C. "Just one more thing."
4. Michael Knight	D. "The little gray cells."
5. Kojak	E. "Works for me."
6. Dan Matthews	F. "Oooh! Oooh! Oooh!"
7. McCloud	G. "He's all lawyered up."
8. Steve McGarrett	H. "Freeze, dirtbags!"
9. Inspector Morse	I. "This is the city.
10. Hercule Poirot	I wear a badge."
11. Gunther Toody	J. "You got it!"
12. T. J. Hooker	K. "Who loves ya, baby?"
13. Hunter	L. "There you go."
14. Richie Brockelman	M. "Make my day!"
15. Andy Sipowicz	N. "I stumble around."
	O. "Ten-four."

SOLUTION
1. M, 2. C, 3. I, 4. J, 5. K, 6. O, 7. L, 8. A, 9. N, 10. D, 11. F, 12. H, 13. E, 14. B, 15. G.

From 1972 to 1976, Michael Douglas starred as Inspector Steve Keller, young partner to Karl Malden's Lt. Mike Stone, on *The Streets of San Francisco.*

Saturday Night Special Veal Stew

½ **pound bacon**
1 **medium onion, coarsely chopped**
1 **cup sliced mushrooms**
½ **pound chicken livers**
2 **pounds veal, cubed**
    Pepper
    Paprika
    Seasoning salt
2 **28-ounce cans peeled whole tomatoes**
1 **lemon, sliced**
4 **cloves**

In a large skillet, fry the bacon until crisp. Drain on paper towels and cut into 1-inch pieces. Sauté the onion, mushrooms, and chicken livers in the bacon fat. Set aside on paper towels. Season the veal with a mixture of pepper, paprika, and seasoning salt to taste. Brown the veal in the bacon fat and drain. Preheat the oven to 350°. Assemble the cooked ingredients in a round casserole dish. Top with tomatoes, lemon slices, and cloves. Bake for 1 hour.

Makes 4 to 6 servings.

Michael Douglas

Archer's Menudo

1 whole calf's foot or 4 pigs feet
2 pounds tripe
   Garlic
   Hot red peppers
   Salt
2 16-ounce cans whole white hominy
   (not grits)
   Mexican oregano
   Lemon or lime juice

For this dish, you should have a *pata* (a whole calf's foot—hoof and all). Mexican groceries have them. Pigs feet are okay, but you'll need 3 or 4 of them. You'll also need 2 pounds of tripe, washed and cut up into 1x2-inch pieces. I use a lot of garlic, but suit yourself. The same goes for the red peppers and salt.

Boil the foot and tripe in plenty of water and skim well. Turn the heat down to simmer until the tripe is very tender and allow it to cool a little. Take out the foot, bone it, chop the meat, and then return the meat to the pot with the tripe. Salt and add red peppers to taste. Add 2 big cans of whole white hominy. Before serving, add crumbled Mexican oregano and squeeze in some fresh lemon or lime juice. Serve tortillas on the side.

It doesn't smell too good while cooking, but it tastes great and is good for stomach problems. (It's the red peppers that do it.)

Makes about 4 servings.

Brian Keith

Fort Apache Mediterranean Stew

1 pound chuck steak, cut into 1½-inch cubes
1 pound sweet Italian sausage, cut into rounds or patties
1½ cups burgundy
2 cups water
1 6-ounce can tomato paste
½ teaspoon salt or to taste
¾ teaspoon pepper
3 garlic cloves, minced
2 teaspoons paprika
1 pound cubed cooked ham
3 medium onions, coarsely chopped
1 sweet red pepper, coarsely chopped
¼ cup chopped fresh parsley
2 1-pound cans garbanzo beans
1 teaspoon grated lemon rind
1 head cabbage, cut into wedges

In a large skillet, sauté the beef cubes and sausage until brown. Drain the meats and cut the sausage into smaller pieces. Transfer the meats to a Dutch oven. Add the wine, water, tomato paste, salt, pepper, garlic, and paprika. Bring to a boil, cover, and simmer 1½ to 2 hours or until the meat is tender.

Brian Keith (right) played a New England chief of police with an international dilemma on his hands in the 1966 film *The Russians Are Coming, The Russians Are Coming.* Jonathan Winters was his deputy.

Add the remaining ingredients, except the cabbage. Cover and cook for 20 minutes. Add the cabbage and cook until it's crisp-tender, about 15 to 20 minutes. Refrigerate overnight to develop the flavors. Skim off the fat. Bring the stew to room temperature. Reheat in a microwave oven for 4 to 5 minutes or on a stove top for 15 to 20 minutes until hot.

Makes 6 to 8 servings.

Edward Asner

Mom's 10-7* Meal in One Pot

1½ **pounds lean ground beef**
2 **teaspoons vegetable oil**
5 **14½-ounce cans Swanson's beef broth**
2 **14½-ounce cans stewed tomatoes**
2 **15-ounce cans mixed vegetables**
1 **15½-ounce can white hominy**
1 **15½-ounce can red kidney beans**
1 **8-ounce can mushrooms (optional)**
4 **green onions or 1 small white onion, chopped**
1 **cup chopped celery with leaves**
1 **teaspoon garlic salt**
2 **bay leaves**
½ **cup uncooked barley (optional)**

In a skillet, brown the ground beef in the vegetable oil. Meanwhile, open all the canned items and dump the contents into a big soup pot. Add the onions and celery. After thoroughly draining the excess fat, add the beef to the soup pot. Add the seasonings (and barley, if desired) and cook over medium heat for 45 minutes. My husband adds Louisiana Hot Sauce before eating, but he's a southerner who loves spicy food! This is a great meal for the busy mom who wants to make sure her family gets their veggies. I serve with homemade biscuits.

Makes 12 or more hearty servings.

Margie Smith
President
Police Chiefs' Spouses Worldwide

*Police officers' ten-code for out of service.

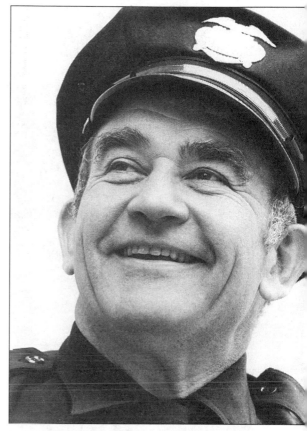

In 1981 Ed Asner played a cop in the feature film *Fort Apache: The Bronx*. He also appeared in blue in an episode of *Police Story*.

Police Chiefs' Spouses Worldwide

Police Chiefs' Spouses Worldwide was established in 1985 to strengthen the bonds of law enforcement families. The organization brings together those interested in the police family—those who believe that love and support are the anchor of every home. One of the group's prime objectives is to establish among the members and their spouses bonds of friendship, confidence, socialization, support, and respect. Organization president Margie Smith may be reached at 1-800-471-7081.

Hal Linden (front) was Capt. Barney Miller, head of New York City's Twelfth Precinct from 1975 to 1982. Filling out Capt. Miller's roster in this mug shot are (left to right) Abe Vigoda as Det. Phil Fish, Jack Soo as Det. Nick Yemana, Ron Glass as Det. Ron Harris, Max Gail as Det. Stanley Wojohowicz (Wojo), and Gregory Sierra as Det. Sgt. Chano Amenguale.

Bundles of Dough

BREADS

Barney Miller's
Cheese Mustard Loaf

1 loaf white bread, unsliced
½ stick butter
⅔ cup minced onion
6 tablespoons French's yellow mustard
3 tablespoons poppy seed
4 teaspoons lemon juice
½ pound (8 slices) Swiss cheese
½ pound (8 slices) American cheese
2 to 3 strips bacon (optional)

Preheat the oven to 350°. Make diagonal cuts almost to the bottom of the bread. Mix the butter, onion, mustard, poppy seed, and lemon juice. Spread a little between each slice of bread. Set aside the rest. Place 1 slice of each cheese in each cut. Press the bread together. Place in a shallow baking pan. Spread the rest of the mixture on the top and sides of the loaf. Place the bacon on top. Bake for 20 minutes or until the bacon is cooked and the loaf is evenly brown. This can be made ahead of time and wrapped in foil. When it's needed, it can be unwrapped and baked a little longer. It's great with a green salad.

Makes 4 to 6 servings.

Hal Linden

Hal Linden's Barney Miller was a wise and patient police captain who coped with a staff of detectives of widely varied personalities—not to mention a bizarre assortment of criminal types that trooped through his Greenwich Village precinct house.

David Birney starred in *Serpico* in 1976 as real-life New York Police Department undercover officer Frank Serpico.

Serpico's Soda Bread

■ This recipe is one my mother used to make, and now I make it with my daughter, Mollie.

3 tablespoons butter
2½ cups all-purpose flour
2 tablespoons sugar
1 teaspoon baking soda
1 teaspoon baking powder
½ teaspoon salt
⅓ cup raisins
   About ¾ cup buttermilk
   Butter, softened

Preheat the oven to 375°. Grease a 5x9-inch loaf pan. In a large bowl, cut 3 tablespoons butter into the flour, sugar, baking soda, baking powder, and salt until fine crumbs form. Add the raisins. Stir in enough buttermilk to cause the dough to leave the sides of the bowl. Knead for 1 or 2 minutes until smooth. Place the dough into the prepared pan and brush with softened butter. Bake for 35 to 45 minutes or until golden brown.
   Makes 1 loaf.

David Birney

J. J. Starbuck's Jerky Gravy and Biscuits

■ This is an old family recipe that Dale really likes from my side of the family.
—*Susan (Mrs. Dale) Robertson*

Bisquick
Beer

Gravy:

½ cup bacon grease
½ cup all-purpose flour
3 cups very dry jerky, ground up in a meat grinder
3 cups whole milk
Salt and pepper to taste

Make biscuits according to package directions, but substitute beer for the liquid.

To make gravy, melt the bacon grease in a skillet. Stir in the flour. Add the jerky. Add the milk all at once and stir. Add salt and pepper to taste. Stir until thickened.

Pour the gravy over the biscuits.

Dale Robertson

While Dale Robertson starred as an eccentric Texas billionaire crime solver on *J. J. Starbuck* from 1987 to 1988, he also made a good government agent as the top man in *Melvin Purvis, G-Man*, the 1974 television movie about the guy who brought down Machine Gun Kelly.

Star Angela Lansbury plays Jessica Beatrice Fletcher, who is quite a good mystery writer but is equally adept at crime solving on *Murder, She Wrote* (1984–96).

Jessica Fletcher's Famous Power Loaf

Recipe, she wrote!

2 cups boiling water
1½ cups cracked-wheat cereal
3 tablespoons soft shortening
2 tablespoons honey

1 tablespoon salt
2 packages active dry yeast
⅔ cup warm water (105° to 115°)
4 cups stone-ground whole wheat flour, divided
2 handfuls bran flakes
2 handfuls quick-cooking oats
½ cup wheat germ

Pour boiling water over the cracked-wheat cereal and stir. Add the shortening, honey, and salt to the cereal. Set the mixture aside to cool until it's lukewarm.

Dissolve the yeast in the warm water and add it to the cereal mixture. Gradually stir in 3 cups of the whole wheat flour. Then stir in the bran flakes, oats, and wheat germ. Mix all the ingredients very well and cover the bowl with a damp cloth. Let the dough rise until it has doubled in bulk. (That takes about 1 hour to 1 hour and 15 minutes, so I sometimes start the dough and then go out to the garden while it's rising.)

When the dough has doubled, punch it down and knead it, blending as much of the remaining flour as you need to keep it from being too runny. Knead the dough until it is fairly elastic and smooth. Then divide the dough in half. Place each half in a 5x9-inch loaf pan. Cover the two loaves and set them in a warm place where they will rise again. When the dough has risen, preheat the oven to 350°. Bake the loaves for 45 minutes, or until the bread is nicely browned.

Serving Suggestion: For a wonderful snack, I love a slice of this bread, still warm from the oven, with some plum jam and a cup of tea.

Makes 2 loaves.

Angela Lansbury

Boise in Blue Batter Bread

■ This recipe produces a heavy, yeasty loaf that is great with soup or salad for a complete meal.

1½ **tablespoons shortening or butter**
1 **cup milk**
1 **tablespoon sugar**
1 **tablespoon salt**
2 **packages active dry yeast**
1 **cup warm water**
4½ **cups all-purpose flour**

Preheat the oven to 400°. Melt the shortening and combine with the milk, sugar, and salt. Dissolve the yeast in the warm water. Combine all the ingredients, alternating flour with liquid until completely mixed without lumps. Immediately pour the batter into a greased 5x9-inch loaf pan. Bake for 45 minutes or until the top is golden brown.

Makes 1 loaf.

Larry Paulson
Chief of Police
Boise, Idaho

NOW STARRING

Match the actor to the film.

1. Dana Andrews	A. *Beverly Hills Cop*
2. Joe Don Baker	B. *Bullitt*
3. Kevin Costner	C. *Chinatown*
4. Clint Eastwood	D. *The French Connection*
5. Morgan Freeman	E. *The Fugitive*
6. Mel Gibson	F. *Laura*
7. Gene Hackman	G. *Lethal Weapon*
8. Bob Hoskins	H. *Magnum Force*
9. Tommy Lee Jones	I. *Seven*
10. Steve McQueen	J. *The Untouchables*
11. Eddie Murphy	K. *Walking Tall*
12. Jack Nicholson	L. *Who Framed Roger Rabbit?*

SOLUTION

1. F, 2. K, 3. J, 4. H, 5. I, 6. G, 7. D, 8. L, 9. E, 10. B, 11. A, 12. C

Captain McEnroe's Family Cornbread

■ This is a recipe that has been handed down through our family, the Bumgarners, for generations.

½ cup all-purpose flour
1 cup yellow cornmeal
½ cup yellow grits
1 teaspoon salt
2 tablespoons sugar
1½ teaspoons baking powder
1 cup buttermilk
3 tablespoons bacon grease or oil
1 egg

Preheat well-greased cast-iron cornstick pans to 400°. Stir together all the dry ingredients. Add all the liquid ingredients. Pour batter into hot cornstick pans. Bake for 20 minutes.
  Makes about 1½ dozen.

Jack Garner

Chief's Cheese Biscuits

3¼ cups all-purpose flour
½ teaspoon baking soda
½ teaspoon salt
2 to 4 tablespoons fresh herbs, chopped fine (optional)
1½ to 1¾ cups buttermilk
    Tillamook sharp cheddar cheese, shredded
    Small amount melted butter or margarine

Preheat the oven to 450°. In a bowl, mix together the flour, baking soda, salt, and herbs. Stir in the buttermilk until the dough is moistened and leaves the side of the bowl. Turn the dough out onto a floured surface and knead gently a few times to smooth. Pat or roll out to ½-inch to ¾-inch thickness. Cut into squares or triangles. Place on a greased baking sheet. Brush with a small amount of melted margarine or butter. Sprinkle with the

On *The Rockford Files,* Jack Garner's (left) Captain McEnroe had more than a few awkward encounters with brother James Garner's Jim Rockford, but all's fair in love and golf when the brothers hit the links.

desired amount of cheese. Bake for 15 to 20 minutes. Remove from the sheet and serve. (These biscuits also freeze well.)

Makes about 2 dozen.

Charles A. Moose, Ph.D.
Chief of Police
Portland, Oregon

Police Academy Garlic Bread

2　sticks butter
2　cloves fresh garlic
1　teaspoon garlic salt
½　teaspoon garlic powder
1　tablespoon prepared
　　minced garlic
　　Fresh French or Italian
　　bread, unsliced
　　Parmesan cheese, grated

Melt the butter in a large skillet. Smash the garlic cloves and mince. Add to the butter and cook over low heat. Combine the garlic salt and garlic powder with the cooked garlic. Let cook over low heat for a couple of minutes, stirring constantly. Cut the whole loaf of bread in half and then slice lengthwise in half again. You should now have 4 equal-sized pieces. Dip each piece in the garlic-butter mixture to coat the top. Sprinkle Parmesan cheese on top and set aside. Turn broiler on or use a toaster oven. Wait until the temperature is very hot and then place the bread under the broiler for approximately 1 minute or until golden brown. Remove from oven, slice, and serve. You'll have a crispy top with soft bread.

Makes 1 loaf.

Michael Winslow

Michael Winslow is a stand-up comic with an incredible array of sounds at his disposal. As Officer Larvelle Jones, Winslow unleashed a barrage of his sound effects throughout six *Police Academy* films.

> *"That is why you'll never be a great detective, Cato. It's so obvious that it could not possibly be a trap."*
>
> —*Jacques Clouseau*
> *(Revenge of the Pink Panther)*

Armed and Dangerous Apple Bread

This smells so good while it's baking!

½ cup vegetable shortening or margarine
1 cup sugar
2 eggs
1 cup sifted all-purpose flour
½ teaspoon salt
1 teaspoon vanilla extract
1 teaspoon baking soda, dissolved in 2 tablespoons sour milk
2 cups of unpeeled apples, cored and cut into small pieces
2 tablespoons sugar
2 teaspoons ground cinnamon

Preheat the oven to 325°. Cream the shortening and 1 cup of sugar together. Add the eggs, flour, salt, and vanilla. Add the baking soda-milk mixture and mix together. Stir in the apples. Place the mixture into a greased 5x9-inch loaf pan. Sprinkle the 2 tablespoons of sugar and the cinnamon on top. Bake for 1 hour. Allow the baked bread to cool for 15 minutes before turning out of the pan.

Makes 1 loaf.

Ben Click
Chief of Police
Dallas, Texas

Walking Tall Diet Banana Bread

It'll help you walk small.

½ cup vegetable shortening
20 packages artificial sweetener
2 eggs, beaten
1 teaspoon baking soda
3 bananas, mashed
2 cups all-purpose flour
1 teaspoon vanilla extract
¼ to ½ cup chopped nuts

Preheat the oven to 325°. Cream the shortening and sweetener together. Add the eggs and mix together. Add the remaining ingredients and mix well. Pour into a greased 5x9-inch loaf pan. Bake for 1 hour and 15 minutes.

Makes 1 loaf.

Sheriff Buford Pusser
Submitted by sister Gail Davis

Legendary Sheriff Buford Pusser.

From 1972 to 1974, Richard Boone starred in *Hec Ramsey*, one of the rotating elements of *The NBC Sunday Night Mystery Movie*. Ramsey was a rugged old gunfighter who had found the science of criminology to be a boon in snaring lawbreakers.

Hec Ramsey's Mango Bread

■ We lived in Hawaii for some years and picked this recipe up there. Enjoy!

2 **cups all-purpose flour**
1 **cup sugar**
½ **cup firmly packed brown sugar**
2 **teaspoons baking soda**
½ **teaspoon salt**
1 **teaspoon ground cinnamon**
3 **eggs, beaten**
1 **cup vegetable oil**
1 **teaspoon vanilla extract**
1 **cup chopped nuts**
¾ **cup raisins**
2 **large, ripe mangoes**

Preheat the oven to 325°. In a large bowl, mix together the flour, sugars, baking soda, salt, and cinnamon. Add the eggs, oil, vanilla, nuts, and raisins and mix well. Over this mixture, slice the mangoes so that the juice drips into the mixture. (If the mangoes are not very juicy, add a little bit of orange juice.) Stir in the mangoes. The mixture will be quite thick. Pour into 2 greased 5x9-inch loaf pans. Bake for about 1 hour. After 45 minutes test with a skewer or toothpick. When it comes out clean, bread is done. Slice and serve warm. Add vanilla ice cream for a delicious dessert. (This also freezes well after cooling.)

Makes 2 loaves.

Richard Boone
Submitted by Claire (Mrs. Richard) Boone

Pat Hingle has played plenty of cops in his career, from Commissioner Gordon in the *Batman* movies to Chief Jannings in Clint Eastwood's *Sudden Impact*. On television, he starred as Deputy Police Chief Paulton on *Stone* in 1979, and he was a friend of Jessica Fletcher as NYPD Detective Lieutenant O'Malley on *Murder, She Wrote*.

Commissioner Gordon's Pumpkin Bread

■ This is not a diet bread, but it's worth it! It's my favorite!

2½ cups all-purpose or self-rising flour
2 teaspoons baking soda
½ teaspoon salt
1 teaspoon ground cinnamon
1 teaspoon ground nutmeg
1 3.4-ounce package lemon pudding mix, instant or regular
1 3.4-ounce butterscotch pudding mix, instant or regular
1 16-ounce can pumpkin

2 cups granulated sugar
5 eggs
1½ cups vegetable oil
1 tablespoon vanilla extract
2 cups chopped pecans

Preheat the oven to 350°. In a large bowl, sift together the flour, soda, salt, cinnamon, nutmeg, and the pudding mixes. In a second large bowl, mix together the pumpkin, sugar, eggs, cooking oil, and vanilla. Combine the two mixtures, and then add the pecans. Pour into 3 greased and floured 5x9-inch loaf pans. (I use sugar instead of flour.) Bake for 1 hour.

Makes 3 loaves.

Pat Hingle

Shamrock Box Bread

1 pound raw potatoes
2 cups cooked mashed potatoes
4 cups all-purpose flour
   Salt and pepper to taste
¼ cup melted bacon fat

Peel and grate the raw potatoes into a cheesecloth. Wring the potatoes over a bowl; save the liquid. Place the grated potatoes in a shallow pan and spread the mashed potatoes over top. Once the starch has settled in the leftover liquid, pour off the water, scrape out the starch, and spread over the mashed potatoes. Stir the flour into the potatoes and mix well. Add salt and pepper to taste. Add the bacon fat. Preheat the oven to 300°. Knead the mixture and roll onto a floured board. Shape into round flat cakes and cut a cross into the top. Bake on a bacon-greased sheet for 40 minutes. Serve hot with butter.

Makes about 2 dozen.

Lt. Patrick F. O'Brien
President
Police Emerald Society

Snoops Molasses Bread

Tim's a health nut!

2   cups whole wheat flour
½   cup soy flour
½   teaspoon ground cinnamon
¼   teaspoon salt
2   teaspoons baking powder
2   eggs, beaten
¼   cup vegetable oil (safflower is great)
¼   cup molasses
6   tablespoons honey
1   teaspoon grated orange rind
¾   cup milk

Preheat the oven to 350°. In a large mixing bowl, stir the first 5 ingredients together. In another bowl, beat the eggs, oil, molasses, honey, orange rind, and milk together. Stir the liquid mixture into the dry ingredients and combine carefully. The batter is going to be very stiff, so get strong! Turn the batter into an oiled loaf pan. Bake for 30 minutes or until a toothpick inserted into the center comes out clean.

Serving Suggestion: Slice the bread thick and serve with soup or fruit.

Makes 1 loaf.

Daphne and Tim Reid

Husband and wife Tim Reid and Daphne Maxwell Reid teamed up as partners against crime in the 1989 television series *Snoops*. Reid also played Detective "Downtown" Brown as he lent a hand to A. J. and Rick Simon on *Simon & Simon*.

Chris Cagney's Skillet Cornbread à la Aunt Ella

■ This offering comes from my grandmother's cookbook. She had three cookbooks published. This recipe is from her second book, entitled *Aunt Ella's Cookbook,* published in 1949. I picked it because it goes well with The Blonde's Baked Beans (p. 91)

2 cups boiling water
2 cups cornmeal
1 teaspoon salt
3 tablespoons bacon drippings
1 cup milk
2 eggs, beaten
3 tablespoons baking powder

Preheat the oven to 450°. In a mixing bowl, pour the boiling water over the cornmeal, stirring constantly. Mix in the salt. Melt the bacon drippings in an iron skillet. Make sure the skillet is well-covered, and pour the rest of the grease over the cornmeal mixture. Add the milk gradually and beat until smooth. Add the eggs and baking powder and mix lightly. Pour the mixture into the greased skillet and bake for 20 minutes.

Makes 8 to 10 servings.

Sharon Gless

Frank Furillo's S-O-S Muffins

No Salt, Oil, Sugar.

2 cups whole wheat flour
1 cup unbleached flour
1 tablespoon cinnamon
3½ tablespoons baking powder
   (preferably salt free)

Daniel J. Travanti as Capt. Frank Furillo.

Sharon Gless as Det. Chris Cagney.

1 cup raisins
2 to 3 cups apples, diced
1 cup (or less) apple juice concentrate
2 to 3 cups pineapple or apple juice

Preheat the oven to 400°. Mix all the ingredients well. The batter should be loose but not runny. Pour the batter into muffin tins. Bake for 35 to 45 minutes.
  Makes about 16.

Daniel J. Travanti

Sweet Magnolia Sweet Potato Bread

2 cups sugar
2 eggs
½ cup vegetable oil
⅓ cup water

1 cup cooked sweet potatoes
¾ cup chopped pecans or walnuts
1¼ cups all-purpose flour
½ teaspoon salt
1 teaspoon baking soda
1 teaspoon ground nutmeg
1 teaspoon ground cinnamon

Preheat the oven to 350°. Beat the sugar and eggs. Add the oil, water, sweet potatoes, and chopped nuts. Mix well. Combine the flour, salt, baking soda, nutmeg, and cinnamon. Add to the sweet potato mixture and mix thoroughly. Pour into a large greased loaf pan (fill half full). Bake for 1 hour or until golden brown.
  Makes 1 large loaf.

Robert L. Johnson
Chief of Police
Jackson, Mississippi

One of the great precinct commanders of television police history was Daniel J. Travanti's Capt. Frank Furillo on *Hill Street Blues* (1981–87). Travanti (center) sits with fellow cast members (left to right) Veronica Hamel as public defender Joyce Davenport, Taurean Blacque as Det. Neal Washington, Rene Enriquez as Lieutenant Calletano, Keil Martin as Det. Johnny LaRue, Michael Warren as Officer Bobby Hill, and Michael Conrad as Sgt. Phillip Esterhaus.

The hippest cops of the 1980s just might have been Philip Michael Thomas (left) and Don Johnson as Ricardo Tubbs and Sonny Crockett respectively (from 1984 to 1989) on *Miami Vice.*

Side Arms

SIDE DISHES AND VEGETABLES

Sergeant Jablonski's Kapusta

■ This recipe for a Polish version of sauerkraut is from Bob's mother. I learned it from her when Bob and I were engaged, and we still make it for holidays. It's great on hot dogs or with kielbasa. —Ida (Mrs. Robert) Prosky

2 28-ounce cans sauerkraut
1 medium onion, chopped
3 sticks butter
   Salt and pepper to taste

Empty the sauerkraut into a large pot and cover with water. Cook over medium heat for 40 minutes. Remove from heat and pour into a colander to drain. Rinse with cold water. Squeeze the water out of the sauerkraut 1 handful at a time (see why I do this only once a year?). Chop the sauerkraut handful by handful. In a large skillet, sauté the onion in 1 stick butter. Add the sauerkraut and the remaining 2 sticks butter to the onion. Cook for 30 minutes. Add salt and pepper to taste. Kapusta is even better when it's made a day ahead, stored (covered) in the refrigerator, and then reheated on top of the stove or in the oven before serving.

These amounts make enough for 12 ordinary people or 4 Proskys.

Robert Prosky

Robert Prosky joined the cast of *Hill Street Blues* in 1984 as Sgt. Stan Jablonski, a rough-hewn veteran cop who took over the opening roll call.

Buddy Ebsen cloaked himself with homespun charm when he starred as veteran private investigator Barnaby Jones (1974–80). One episode (pictured here) featured Ebsen's real-life daughter Bonnie Ebsen. For his portrayal as an intellectual detective, Ebsen was inducted into the worldwide Sherlock Holmes Society, an organization comprised of devotees of Sir Arthur Conan Doyle's cerebral sleuth.

Barnaby Jones Potato Casserole

1½ pounds shredded hash browns
1 bunch green onions, chopped
8 ounces plain yogurt or sour cream
1½ cups grated cheddar cheese
1 10¾-ounce can cream of broccoli (or cream of chicken) soup
1 sliver butter, melted
3 to 4 ounces (about ½ package) seasoned poultry-flavored stuffing mix
1 additional stick butter, melted

Preheat the oven to 325°. Mix together the hash browns, onions, yogurt or sour cream, cheese, soup, and sliver of butter. Put in a 9x13-inch baking dish. Mix the stuffing and the melted butter with a fork. Sprinkle on top of the casserole. Bake, uncovered, for 1½ hours.

Makes 8 servings.

Buddy Ebsen

Hart to Hart Pierogie

It has wonderful powers.

Cheese Mix:

2 big potatoes, cooked and mashed
1 stick margarine
   Salt and pepper to taste
2 pounds pot or hoop cheese
3 eggs

Sauerkraut Mix:

16 ounces sauerkraut
    Water
1 onion, chopped
1 stick margarine
   Salt and pepper to taste

Dough:

2½ pounds all-purpose flour
 4 eggs
16 ounces sour cream
    Salt to taste
    Warm water (to mix the flour)

In a large bowl, combine all the cheese mix ingredients, and mix together well. Set aside.

Rinse off the sauerkraut with water and pour off the water. Put the sauerkraut into a saucepan and add enough water to cover. Cook for 20 minutes. Rinse off and squeeze dry. Fry the chopped onion in the margarine until the onions are translucent. Add to the sauerkraut and mix. Add salt and pepper to taste and mix well. Set aside.

Mix together all of the dough ingredients and knead in a bowl. Cover with a towel and let stand for 10 minutes. Knead until smooth. Cut off a piece of dough, place on a floured board, and roll out to a ⅛-inch thickness. Cut into 2½-inch squares. Put dabs of cheese mix and sauerkraut in the center of a square. Place another square on top and pinch the edges all the way around to seal in the mixture. Repeat until all dough is used. Cook in salted water over medium heat. When pierogies float, they are done.

Makes 4 servings.

Stefanie Powers

Stefanie Powers and Robert Wagner were jet-setting supersleuths Jennifer and Jonathan Hart in *Hart to Hart* from 1979 to 1984. Lionel Stander, left, served as the Harts's chauffeur and confidant Max, and their favorite hound was named Freeway.

Frances McDormand won an Academy Award for her on-target portrayal of Brainerd, Minnesota, Police Chief Marge Gunderson in the 1996 Cohen Brothers film *Fargo*.

Marge's Mashed Perpotaters

"Yah!"

2 pounds small red potatoes, halved
4 ounces cream cheese, softened
¼ cup milk, plus more as needed
½ stick butter, softened
   Salt and pepper to taste
¼ cup chopped chives or scallions
¼ pound smoked salmon

In a large pot of salted water, boil the halved potatoes with the skins on until tender. Drain and return to the pot. In a small saucepan over low heat, combine the milk, butter, and cream cheese. Mash the potatoes with a hand masher. Pour the milk mixture in a little at a time until incorporated. Add extra milk if too dry. Add salt and pepper to taste. Just before serving, fold in the chives and salmon.

Makes 8 servings as a side dish or 4 servings as a main dish.

Frances McDormand

Cop's Kugelis (Lithuanian Potato Pudding)

3 pounds red potatoes
3 pounds white potatoes
½ pound bacon
1 large onion
2 teaspoons salt
½ teaspoon pepper
6 eggs
   Sour cream

Preheat the oven to 400°. Peel the potatoes and place in ice water to prevent discoloration. Cut the bacon crosswise into narrow strips and fry until it begins to crisp. Remove from heat. Grate the onion and potatoes with a food processor or hand grater. (We like a coarse texture, but experiment with the coarseness of the grating disc to get the consistency that you like.)

In a large mixing bowl, pour the bacon with fat over the grated onions and potatoes. Lightly beat the eggs, add to the potatoes, and mix together. Add the salt and pepper and mix well. Place in a loaf pan and bake for about 15 minutes. Reduce temperature to 375° and bake for 45 minutes more, or until the top is crisp and medium brown. (Make sure the mixture is at least 2½ inches deep in the loaf pan.) Serve with sour cream.

Makes about 4 servings.

Dennis E. Nowicki
Chief of Police
Charlotte-Mecklenburg, North Carolina

Holster Hash Browns

■ This recipe was designed for the camper who has brought plenty of food but only one frying pan. I've made this many times out on a riverbank over an open fire. Slide some bread onto a coat hanger and hold it over the fire to make toast. (This is making me hungry!)

½ stick butter
2 or 3 cups frozen hash browns (or chopped up potatoes cooked until brown)
½ cup chopped onions
2 eggs
1 cup grated cheese
  Sausage or bacon, cooked and drained (optional)

In a skillet over medium heat, melt the butter. Toss in the hash browns and the onions. Crack eggs into the mixture and stir the same as you would scrambled eggs. When the eggs have cooked, add the cheese and turn the heat to low. Serve when the cheese is melted.

Note: If you're cooking over an open fire and decide to add bacon or sausage, you can use the grease instead of the butter.

Makes 1 or 2 servings.

Gerald Ownby
Chief of Police
The North Pole, Alaska

Since 1993, Melissa Leo has portrayed Det. Kay Howard, whose character holds the record for most cases solved in *Homicide: Life on the Street*. She also appeared with Lou Gossett Jr. in episodes of *Gideon Oliver* and in the television movie *Carolina Skeletons*.

Interrogation Room Garlic Mashed Potatoes

But there's no 'box' involved here.

■ This recipe from my good friend Kevin McGowan goes well with Sergeant Howard's Stuffed Chicken with Tapenade (page 164).

1 bulb fresh peeled garlic
3 pounds red potatoes or "new" potatoes
1 stick unsalted butter
  Salt and white pepper to taste
1 cup milk or heavy cream

Preheat the oven to 400°. Place the peeled garlic in a lightly greased baking dish. Place the dish in the oven until the garlic is soft (about 20 minutes). Remove the garlic from the oven and place in a food processor or blender. Pulse to a purée.

Boil the potatoes in a pot until tender. Strain. Add the garlic, salt, and pepper. Mash until smooth. Add the butter and half of the milk or cream and mix well. The remaining milk is available, if needed.

Makes 4 servings.

Melissa Leo

Awesome Austin Candied Sweet Potatoes

6 medium sweet potatoes
1 cup packed brown sugar
1 stick margarine
¼ cup water

Clean and boil the potatoes until tender. Cool, peel, and cut the potatoes in half lengthwise, then place in a baking dish. Combine the remaining ingredients in a small saucepan and bring to a boil. Boil for 5 minutes. Pour the mixture over the potatoes. Preheat the oven to 375°. Bake for 45 minutes, basting occasionally.
   Makes 4 to 6 servings.

Elizabeth M. Watson
Chief of Police
Austin, Texas

NEW BEATS

Match the movie stars to their television series.

1. Kim Basinger	A.	*Adams of Eagle Lake*
2. Charles Bronson	B.	*Bronk*
3. Melvyn Douglas	C.	*Cade's County*
4. Glenn Ford	D.	*Colonel March of Scotland Yard*
5. James Earl Jones	E.	*The Blue Knight*
6. Louis Jourdan	F.	*Dog and Cat*
7. Boris Karloff	G.	*Half Nelson*
8. Lee Marvin	H.	*Hollywood Off Beat*
9. Walter Matthau	I.	*I'm the Law*
10. Ray Milland	J.	*Madigan*
11. Roger Moore	K.	*Man With a Camera*
12. Nick Nolte	L.	*Markham*
13. Jack Palance	M.	*M Squad*
14. Joe Pesci	N.	*Paris*
15. George Raft	O.	*Paris Precinct*
16. Burt Reynolds	P.	*The Saint*
17. Richard Widmark	Q.	*Tallahassee 7000*
18. George Kennedy	S.	*Dan August*

SOLUTION
1. F, 2. K, 3. H, 4. C, 5. N, 6. O, 7. D, 8. M, 9. Q, 10. L, 11. P, 12. A, 13. B, 14. G, 15. I, 16. S, 17. J, 18. E

Jake Axminster's Zesty Pinto Beans

2 cups pinto beans
6 cups water, plus 6 more for soaking beans
1 teaspoon salt
1 teaspoon black pepper
1 teaspoon chili powder
1 teaspoon Lawry's seasoning salt
1 teaspoon ground oregano
2 tablespoons vegetable oil
1 large or 2 medium yellow or white onions, diced
4 green chili peppers, diced (optional)
4 to 6 cloves garlic, diced
1 medium green bell pepper, diced (optional)
4 medium red tomatoes, diced

Using a 4-quart soup pot, soak the pinto beans overnight in 6 cups of water. Rinse the presoaked beans and put them in a 4-quart soup pot filled with 6 cups of fresh cold water. Cook the beans on medium heat. Add the salt, pepper, chili powder, seasoning salt, and oregano after the beans start to boil.
   In a medium skillet add the vegetable oil; fry the onions, green chilies, garlic, and green bell peppers until lightly browned, then pour into the pot with the beans. Add the diced tomatoes and stir. Cover the beans and cook for 2 hours on medium heat.
   Serving Suggestion: Serve with cornbread or a nice loaf of sourdough bread. They also may be served over white rice.
   Makes 10 to 15 servings.

Wayne Rogers

Wayne Rogers starred as Jake Axminster in *City of Angels,* a 1976 detective series set in 1930s Los Angeles. He also played a good-guy police chief in the CBS miniseries *Chiefs.*

Mexican Jumping Bail Beans

3   cups dried pinto beans, sorted, debris
    removed, and washed
½   onion, quartered
4   cloves garlic
    Vegetable oil
    Grated cheese

For regular beans: Place the beans in a 6-quart pot and add enough water to cover the beans by about 1 inch. Bring to a boil and then reduce the heat to medium. Add the onion and garlic and cook for 2 hours, or until the beans are tender. (To cook a bit faster, you can soak the beans overnight.) You can serve the beans directly from the pot.

For refried beans: Use a slotted spoon to remove the onion and garlic from the beans. Heat a 10-inch skillet to medium hot with enough oil to cover the bottom of the pan. Add the amount of beans desired, minus any liquid. Allow the beans to simmer in the oil for about 3 minutes, then mash until creamy with a potato masher. If the beans are too dry, add liquid from the pot to satisfaction. Top with grated cheese, if desired, cover until the cheese is melted, and serve.

Makes about 4 servings.

Arturo Venegas Jr.
Chief of Police
Sacramento, California

Rockford's Refritos

■ James Garner (or "Mr. G" as he is known) cannot eat onions or garlic, but they are included for those who can enjoy them.

2   16-ounce cans pinto beans, drained
    and well rinsed
⅛   teaspoon garlic powder
¼   teaspoon cumin
¼   teaspoon chili powder
1   tablespoon diced green chilies
¼   cup salsa
½   cup chicken broth
2   tablespoons olive oil, divided
¼   large onion

It looks like breakfast time for Jim Rockford as he visits one of his favorite eateries, the taco stand conveniently located across the parking lot from his Malibu trailer. That's Sam (Al Checco) providing service with a smile. In the world beyond television, the taco stand is really the back side of the Sand Castle restaurant, another of the bachelor P.I.'s favorite hangouts.

Place the beans into a mixing bowl. Sprinkle with the garlic powder, cumin, and chili powder. Mash the ingredients with a potato masher. Add the green chilies, salsa, chicken broth, and 1 tablespoon of the olive oil. Mince the onion and sauté it in the remaining tablespoon of olive oil in a large skillet. When the onion is completely soft and golden brown, add the beans to the skillet. Cook the mixture over medium-low heat for about 10 minutes while stirring and scraping with a wooden spatula.

Makes 3 servings.

James Garner

The Blonde's Baked Beans

■ I make this for every family barbecue, and it's really a hit. It's so easy, and when they see you bring it out of the oven, they assume that you started from scratch. The problem about it is that I have never measured the ingredients. So, here goes...

2 **huge cans baked beans**
1 **or 2 huge red onions, chopped**
   Quite a lot of brown sugar
   Tons of Worcestershire sauce
   Lots of raw bacon strips

Sharon Gless played Det. Chris Cagney on the ground breaking, Emmy-winning 1980s police drama *Cagney & Lacey*.

Preheat the oven to 350°. Empty the cans of beans into a large ovenproof pot. (If the pot is really old and kind of beat up, it sells the authenticity of your family recipe from generations ago.) Add the onions. It's important to have lots of onions. Lots! Add the brown sugar. Just shake it out of the box—lots. Add the Worcestershire sauce. Just shake it right onto the beans. It will give the beans a darker color, plus real bite. Don't forget—lots! The trick here is to really put tons of the above ingredients in. Don't be shy. Then cover the whole dish with strips of raw bacon. You shouldn't be able to see the beans because there is so much bacon covering them.

Cover the pot and put it in the oven. Leave it in there for about 45 minutes, or until it is really bubbling. When it is hot all the way through, take off the cover, remove the bacon, and throw the bacon away.

Serving Suggestion: Set the pot out on the table with a big spoon. It's good with barbecued burgers. This recipe is not for the cholesterol conscious, but it tastes awfully good!

Makes tons of servings.

Sharon Gless

Richard Denning and Barbara Britton played Jerry and Pamela North, a husband-and-wife team of crimebusters who lived in New York's Greenwich Village on *Mr. and Mrs. North* (1952–54). In 1960 Denning starred in *Michael Shayne, Private Detective;* and he played the governor on *Hawaii Five-O.* Among Denning's mystery-film credits are *The Glass Key* with Alan Ladd and Veronica Lake, *Quiet Please, Murder,* and *The Glass Web.*

Mr. North's Corn Pudding

2 cups corn, canned, creamed, or
  cut off cob
2 eggs slightly beaten
2 tablespoons melted butter or margarine
1 teaspoon sugar
2 cups scalded milk
1 teaspoon salt
¼ teaspoon pepper

Preheat the oven to 325°. Combine all of the ingredients and thoroughly mix. Pour into a greased casserole dish. Place the casserole in a pan of hot water. Bake for about 45 minutes, or until firm.

Makes 6 servings.

Richard Denning

Commissioner's Cranberry Relish

12 ounces fresh cranberries
¾ cup confectioners' sugar
  Rind and juice of 1 orange
½ cup water or ½ cup orange juice
1 stick cinnamon
¼ teaspoon ground ginger
3 cloves
2 tablespoons port or Grand Marnier

Place all the ingredients in a saucepan, stir until the sugar dissolves, then bring to a boil. Reduce heat and simmer without a lid until the cranberries pop—about 4 to 5 minutes. Remove from heat. Serve hot or cold. It can be made in advance and refrigerated for Thanksgiving or Christmas dinner. It is also wonderful with roast chicken and pork almost any time of year.

Makes about 3 cups.

*Gil Kerlikowske
Commissioner of Police
Buffalo, New York*

Lieutenant Gerard's Baked Apples

4 cooking apples
1 tablespoon mixed candied citrus peel,
  chopped
1 tablespoon raisins or currants
1 tablespoon brown sugar
1 teaspoon lemon juice
1 teaspoon cinnamon
8 cloves
¼ cup corn syrup or honey
  Ground cinnamon
½ stick butter

Preheat the oven to 350°. Wash and core the apples. Combine the candied peel, raisins, brown sugar, lemon juice, and cinnamon. Stuff the apples with this mixture. Slash the apple peel in a few places to prevent bursting. Stud each with 2 cloves. Place in a baking dish and add just enough water to cover the bottom. Drizzle the syrup over the apples and sprinkle with a little cinnamon. Place a dollop of butter on top of each apple. Bake for 40 minutes, or until the apples are tender.

Makes 6 servings.

Barry Morse

Ricardo Tubbs's Macaroni and Cheese

1 teaspoon salt
Water
8 ounces macaroni noodles, uncooked
8 ounces evaporated milk
2 teaspoons margarine or butter
4 ounces sour cream
4 ounces cream cheese
Garlic salt
Seasoned salt
Pepper
8 ounces shredded jalapeño Jack cheese
8 ounces shredded Colby cheese
4 ounces shredded medium cheddar cheese

Boil the water and salt in a big enough pot to handle the noodles. Cook the noodles according to package directions. Rinse with hot water when done. In a saucepan over medium heat, combine the milk and the margarine or butter. Add the sour cream and cream cheese, and cook until blended together. Add the garlic salt, seasoned salt, and pepper to taste. Set aside.

Preheat the oven to 350°. In a large baking pan, layer half the macaroni over the bottom. Cover with half of the cheese mixture. Then make a layer with the rest of the macaroni and top it with the cheese mixture. Sprinkle the 3 shredded cheeses over all. Bake, covered, for about 20 to 30 minutes.

Makes 4 servings.

Philip Michael Thomas

Philip Michael Thomas played Ricardo Tubbs in the 1980s police drama *Miami Vice.*

Colorado Cops Casserole

2 16-ounce cans Veg-All, drained
1 cup mayonnaise
1 medium onion, chopped
1 cup grated cheddar cheese
1 10½-ounce can cream of celery soup
½ soup can of milk
1 sleeve, Ritz crackers, crushed
¾ stick butter, melted

Preheat the oven to 350°. Combine the vegetables, mayonnaise, onion, and cheese. Dilute the soup with the milk and fold into the vegetable mixture. Pour into a buttered casserole dish. Top with the crushed crackers and pour the melted butter over all. Bake for 20 minutes. The leftovers are delicious too!

Makes about 6 servings.

David L. Michaud
Chief of Police
Denver, Colorado

For more than fifteen years, James Reynolds's Abe Carver has preserved law and order on NBC's *Days of Our Lives*. As Police Commander, Abe Carver is the top cop in Salem.

Abe Carver's Spicy Apple Sausage Dressing

6 green apples (Pippin, if available), chopped
2 large white onions, chopped
5 to 6 ribs celery, chopped
2 sticks butter, divided
2 loaves bread (wheat, white, or egg)
6 hot Italian sausages, with skins removed, and then crumbled and browned
1 tablespoon sage
   Tabasco sauce
   Salt and pepper

In a large skillet, sauté the apples, onions, and celery in 1 stick of the butter (or less, as needed) until the onions are translucent. Preheat the oven to 350°. In a separate bowl, crumble the bread. Stir in the cooked sausage, 1 stick of melted butter, and sage. Add the bread mixture to the apple mixture and stir. Liberally dash on Tabasco sauce to taste. Salt and pepper to taste. Place in a baking dish. Bake for about 20 minutes or until lightly browned.

Makes 6 servings.

James Reynolds

HARD-BOILED DETECTIVES

Match the actor to the detective.

1. Don Adams   A. Stuart Bailey
2. Buddy Ebsen   B. Richard Diamond
3. Jim Hutton   C. Byron Glick
4. David Janssen   D. Peter Gunn
5. Stacy Keach   E. Mike Hammer
6. Joe Penny   F. Barnaby Jones
7. Craig Stevens   G. Ellery Queen
8. Mario Van Peebles   H. Sonny Spoon
9. Ben Vereen   I. Jake Styles
10. Efrem Zimbalist Jr.   J. Tenspeed

SOLUTION
1. C, 2. F, 3. G, 4. B, 5. E, 6. I, 7. D, 8. H, 9. J, 10. A

Rockford's Trailer Dressing

It's without pier!

■ We have this dressing every Thanksgiving and Christmas. It originates from Lois's mother, Sara.

2 dozen kaiser rolls
1 onion, very finely chopped
1 head celery hearts, finely chopped
2 raw eggs
   Salt and pepper to taste
   Chicken fat to taste

Preheat the oven to 350°. Soak the rolls in water just long enough to moisten. Squeeze out the water and crumble the rolls. Mix all the ingredients together in a large wooden bowl. Place in a round casserole dish. Bake, uncovered, for 1 hour. Stir to prevent crusting.
   Makes 6 to 8 servings.

James Garner

Top Secret Dilly Brussels Sprouts

Declassified: Delicious

1 10-ounce package frozen
   brussels sprouts
½ cup Italian dressing
1 tablespoon sliced green onion
½ teaspoon dill seed

Cook the sprouts in a saucepan of water over medium heat. Drain the water off. Mix all the other ingredients together and pour over the sprouts. Chill for several hours. Serve either as a side dish, or with toothpicks, as an appetizer.
   Makes 4 servings as a side dish.

David D. Whipple
Executive Director
Association of Former Intelligence Officers

> *"That Number four you just picked up from Angelo's Pizza? Some scouring powder fell in there. Don't eat it! Hey, I hope you try your phone machine before dinner."*
>
> —Message on Jim Rockford's Answering Machine

James Garner starred in *The Rockford Files* (1974–80) as Jim Rockford, a hard-luck private eye once wrongly imprisoned for a crime he didn't commit and a man with many ex-cons for friends. Several CBS movies based on *The Rockford Files* have picked up the detective's trail in the 1990s.

Goode Guy's Bunco Squash

■ This is one meal I can never turn down!

5 good-sized yellow or zucchini squash
1 medium onion
1 cup all-purpose flour
  Salt and pepper to taste
4 tablespoons margarine or vegetable oil

Wash the squash and slice them ¼-inch thick, or less. Put in a large bowl and run the slices under water and then drain. Chop the onion and mix with the squash. Add the flour and the salt and pepper to taste. Mix well until the squash is covered with flour. Some folks prefer to have the flour, salt, and pepper in a separate bowl and cover the squash piece by piece. If you've got all day, have at it. Otherwise, go ahead and coat the bottom of a warm skillet (I prefer cast-iron) with melted margarine or oil. Put the floured squash into the skillet and cook over medium or medium-low heat. Turn the squashes from time to time with a spatula until good and brown. Serve with corn bread.
  Makes about 4 servings.

Randall Franks

He's a bluegrass musician and southern humorist from Georgia, but Randall Franks played it straight as Officer Randy Goode on *In the Heat of the Night*, set in Sparta, Mississippi.

Spanakopita (Spinach Pie) à la Telly

This dish is a Telly vision!

3 pounds spinach
1 large onion, finely chopped
½ cup olive oil, divided
½ cup parsley
8 eggs, beaten
1 pound feta cheese, crumbled
½ cup chopped fresh mint or dill
  (optional)
  Salt
½ pound phyllo pastry leaves
1 stick butter, melted

Wash the spinach thoroughly, dry completely with paper towels, cut off the stems, and chop. Brown the onion in 3 tablespoons of the olive oil. Combine the spinach, parsley, eggs, cheese, and mint or dill. Add the cooked onions. Season lightly with salt and mix well. Preheat the oven to 350°. Grease a 9x13-inch baking pan and line it with 5 of the phyllo sheets, brushing each sheet with the melted butter and remaining olive oil. Spread the spinach mixture over the phyllo and top with the remaining sheets of phyllo, again brushing each with the butter and oil. Brush the top sheet. Bake for 45 minutes. Cool and cut into squares.
  Serving Suggestion: This dish is wonderful as a main course, with a fresh horiatiki salata (Kojak's Greek Village Salad, p. 42) to accompany it. Yasou!
  Makes 8 to 10 servings.

*Telly Savalas
Submitted by Julie
(Mrs. Telly) Savalas*

Francis McDormand takes aim as Chief Marge Gunderson in *Fargo*.

Fargo Roadblock Red Peppers

You'll stop for these. "You betcha!"

  6 **red peppers**
     Juice of 2 lemons
  2 **large cloves garlic, crushed**
     Pinch red pepper flakes (optional)
  1 **cup olive oil**
 10 **large basil leaves**
  2 **sprigs rosemary**

Clean, dry, and halve the red peppers. Discard the stems and seeds.

Roasting Method #1: Place the pepper halves, skin side up, on a broiler pan that's close to the heat. Roast for 20 to 25 minutes until the skin is blackened.

Roasting Method #2: Take the whole pepper, skewer it on a fork, and rotate over a high gas flame or stove top until the skin is blackened.

Place the roasted peppers in a plastic bag and seal tightly. Set aside for about 15 minutes, or until cool enough to handle. (This steams the skin loose.) In a 1-quart sealable jar (old glass Mason canning jars are perfect and make a good-looking present), combine the lemon juice, crushed garlic, and pepper flakes, if desired.

Take the peppers out of the bag one at a time and keep the bag sealed on the remaining peppers. Peel off the blackened skin, cut into strips, and place in the container with lemon juice mixture. Cover with the olive oil. Add the basil and rosemary. Stir with a spoon to incorporate the lemon juice and oil. Let cool, unsealed, and then seal and refrigerate. The peppers will keep for up to 3 weeks.

Makes 1 quart.

Frances McDormand

One of television's most colorful police dramas was *The Untouchables* (1959–63), starring Emmy winner Robert Stack as Eliot Ness. Ness was a real-life federal agent determined to defeat Prohibition-era gangsterism. In the 1990s Stack wrestles with crimes and mysteries by hosting *Unsolved Mysteries*.

Eliot Ness's Creamed Spinach

Your whole gang will love it!

1 10-ounce package frozen chopped
    spinach
1 teaspoon A-1 Steak Sauce
¼ teaspoon curry powder
½ can Aunt Penny's White Sauce (or
    make 1 cup of your own white sauce)
    Squeeze of fresh lemon
    Salt and pepper to taste

In a large saucepan, bring the spinach to a boil in water according to package directions. Pour off the water and reduce heat. Stir in the remaining ingredients and heat through. That's it—very easy and good!

Makes 2 to 3 servings.

Robert Stack

Harper's Creamed Spinach

1 pound fresh spinach
⅛ teaspoon ground nutmeg
3 ounces cream cheese, softened
½ cup heavy cream
1 egg

Wash the spinach and trim the ends. Place the spinach in a saucepan with just the water that clings to the leaves. Sprinkle with nutmeg. Cover and steam for 2 to 3 minutes or just until the leaves are wilted. Drain any excess liquid. Finely chop the spinach and return to the saucepan.

Beat the cream cheese in a small bowl until fluffy. Gradually beat in the heavy cream and egg until well blended. Stir the cream cheese mixture into the chopped spinach. Heat over medium heat, stirring frequently until well blended and creamy. Serve immediately.

Makes 4 servings.

Paul Newman

Naked City Red Beans and Rice

2 pounds red beans
2 cups chopped onions
1 teaspoon minced garlic
2 cups chopped celery
1 cup chopped green pepper
¼ cup olive oil
3 teaspoons salt
    Pepper to taste
2 smoked ham hocks
2 large bay leaves
6 cups water
    Hot pepper sauce to taste
6 cups cooked rice

Rinse the beans and place in a large pot and cover with water, plus about 3 more inches of water. Bring to a boil, and continue to boil for 3 minutes. Remove from heat, cover, and let stand for 1 hour. Do not drain. In a skillet, sauté the onion, garlic, celery, and pepper in olive oil until wilted. Season with salt and pepper. Add the ham hocks and bay leaves to the beans, stir in the vegetable mixture, and add 6 cups of water (or beef broth, if you prefer). Bring to a boil and simmer, uncovered for approximately 1 hour to 1½ hours. Add hot pepper sauce to taste.

Serving Suggestion: This dish should be on the soupy side as it is served over rice. If the beans are a bit thick, add more water or broth as needed. You can also serve grilled andouille sausage or some other smoked sausage. This makes a very good meal with iced tossed salad and French bread.

Makes 6 to 8 servings.

Paul Burke

Frank McBride's Risotto

A nice switch.

1¾ cups dried porcini mushrooms
 1 cup warm water

6 cups beef stock
1 stick unsalted butter
1 medium white onion, chopped
4 fresh sage leaves
2 cups Arborio rice
¾ cup dry red wine
3 tablespoons chopped parsley
¾ cup fresh grated Parmesan cheese

Soak the mushrooms in warm water for 40 minutes. Strain the liquid and reserve. Bring the beef stock to a boil and continue to simmer. In a large saucepan, melt 3 tablespoons of the butter. Add the onion and sage. Cook until the onion is translucent. Add the rice and cook until well toasted. Add the wine and cook until absorbed. Stir in the mushroom juice and then the mushrooms. Add the beef stock, 1 cup at a time, until absorbed. Remove from heat and add the parsley, cheese, and the rest of the butter. Mix well and serve.

Makes 4 servings.

Eddie Albert

Eddie Albert, Robert Wagner, and Sharon Gless starred in *Switch*, the 1975–78 television series about a retired bunco-squad cop turned private detective who is partnered with his former nemesis, a charming ex-con man. Albert was Frank MacBride, Wagner was Pete Ryan, and Gless portrayed Maggie, an all-around girl Friday. (Several years later she starred in *Cagney & Lacey* as Det. Chris Cagney.)

San Diego Spicy Rice

1 cup uncooked rice
3 tablespoons vegetable oil
1 small purple onion, chopped
½ teaspoon chopped garlic, chopped
1 medium tomato, chopped
1 jalapeño pepper, chopped
½ cup chopped cilantro, chopped
2½ cups chicken broth
½ teaspoon black pepper
  Avocado
  Leafy cilantro

In a saucepan on high heat, brown the rice in the oil. Add the onion, garlic, tomato, jalapeño pepper, and cilantro to the rice. Add the broth and black pepper and bring the mixture to a boil. Lower the heat and simmer for about 35 minutes. Garnish with avocado and leafy cilantro. Enjoy!

Makes 2 to 3 servings.

Jerry Sanders
Chief of Police
San Diego, California

Twelve O'Clock High Creole Rice

3 cups tomato juice
3 cups chicken broth
¼ cup olive oil
1 large onion, diced
1 teaspoon minced garlic
  (don't be afraid)
1 medium green pepper, diced
1 large tomato, diced
1 tablespoon capers
8 ounces chopped black olives
2 tablespoons chopped parsley
  Salt and pepper to taste
½ stick butter
2 cups uncooked rice
  A few drops of hot sauce

Heat the tomato juice and broth and set aside. In a skillet, add the olive oil and sauté the onion until wilted. Add the gar-

Paul Burke starred as Det. Adam Flint in *Naked City* (1960–63), which was shot on location in New York City. He starred in *The Thomas Crown Affair* (1968) as a detective trying to pin a bank robbery on a supercool millionaire played by Steve McQueen. In 1986 Burke played Nicholas Broderick, the editor of *CrimeWorld* magazine, in the television series *Hot Shots*.

Burke is an amateur chef who has long enjoyed preparing gourmet dishes for which his mother was famous when his parents operated a number of nightclubs in New Orleans.

lic and green pepper and sauté for 2 to 3 minutes. Add the tomato, capers, olives, parsley, salt and pepper to taste, and sauté for 2 to 3 minutes and set aside.

In a deep skillet, melt the butter and then add the rice and toss. Sauté until golden. (Be careful not to burn the butter or the rice.) Add the vegetable mixture and blend. Pour in 3 cups of the liquid and a few drops of hot sauce to your liking, and stir. Cover and simmer until most of the liquid is absorbed. Continue to add liquid 1 cup at a time until the liquid is absorbed and the rice is almost done. Turn off the heat. Cover and allow to sit for five minutes. Fluff with a fork and serve.

Makes 4 servings.

Paul Burke

North of the Border Mexican Rice

¼ cup vegetable oil
1 cup long-grain rice
½ white or yellow onion, finely diced
3 cloves garlic, minced
¼ teaspoon cumin
2 cups water
2 chicken bouillon cubes, or 2 teaspoons
   chicken bouillon granules
4 ounces tomato sauce

Heat the oil in a 10-inch skillet and add the rice and diced onion. When the rice is browned and the onion is soft, add the garlic and cumin, and sauté. Stir in the water, bouillon cubes, and tomato sauce. Simmer until steam vents form and the liquid is absorbed by the rice. Cover and turn the heat to low and simmer for 14 minutes. Take the pan off the heat and allow it to sit for 5 minutes, still covered.

After 5 minutes, remove the cover and fluff the rice. Enjoy!
    Makes 2 servings.

Arturo Venegas Jr.
Chief of Police
Sacramento, California

Schanke's Spanokorizo Surprise

1 small onion
1 clove garlic
1 tablespoon olive oil
1 20-ounce can unseasoned stewed
   tomatoes
   Pinch oregano
1 cup Uncle Ben's converted (or other
   parboiled) rice
1 cup water
1 10-ounce bag spinach, washed and
   finely chopped

Chop the onion and garlic and gently brown them in a good saucepan with the olive oil over medium heat. Add the tomatoes and oregano and gently bring to a boil. Add the rice and the water, and bring to a boil again. When the rice is cooked (in less than 20 minutes), fold in the spinach and cook gently for another 5 minutes, or until the spinach is cooked. Serve with fresh bread. Enjoy!
    Makes 2 to 4 servings.

John Kapelos

John Kapelos played as swell a partner as a vampire cop could ever have when he co-starred as Det. Don Schanke, pal to everlasting Nick Knight, on *Forever Knight* from 1992 to 1996.

Angie Dickinson as Sgt. Pepper Anderson in *Police Woman*.

The Precinct

ENTRÉES

Smith Family Swedish Meatballs

½ cup bread crumbs
½ cup milk
½ cup finely minced yellow onion
3 tablespoons sweet butter, divided
1 pound lean ground beef
1 pound ground veal
1½ teaspoons salt
⅛ teaspoon freshly ground black pepper
½ teaspoon ground cinnamon or ¼ teaspoon ground nutmeg
2 eggs, lightly beaten
Several teaspoons milk
Heavy cream (for optional sauce)

Soak the bread crumbs in the ½ cup milk until the liquid is absorbed. Mix with a fork to form a smooth texture. Sauté the onion slowly in 1 tablespoon butter until golden brown; remove the onion to a mixing bowl. Add the beef, veal, salt, pepper, cinnamon, and eggs to the bowl. Mix well with your fingers. Place the bowl, tightly covered, in the refrigerator for several hours.

Preheat the oven to 350°. When the mixture is chilled, shape it into 2-inch balls. Heat the remaining butter in a large skillet until it begins to sizzle. Over medium heat, brown the meatballs quickly on all sides by shaking the pan.

Transfer the meatballs to an ovenproof baking dish.

Add a few teaspoons of milk to the skillet and deglaze over medium heat while stirring. Pour the milk mixture over the meatballs in the baking dish. Bake for about 15 minutes or until the meatballs are heated through.

Serving suggestion: Serve with mashed potatoes and sauce made from the juices in the casserole. Blend with a little heavy cream over direct flame until slightly reduced in volume to make a thin sauce. Season to taste.

Makes 4 to 6 servings.

Henry Fonda
Submitted by Shirlee (Mrs. Henry) Fonda

Henry Fonda was a family man and a Los Angeles plainclothesman, Sgt. Chad Smith, as the star of *The Smith Family* in 1971. He also played a big-city police commissioner in the 1968 film *Madigan*.

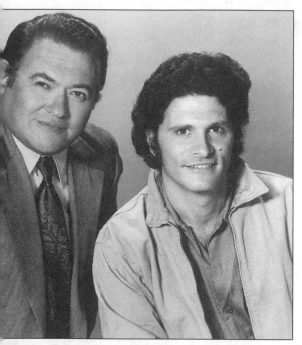

Tony Musante (right) starred as Det. Dave Toma and Simon Oakland played his boss, Inspector Spooner, in *Toma* in 1973. The series was based on the real-life exploits of New Jersey detective Dave Toma, who achieved an impressive arrest-and-conviction record by wearing various disguises and mingling with street people.

Toma's Flank Steak Antonio

■ With this recipe, I won first prize at a delightful celebrity cookout called "Uomo in Cucina" (Man in the Kitchen) in Florence, Italy. The recipe came originally from friend and fellow actor Pierre Olaf.

Flank steak (have the butcher give you enough for the number of guests you plan to serve)
4 to 6 garlic cloves, finely minced
2 to 4 tablespoons dried oregano
2 to 4 tablespoons basil
2 to 4 tablespoons thyme
Salt and pepper to taste
About ½ cup mixture of half olive oil and half safflower (or corn) oil (if you use all olive oil, it may taste better, but it tends to flare more on the grill)

Score the flank steak with about 3 to 4 evenly spaced horizontal slashes. Sprinkle the minced garlic evenly over the surface of the steak. Then sprinkle the 3 herbs over the surface to cover evenly. Add salt and pepper. Drizzle the combined oils over the meat to moisten the meat, leaving the steak totally covered with the oil. Turn the flank steak over and repeat the process. Place the steak in an ovenproof glass dish large enough to hold it. Cover tightly with foil or plastic wrap and let it marinate overnight in the refrigerator. If you don't have time for that, let it marinate at room temperature for at least 4 hours.

Prepare your grill by using either mesquite charcoal or regular charcoal with some hickory wood chips added for flavor. When the fire is hot, just after the charcoal has turned to a gray-white ash, grill the steak 5 minutes on each side, turning once. Remove from grill and let it sit, covered, for 5 to 10 minutes before slicing thinly against the grain. The slices should be slightly crusty on the outside but pink inside. It will be juicier if you let it sit before carving, allowing the juices to settle back into the meat.

The steak is especially good served with corn on the cob that has been cooked for about 25 minutes on the grill in its husk (with the corn silk removed before and the corn cob wrapped in the husk and soaked in salted water for a few hours prior to grilling, allowing the corn to steam inside the husk). Another good side dish is Insalata Caprese—slices of good summer-ripe tomatoes interspersed with slices of fresh Buffalo mozzarella cheese and dressed with salt, freshly ground pepper, olive oil, balsamic vinegar, and lots of fresh basil leaves.

Makes 4 to 8 servings, depending on the size of the steak.

Tony Musante

the meat (not into it). Place the steaks on the grill, about 4 inches from the hot coals, to scar. For a 1½-inch steak, sear on high, direct heat for 3 to 5 minutes on the first side. Turn with tongs and cook the second side on medium to low heat. Cook 5 to 8 minutes for medium and 12 to 15 minutes for well done. Because grills and broilers vary, it is best to check for doneness by slitting close to the bone or in the thickest part of the meat to peek. Enjoy!

Burt Reynolds

Burt Reynolds has played a cop in three television series. First he was Lt. John Hawk, a full-blooded Iroquois serving in New York City in the 1966 series *Hawk* (left). In 1970 he starred as Santa Luisa, California, Det. Dan August (below). In 1989 he returned to star as B. L. Stryker, a New Orleans cop turned Palm Beach private eye. On the big screen, Reynolds played a cop in *Fuzz* in 1972, a private eye in *Shamus* in 1973, and a tough vice cop in the 1981 film *Sharky's Machine*, which he directed.

Sharky's Machine
Marinated Steak à la Burt

1   tablespoon lemon juice
½ cup soy sauce
½ teaspoon Worcestershire sauce
1   teaspoon sugar
½ clove garlic, crushed
2   tablespoons of your best brandy or
    bourbon
    Dash of liquid red pepper seasoning
    Dash of ground ginger
    Thick-cut steaks (your choice)

Combine the first 8 ingredients. Let the steaks marinate in this mixture for at least 30 minutes—1 hour is even better. To broil or barbecue the steaks, trim the excess fat. Slash the remaining fat just to

Ethan Wayne, John Wayne's youngest son, played a cop in the films *McQ* and *Brannigan,* but he is best known as Officer Matt Doyle in *Adam 12* (1989–90).

> *"For a fugitive, there are no freeways. All roads are toll roads to be paid in blood and pain."*
>
> —William Conrad, the narrator
> *(The Fugitive)*

Matt Doyle's Adam-12 Steak Out

I love steak!

New York strip steak
Balsamic vinegar
Olive oil
Salt
Pepper

Take a large New York strip. (I like it butter-flied, but either way is fine.) Leave plenty of fat on the edge of the meat. Cover the meat with balsamic vinegar, and then splash with olive oil. Poke the meat repeatedly with a fork to tenderize it and let the marinade in. Salt and pepper to taste (I like a lot of salt and pepper); barbecue it.

Serving suggestion: I usually barbecue some hot Italian sausage, bell peppers, onion, and asparagus—all covered lightly with olive oil. I use some lemon slices for the sausage and serve with a nice slice of jalapeño bread. That's it!

Ethan Wayne

Bangor Cranberry Meatballs

■ These are the first things to be eaten at any family gathering.

1 12-ounce can whole-berry cranberry sauce
1 10-ounce bottle chili sauce
1 pound lean ground beef

Put the cranberry sauce and the chili sauce into a 6- to 8-quart pot and bring to a slow boil over medium heat. Meanwhile, roll the ground beef into 1-inch meatballs and place in the kettle with the sauce. Simmer the meatballs in the sauce over medium heat until the sauce thickens and the meatballs are cooked through (about 40 to 50 minutes). Serve hot by themselves or over rice.

Note: The recipe may be increased proportionately to make as many meatballs as needed. These proportions must be strictly followed. Increasing the proportion of ground beef will result in a greasy and thin sauce. Do not use ground beef that is less than 80 percent lean.

Makes about 3 dozen.

Randy Harriman
Chief of Police
Bangor, Maine

Manhunt Steak and Kidney Pie

2½ pounds top round steak, cut into small pieces
2 lamb or beef kidneys, cut into small pieces
¼ cup all-purpose flour
Salt
Freshly ground black pepper
1 teaspoon powdered mace
2 tablespoons vegetable oil
½ pound fresh mushrooms, sliced
3 medium onions, chopped
1 small clove garlic, chopped
2 cups meat stock or 1 8-ounce can beef consommé
1 cup port
Dash Worcestershire sauce
1 teaspoon dry mustard
1 bay leaf
Pastry for 1-crust pie
1 egg
2 tablespoons milk

Preheat the oven to 300°. Dredge the steak and kidney pieces in flour seasoned with salt, pepper, and mace. In a large, ovenproof casserole dish, heat the oil. Sauté the meat just to brown both sides. Add the mushrooms, onion, and garlic; continue cooking for about 5 minutes. Add the meat stock, port, Worcestershire sauce, dry mustard, and bay leaf. Cover and cook in the oven for 2½ hours. Remove from oven; chill and skim off the surface fat.

Preheat oven to 400°. Place the steak and kidney mixture in a deep 9-inch casserole dish or pie plate or into individual baking dishes. Cover with pastry, cutting slashes to allow steam to escape. In a small bowl, beat together the egg and milk and brush over the pie crust. Bake in the oven until the pie crust is golden brown.

Makes 6 to 8 servings.

Barry Morse

Barry Morse was the relentless Indiana police lieutenant Philip Gerard who pursued the fleeing Dr. Richard Kimble (David Janssen) in television's longest chase scene, on *The Fugitive* from 1963 to 1967. Morse's brother was a real-life bobby at London's Old Bailey.

Adam West may be world famous for his role in the mid-1960s as the Caped Crusader, but he starred as policemen in two other television series. West was Capt. Rob Wright on *The Last Precinct* in 1985, and he was Sgt. Steve Nelson on *The Detectives* in 1959. *Photograph courtesy of Steve Cox Collection.*

Caped Crusader Cast-Iron Skillet Pot Roast

■ I hang my skillet at home on my ranch in Idaho. This is my humble recipe, but it's not for humble pie!

1 **large chuck or 7-bone roasting cut of beef, elk, moose, or other meat**
   Herb salts and seasonings to taste
   Extra virgin olive oil and butter
4 **large onions, halved**
   Several large, fresh cloves garlic, peeled

Dried pepper flakes
Hot water
Potatoes (at least 1 per serving), cut into chunks
Carrots (at least 1 per serving), cut into strips
2 **ribs celery**
1 **apple, cut up but not peeled**
   A few dates or raisins
   Red wine (optional)
   Worcestershire sauce
1 **16-ounce package frozen green peas**

Season the roast well. Braise the meat in the olive oil and butter in a cast-iron skillet while adding the onion and garlic. The onion and garlic should be cooked until golden brown, not burned. Insert some of the garlic into the roast. Sprinkle some of the pepper flakes here and there. Preheat the oven to 400°. When the meat is well braised on the stove, turn heat off and add enough hot water (seasoned a bit) to submerge the celery ribs, some potato chunks, and carrot strips. The rest you will parboil and add later once the meat shrinks to give you more room in the skillet.

Add the apple pieces to the top of the roast and in the liquid. Slip a few dates and/or raisins into cracks in the meat. Carefully transfer the skillet to the oven. (The skillet will be heavy and quite hot by this time.) Cover the roast loosely with foil. Cook for about 4 hours or until the meat falls apart with a fork. Add water when needed in order to keep the vegetables mostly covered. About an hour before the roast is done to taste, add the parboiled vegetables to cook further in the juices. Season a bit more if you wish. Add some red wine and Worcestershire sauce to taste. Remove the foil for a bit to further brown the contents. About 10 minutes before serving, add the mostly thawed green peas to the center of the roast in an attractive heap. Recover with foil. The dog will be howling by now!

Serving suggestion: Serve from the skillet with some sourdough biscuits, which you can dip in the juices. Or you can make gravy. It is exciting to anticipate that there is little cleanup!

Makes 6 to 8 servings.

Adam West

.38 Caliber Meatballs

¾ **pound ground beef**
¼ **pound ground pork**
1 **cup Italian bread crumbs**
½ **cup grated Parmesan or Romano cheese**
1 **tablespoon parsley, minced**
3 **cloves garlic, finely chopped (reserve about 1 clove's worth)**
½ **cup milk**
2 **eggs, beaten**
1½ **teaspoons salt**
⅛ **teaspoon freshly ground pepper**
Vegetable oil seasoned with the reserved garlic and some minced onion
Your favorite meatball sauce

Combine the first 10 ingredients and form into 1-inch meatballs. Pan fry in the oil mixture until brown. Place the meatballs in your favorite sauce and simmer for about 1 hour.

Makes about 3 dozen.

Ernest A. Williams
Chief of Police
Trenton, New Jersey
Submitted by Det. Sgt. John P. Schroeder Sr.

MYSTERY MENAGERIE

Match the pet with the television series.

1. *Baretta*
2. *The Blue Knight*
3. *Columbo*
4. *Due South*
5. *Honey West*
6. *Hooperman*
7. *Longstreet*
8. *The Thin Man*
9. *Magnum, P.I.*
10. *Miami Vice*

A. Asta, a dog
B. Bijoux, a dog
C. Bruce, an ocelot
D. Diefenbaker, a wolf
E. Elvis, an alligator
F. Zeus and Apollo, Dobermans
G. Leo, a dog
H. Pax, a dog
I. Fred, a cockatoo
J. Dog, a dog

SOLUTION
1. I, 2. G, 3. J, 4. D, 5. C, 6. B, 7. H, 8. A, 9. F, 10. E.

Alien Nation Steak

2 pounds flank steak
½ cup cooking sherry
½ cup soy sauce
   Lots of crushed garlic
2 tablespoons honey
   Some fresh ginger, peeled and chopped

Marinate the steak for 24 hours in a sauce made from combining all the other ingredients. Broil the meat to a perfect medium rare. Use the drippings to pour over rice.
   Serving suggestion: Serve with Caesar salad.
   Makes about 4 servings.

Eric Pierpoint

Eric Pierpoint portrayed an out-of-this-world member of the Los Angeles Police Department as Det. George Francisco, a Newcomer from the planet Tencton, from 1990 to 1991 on Fox's *Alien Nation*. He also has appeared in other cop shows, such as *Hill Street Blues*, *Hot Pursuit*, and *In the Heat of the Night*.

Jailhouse Flank Steak

¼ cup vegetable oil
½ cup beer
2 tablespoons lemon juice
1 clove garlic, minced
1 teaspoon salt
1 bay leaf
½ teaspoon pepper
½ teaspoon dry mustard
½ teaspoon basil
½ teaspoon oregano
½ teaspoon thyme
1 flank steak, approximately 1½ pounds

Combine all the liquids, herbs, and spices, and pour over the steak. Refrigerate for several hours or overnight. To cook the steak, grill approximately 10 minutes per side. To serve, cut on a diagonal across the grain in slices.
   Makes 4 servings.

Gayle Ray
Davidson County Sheriff
Nashville, Tennessee

Kato's Oyster Sauce Beef

■ Bruce's favorite cuisine was, of course, Chinese, and I used to prepare the following recipe for him frequently. When we were dating and attending the University of Washington, almost every day we would go to a favorite Chinese restaurant and order this dish, plus perhaps one other and steamed rice. This dish is Cantonese and is found on many menus but is much tastier when prepared at home.

—*Linda Lee Caldwell*

1　**pound beef flank steak, sliced***
1　**tablespoon cornstarch**
1　**tablespoon rice wine or sherry**
1　**tablespoon dark soy sauce or regular soy sauce**
2　**teaspoons sugar**
2　**tablespoons canola, peanut, or other vegetable oil (or less if using a nonstick pan), divided**
1　**large onion, sliced vertically (Vidalia, Maui, or Walla Walla sweets, if available)**
2　**slices unpeeled ginger root about the size of a thick quarter**
2　**cloves garlic, peeled and mashed**
¼　**cup water**
4　**tablespoons oyster sauce**

The good guy in a number of martial arts feature films, such as *Enter the Dragon* and *Fists of Fury*, Bruce Lee first leapt to fame as Kato on *The Green Hornet* from 1966 to 1967.

Mix the beef slices well with the cornstarch, wine, soy sauce, and sugar. Set aside. Heat half the oil in a wok or frying pan over high heat until hot but not smoking. Add the onion, ginger slices, and garlic. Stir constantly for about 1 minute; then reduce the heat and stir until the onion is partially cooked but not brown. Remove from the pan.

Heat the remaining oil over high heat and add the beef slices. Cook and stir constantly for about 2 minutes; add the onion mixture and continue stirring for about 1 minute or until most of the pink of the meat is gone. Add the water and oyster sauce and then cook and stir until the beef is done and the mixture is thickened. Discard the garlic and ginger slices if desired. Serve immediately with a steamed or stir-fried green vegetable (spinach or broccoli is great) and steamed white or brown rice on the side. When combined with other dishes, it could also form part of a Chinese meal for more guests.

Makes 2 to 3 servings.

*To slice flank steak: Cut the steak lengthwise with the grain into long pieces about 2 inches wide. Then slice each piece against the grain into thin, 1/8-inch slices.

Bruce Lee
Submitted by Linda Lee Caldwell
(formerly Mrs. Bruce Lee)

Chief Inspector's Cottage Cheese Meat Loaf

1　pound lean ground beef or ground veal
1　cup cottage cheese
1　egg
1　cup quick-cooking rolled oats
¼　cup catsup
1　tablespoon prepared mustard
2　tablespoons chopped onion
¾　teaspoon salt
⅛　teaspoon pepper
⅓　cup grated Parmesan cheese

Preheat the oven to 350°. Combine the ground meat with the cottage cheese, egg, rolled oats, catsup, mustard, onion, salt, and pepper. Mix all the ingredients lightly until well blended. Press the mixture loosely into a shallow baking pan that is about 8 inches square. Bake, uncovered, in the oven for 20 minutes. Remove from the oven and sprinkle the Parmesan cheese evenly over the top. Return to the oven and continue to bake for 10 minutes. Let stand for 5 minutes before cutting into squares. (You can double the quantity and put one loaf in the freezer.)

Makes about 4 servings.

Blake Edwards

Meat Loaf Clouseau

■ This is sort of a cross between meat loaf and shepherd's pie.

2　pounds minced meat
2　eggs, slightly beaten
2　scant teaspoons salt
⅛　teaspoon pepper
6　ounces soft bread crumbs
2　ounces minced onion
½　teaspoon dried oregano or 1½ teaspoons freshly chopped
½　teaspoon dried basil
2　tablespoons minced parsley
3　pounds fresh mashed potatoes
2　egg yolks

Paprika
Parmesan cheese, grated

Preheat the oven to 400°. In a mixing bowl, blend the meat, 2 whole eggs, salt, pepper, crumbs, onion, and the herbs. Pack firmly into a round ovenproof bowl. Bake for 1 hour and 20 minutes. Completely drain off the liquid that accumulates by inverting the bowl on a wire rack. Pat the loaf dry and slide into a casserole dish or pie plate that is larger than the loaf.

In the meantime, prepare the mashed potatoes. Beat until fluffy and beat in the egg yolks. Frost the meat loaf with the potatoes. Sprinkle with paprika and Parmesan cheese and return the loaf to the oven for 25 to 30 minutes or until golden.

Makes about 6 servings.

Peter Sellers
Submitted by mother-in-law Iris Frederick

Slammer Stroganoff

1½　pounds round steak, cut into ½-inch strips
1½　cups chopped onion
3　tablespoons all-purpose flour
1　teaspoon garlic salt
1　6-ounce can diced, stewed tomatoes
1　4-ounce jar mushroom stems and pieces
½　cup water
1　tablespoon sugar
½　teaspoon Worcestershire sauce
8　ounces sour cream

Preheat the oven to 350°. In a 2-quart casserole dish, sprinkle the meat and onion with flour and salt and toss to coat. Bake for 30 minutes. Stir in all the remaining ingredients except the sour cream. Cover and bake for 1½ hours. Stir in the sour cream. Let stand for 15 minutes.

Serving suggestion: Serve on buttered noodles or rice.

Makes 4 to 6 servings.

Richard B. Zortman
Chief of Police
Ouray, Colorado

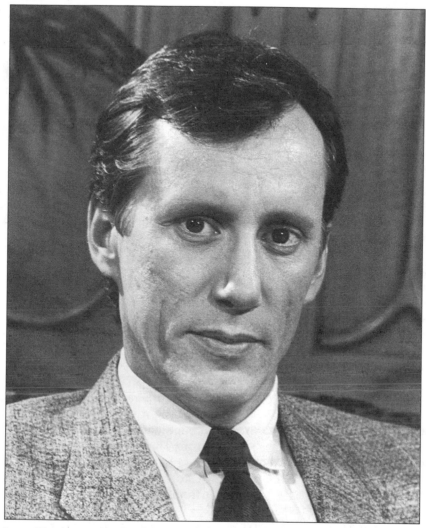

James Woods starred in *Cop* (1987). In 1991's *The Hard Way* he played a New York City cop assigned to brief an actor (played by Michael J. Fox) on how to be a police detective.

Not-So-Hard-Way Hungarian Goulash

■ This recipe is from James Woods's mother, Martha Dixon, but she says every time he comes to visit, he makes it for her.

1 **pound lean ground beef**
1 **medium onion, chopped**
1 **16-ounce can red kidney beans**
1 **16-ounce can stewed tomatoes**
  Mrs. Dash, salt, and pepper to taste
1 **cup cooked rice**

Brown the beef in a skillet with the onion. Drain off excess grease. Add the kidney beans, stewed tomatoes, spices, and heat through. Serve over the rice.

Makes 4 to 6 servings.

James Woods

Number One Son's Beef and Asparagus Stir Fry

■ Keye did not do much cooking because my mother was a great cook, and he liked everything she fixed. Nevertheless, this was one of the few dishes he always prepared for special friends, including Warner Oland, who particularly enjoyed it.   —Ethel Longenecker

Marinade:

2 **tablespoons soy sauce**
1 **tablespoon Worcestershire sauce**
¼ **cup red table wine or sodium-reduced beef broth (Keye used burgundy, never cooking wine, which is too salty)**
2 **teaspoons cornstarch dissolved in 2 tablespoons water**
2 **tablespoons peanut oil**
2 **cloves garlic, peeled and crushed**

Main Dish:

1 **pound flank steak**
1 **large yellow onion**
½ **pound asparagus (½ pound bok choy may be substituted)**
½ **pound brown or white mushrooms with short stems and closed caps**
5 **tablespoons peanut oil**
 Salt (or seasoning salt) to taste, after the dish is cooked and ready to serve

Sauce:

1 **tablespoon soy sauce**
½ **cup red table wine or sodium-reduced beef broth**
¼ **teaspoon black pepper**
 Pinch of crushed red pepper flakes

The steak should be prepared the day before and marinated in the refrigerator until 1 hour before cooking. Prepare the marinade by mixing all the marinade ingredients in a medium-sized mixing bowl. Wipe both sides of the steak with damp paper towels and place on a metal cookie sheet. To aid in making thin slices,

place in the freezer until firm but not frozen (approximately 20 minutes). Remove from the freezer, transfer to a cutting board, and cut along the grain of the meat into approximately 2-inch-wide strips through the whole length of the steak. Remove any visible fat. Slice each strip, across the grain, into thin strips (approximately ¼ inch thick). Add to the marinade and stir or toss until the meat is well covered. Cover the bowl and refrigerate but stir or toss occasionally until ready to cook. Always re-cover the bowl.

Assemble and mix the ingredients for the sauce and refrigerate, covered. About 1 hour before cooking, remove the steak and sauce from the refrigerator and place the steak on a plate (not paper, which absorbs the juices). Discard the marinade. The steak and sauce should be room temperature at cooking time.

Next, slice the onion into half rings. Slice the asparagus and mushrooms and reserve separately.

Use asparagus with medium-sized stalks and tightly closed tips. Break off the tough ends and cut the stalks diagonally into 1¼-inch-long pieces. (If you substitute bok choy, choose a leafy bunch. Discard the bottom core. Separate the leaves from the stalks and wash both. Cut the large stalks lengthwise and then diagonally across in ½-inch-slices. Cut the leaves into narrow bite-sized slices. Reserve the leaves and stalks separately.)

Remove the stem tips from the mushrooms and wipe the mushrooms with damp paper towels. (Avoid water. Mushrooms absorb it.) Slice as thinly as possible. Reserve separately.

To stir-fry, use a wok or very deep 12-inch diameter frying pan. Over medium-high heat, bring the sauce to a boil while stirring. Reduce the heat and simmer, covered, for approximately 3 minutes. Pour into a previously heated large serving bowl and cover. Return heat to medium high and add 2 tablespoons of the peanut oil to the pan. Tilt pan to

A native of Canton, China, Keye Luke became Number One Son to Warner Oland's Charlie Chan (left) in *Charlie Chan in Paris* in 1935. Over a period of fifteen years, Luke appeared in eleven Chan movies opposite Oland and his successors, Sidney Toler and Roland Winters.

cover with oil. Add the beef and stir constantly until light brown (3 to 4 minutes). Leave the meat slightly pink because it will continue to cook after it is removed from the heat. Add the meat to the serving dish and stir or toss with the sauce. Re-cover the bowl.

Cook all the remaining vegetables separately, adding 1 tablespoon of peanut oil to the pan before cooking each vegetable. Stir-fry all the vegetables until crisp but slightly tender. Allow the onion 5 to 7 minutes or until golden brown; the asparagus (or bok choy), 5 to 7 minutes; the mushrooms, about 3 minutes. As each is cooked, add it to the serving bowl with the meat; stir and re-cover the bowl.

After all the ingredients have been mixed in the serving dish, season to taste with salt or seasoned salt. Ladle the completed mixture over hot rice and enjoy.

Note: You may wonder why Keye didn't use "traditional" soy sauce for final seasoning. He felt he could season more uniformly with conventional salt. He also prevented steaming by avoiding liquids other than natural juices and by keeping the pan uncovered.

Cornstarch added to the marinade is not to thicken the sauce but to tenderize the meat. It should be used sparingly or it will unfavorably alter the flavor.

Makes 4 servings.

Keye Luke
Submitted by daughter Ethel Longenecker

Jack Webb (left) shows his friend, actor Tom Williams (center), how to act on the set of the 1967 *Dragnet* television movie. Recalled Williams, "I played Harry Morgan's nephew who was going to dental school and was making him a bridge. My first line reading was a dead-on imitation of Harry's voice, but Webb thought it was 'too cute, palley. Just read the lines.'"

Dragnet Tamale Pie

Just the food, ma'am!

■ Jack loved cooking this meal and gave me the recipe.

1½ **cups cornmeal**
1½ **teaspoons salt**
4½ **cups boiling water**
 2 **tablespoons butter**
 1 **cup shredded cheddar cheese, divided**
 2 **pounds lean ground beef**
 1 **tablespoon vegetable oil**
 1 **clove garlic, minced**
¾ **cup chopped onion**
1½ **cups sliced celery**
2½ **cups cooked tomatoes**
 2 **cups kernel corn**
 1 **tablespoon salt**
 1 **tablespoon chili powder**
 1 **tablespoon Worcestershire sauce**
½ **cup additional cornmeal**
1½ **cups pitted ripe olives**

Stir the 1½ cups of cornmeal and 1½ teaspoons salt into the boiling water. Cook over low heat or in double boiler over boiling water for 30 minutes. Remove from heat. Stir in the butter and ¾ cup of the shredded cheese. Cool lightly. In a large skillet, cook the beef in the oil. Drain off excess grease. Stir in the next 8 ingredients. Slowly stir in the ½ cup of cornmeal. Cover and cook slowly for 10 minutes. Preheat the oven to 350°.

Cut some of the olives into quarters. Stir both the whole olives and the cut olives into the meat mixture. Line the bottom of a greased 3-quart casserole dish with three-fourths of the cooled cornmeal mixture. Pour in the meat filling. Top with the remaining cornmeal mixture and cheese. Bake for 1 hour.

Makes 6 to 8 servings.

Jack Webb
Submitted by Jean Miles
Longtime executive assistant to Mr. Webb

Joe Friday's Beef and Tomatoes

2 tablespoons cornstarch
3 tablespoons soy sauce
2 tablespoons sherry
1 pound beef sirloin, cut into 1-inch-wide strips
1 clove garlic, chopped
1 cup chopped onion
1 cup beef stock
1½ cups tomatoes, cut into wedges
2 tablespoons vegetable oil
Salt and pepper to taste (optional)

Combine the first 3 ingredients in a bowl or saucepan and set aside. In a skillet, sauté the meat, garlic, and onion. Add the stock. Simmer for 5 minutes. Add the sauce and the tomatoes. Cover and cook for 2 minutes. Serve with rice.

Note: More vegetables can be added, but this is the way I made it.

Makes 2 servings.

Jack Webb

The Legend of the China Trader Restaurant

The story goes that film editor Willie Shenker loaned ten grand to producer and director Stanley Kramer to make a movie, only to see the film bomb miserably.

When Kramer later scored a knockout with a Kirk Douglas boxing flick called *Champion*, Kramer felt so bad about losing Shenker's investment in the earlier film that he gave Shenker a few of the points from the film. That action resulted in a return of about a hundred grand.

Shenker used the money to open a Polynesian restaurant called the China Trader in Toluca Lake. It became Jack Webb's favorite restaurant. However, in the mid-1960s, business tapered off, and Shenker discussed his situation with his top customer—Jack Webb.

Webb liked the food, so he bought a quarter interest in the restaurant, and he suggested that Shenker arrange entertainment to liven up the joint. Webb suggested singer Bobby Troup, who sang the hit "Route 66" from the early 1960s television show. Troup joined Shenker and Webb, and bought a quarter interest in the China Trader; his performances drew such good crowds that the restaurant again became very successful. (Later, Troup and his wife Julie London joined the cast of *Emergency.*)

In the late 1960s, Shenker, Webb, and Troup sold the restaurant, and today a dry cleaners stands in the place of the China Trader.

Jack Webb's China Trader Restaurant in Toluca Lake, which is near Los Angeles, California.

Peter Weller was a cyborg cop as the star of *Robocop* and *Robocop 2*, but you could see his face a lot better when he played a New York City detective in the cable television movie *Apology*.

Robo Tacos

8 to 12 taco shells
1 smudge of vegetable shortening
3 cloves garlic, pressed
1 bunch green onions, chopped
3 pounds finely ground chuck
1 28-ounce can Herdez Ranchero salsa
2 teaspoons cumin
1 teaspoon chili powder
2 teaspoons ground cayenne pepper
   Lettuce, shredded
   Tomatoes, chopped
   Cheese, grated

Heat the taco shells in a 150° oven for approximately 10 minutes or microwave until warm. Place the smudge of shortening in a skillet and sauté the garlic and green onions for 5 minutes. Add the ground chuck and brown over medium heat. Add the salsa and cumin to the mixture. After 3 minutes, add the chili powder and cayenne pepper. Simmer and then drain off all the grease from the mixture. Place the beef mixture in taco shells topped with the lettuce and tomato.

Note: As a Texan, I'm a taco freak. The Herdez salsa is the best in the west from Texas. It can be hard to find but important. Tacos are best served with ground beef, not shredded, and spicy hot. Mucho gusto!

Makes 8 to 12 servings.

Peter Weller

Maine Street Meat Pie

1 9-inch pie crust with top crust
1¼ pounds lean ground beef
1 medium onion, diced
1¾ pounds potatoes
   Milk

Preheat the oven to 450°. Place the pie crust bottom in a pie dish and brown in the oven. In a skillet, brown the ground beef with the onion. Drain the excess grease from the skillet. Peel the potatoes, boil them in a pot, and then mash or whip them to a creamy texture, adding the milk as needed. Combine the ground beef and potatoes and stir to form an even mixture. Pack the mixture into the bottom crust and cover with the top crust. Bake until the top crust is golden brown. Enjoy plain or with brown gravy. It's even good served cold after baking.

Makes 4 to 6 servings.

Wayne McCamish
Chief of Police
Augusta, Maine

Patty's Nashville Beat Mexican Casserole

Number one with a bullet.

2 to 3 pounds extra-lean ground beef
1 medium onion, chopped
  Salt to taste
  Pepper to taste
  Tabasco to taste
  Worcestershire sauce to taste
  Garlic powder to taste
1 15-ounce can chili with beans (I use
  Vietti and sometimes use 2 cans)
1 16-ounce container sour cream
2 cups grated sharp cheddar or American
  cheese
1 16-ounce bag plain tortilla chips

Preheat the oven to 400°. In a large skillet, brown the meat and onion together, then drain off the excess grease. Season lightly with a dash of each of the salt, pepper, Tabasco, Worcestershire sauce, and garlic powder. (Some may be eliminated according to taste.) Stir the chili into the mixture. Put the entire mixture into a 9x13-inch casserole dish. Spread the sour cream evenly over the entire mixture. Spread the cheese over the sour cream, then crumble the bag of chips and spread over all. Bake uncovered for 15 minutes. Serve with a mild taco sauce.

Makes 6 servings.

Emmett H. Turner
Chief of Police
Nashville, Tennessee

Meaty Madison Cheese and Macaroni

1 pound ground chuck
  Small amount of olive oil
6 cups cooked macaroni
½ teaspoon hot sauce
1 bell pepper
1 pound sharp cheddar cheese
1½ pounds Monterey Jack cheese

2 eggs
½ cup skim milk
  Salt and pepper

Preheat the oven to 375°. Sauté the ground chuck in a small amount of olive oil. Drain, crumble, and set aside. Soak the bell pepper a few minutes in a small amount of olive oil, pat dry, and sauté. Cut the cheeses into small wedges and set aside. Place the cooked macaroni in a large bowl. Add the ground chuck and sautéed peppers. Mix thoroughly. Beat the two eggs and add to the mixture. Add ½ cup skim milk and salt and pepper to taste. Add the cheeses to the mixture and mix in. Grease or spray a 10x12-inch glass baking dish and place the mixture in the dish. Bake for 30 minutes. Remove and enjoy.

Makes 6 servings.

Richard Williams
Chief of Police
Madison, Wisconsin

COOL COPS

Match the actor to his police character.

1. Alan Autry	A. Detective Sonny Crockett
2. Ray Collins	B. Captain Frank Furillo
3. Broderick Crawford	C. Officer Bill Gannon
4. Fred Dryer	D. Lieutenant Philip Gerard
5. Erik Estrada	E. Chief Bill Gillespie
6. Max Gail	F. Sergeant T. J. Hooker
7. Don Johnson	G. Sergeant Rick Hunter
8. Hal Linden	H. Detective Ken Hutchison
9. Jack Lord	I. Officer Pete Malloy
10. Martin Milner	J. Chief Dan Matthews
11. Al Molinaro	K. Detective Steve McGarrett
12. Richard Moll	L. Captain Barney Miller
13. Harry Morgan	M. Officer Murray Greshner
14. Barry Morse	N. Officer Frank Poncherello
15. Carroll O'Connor	O. Sergeant Bubba Skinner
16. William Shatner	P. Detective Dave Starsky
17. Jack Soo	Q. Bailiff Bull Shannon
18. David Soul	R. Lieutenant Arthur Tragg
19. Daniel J. Travanti	S. Detective Wojohowicz
20. Paul Michael Glaser	T. Detective Nick Yemana

SOLUTION

1. O, 2. R, 3. J, 4. G, 5. N, 6. S, 7. A, 8. L, 9. K, 10. I, 11. M,
12. Q, 13. C, 14. D, 15. E, 16. F, 17. T, 18. H, 19. B, 20. P

Carol's Cincinnati Birthday Lasagna

■ We wanted something different from ham or turkey for our Christmas dinner, so I began to tinker with a lasagna recipe. I created this lasagna recipe after many trial-and-error efforts. This final version was perfected for my wife's birthday, so I call it Carol's Cincinnati Birthday Lasagna.

    1½ pounds ground beef
    1   cup chopped onion
    2   tablespoons olive oil
    1½ tablespoons parsley
    3   teaspoons salt
    ¾   teaspoon pepper
    1½ teaspoons garlic powder
    1½ teaspoons sugar
    1½ teaspoons oregano
    1   26-ounce can whole tomatoes
    3   6-ounce cans tomato paste
    3   cups water
    1   8-ounce package lasagna noodles
    1   pound ricotta cheese
    12 ounces mozzarella cheese, grated
    1½ cups grated Parmesan cheese
    1   tablespoon olive oil

In a skillet, brown the beef and onion in 2 tablespoons olive oil. Meanwhile, in a small bowl, combine the parsley, salt, pepper, garlic powder, sugar, and oregano. Drain the fat from the beef and onion. Add the spices. Using the edge of a spoon, cut the whole tomatoes into wedges and add to the beef mixture along with the tomato paste and water. Simmer, uncovered, for 25 minutes, stirring occasionally.

While the sauce is simmering, prepare the noodles according to package directions. (Hint: Add 1 tablespoon of olive oil to the water to prevent the noodles from sticking together.) When the noodles are cooked, drain and place flat on a plate to cool. Be careful not to overcook the noodles.

Preheat the oven to 350°. Place a few tablespoons of sauce on the bottom of the lasagna pan and spread over the pan. Lay a third of the noodles in the pan, overlapping them lengthwise. Add a third of the sauce, half of the ricotta, a third of the mozzarella, and a third of the Parmesan cheese. Repeat the process using another a third of the noodles, a third of the sauce, half of the ricotta, a third of the mozzarella, and a third of the Parmesan. The final layer consists the last a third of the noodles and the remaining sauce, mozzarella, and Parmesan.

Bake for 35 to 40 minutes or until the sauce is bubbly and the cheese is melted. Let it cool for a few minutes and then cut it into squares and enjoy.

Serving suggestion: This lasagna is especially good with fresh garlic bread, salad, and a glass of wine.

Makes about 6 servings.

Michael C. Snowden
Chief of Police
Cincinnati, Ohio

Poor Man's Lasagna

■ For lack of a better name for this recipe (origin unknown), we have always called this dish by the above name.

    2   pounds lean ground meat
    2   tablespoons good olive oil
        Salt and pepper to taste
    1   onion, minced
    1   or 2 pinches oregano
        Fresh chopped or dried parsley to
        taste
    24 ounces tomato sauce
    16 ounces wide egg noodles
    16 ounces cream cheese, softened
    8   ounces cottage cheese
    8   ounces sour cream
        Pinch of garlic powder

In a skillet, brown the ground beef in the olive oil. Drain off excess grease. Add the salt, pepper, onion, oregano, and parsley to the meat as it simmers. Once the meat is cooked, add the tomato sauce. Mix well and set aside.

In his portrayal of Lt. Doug Chapman on *The Rockford Files,* James Luisi was the perfect by-the-book police nemesis for Jim Rockford. Chapman had little use for private eyes like Rockford meddling in police business. The only P.I. who won favor with the cranky Chapman was Lance White (Tom Selleck), who was chummy enough to call the hard-boiled lieutenant Chappy.

Meanwhile, cook the egg noodles according to the package instructions. When fully cooked (approximately 8 minutes), rinse thoroughly and set aside. In a mixing bowl, blend the cream cheese, cottage cheese, sour cream, and garlic powder. Preheat the oven to 350°.

Place half of the noodles in the bottom of a large, greased casserole dish. Spoon the cheese mixture on top of the noodle layer. Layer with the rest of the noodles and top all with the meat sauce. Cover the dish with foil and bake for about 45 minutes to 1 hour.

Serving suggestion: This recipe is good for company because it can be made a day ahead and then popped in the oven the day of serving. Serve with a green salad, garlic bread, and some red wine; you have not only a tasty dish, but one that leaves the host and hostess free to enjoy their friends.

Makes 6 servings.

James Luisi

Dirty Harry Spaghetti, aka Spaghetti Western

■ A few years ago, Clint Eastwood participated in a foods gala, the Flavors of Monterey, to benefit the March of Dimes. His edible Spaghetti Western brought him top honors.

Juice of 1 lemon, divided
12 tablespoons olive oil, divided
12 baby artichokes
 1 8-ounce package spaghetti
 2 large cloves garlic, diced
¼ cup finely chopped celery
¼ cup chopped shallots, divided
½ cup tomato purée
½ cup fish stock
   Salt and fresh ground pepper to taste

¼ teaspoon thyme
 1 bay leaf
 2 tablespoons chopped parsley
   Saffron
 2 tablespoons tomato paste
½ teaspoon anchovy paste
 4 clams, chopped
 4 Monterey Bay prawns or jumbo shrimp
12 large mussels
½ cup brandy
 1 red bell pepper, thinly sliced
 1 yellow bell pepper, thinly sliced
2½ tablespoons Pernod
½ cup heavy cream
 8 large sea scallops, quartered

Stir the juice from half of the lemon and 2 tablespoons of the olive oil into a large

Clint Eastwood slipped into his quintessential role, Lt. Harry Callahan, in 1971's *Dirty Harry*. He followed up with four more films as the ultracool, independent San Francisco cop and made "make my day" an international catchphrase.

pot of salted boiling water. Add the artichokes and boil for 5 minutes or until almost tender. Remove the artichokes and cool under cold running water. Reserve the artichoke cooking water. Peel the outer leaves from 8 artichokes down to the most tender part (leave 4 artichokes with leaves intact). Cut off the stems. Cut the peeled artichokes into bite-sized pieces (about 1½ inches long). Set aside.

Add additional salted water to the leftover artichoke water. Bring to a boil and cook the pasta. Drain and return to the pot.

In a large pan, heat 7 tablespoons of the olive oil and sauté the garlic, celery, and 2 tablespoons of the shallots until golden. Add the tomato purée, fish stock, salt, pepper, thyme, bay leaf, parsley, 2 generous pinches of saffron, tomato paste, anchovy paste, and clams. Bring to a low simmer and cover.

In a large sauté pan, heat 3 tablespoons of the olive oil and sauté 2 tablespoons of the chopped shallots. Season with black pepper. Add the prawns and mussels, cover with brandy, and ignite. Remove from heat; when the flame subsides, set aside.

Add the red and yellow peppers, artichokes, mussels, and brandy to the sauce and simmer for 5 minutes. Add the Pernod and cream to the sauce and cook for 1 minute, stirring constantly. Remove from heat. Use a slotted spoon to remove the bay leaf and the peppers from the sauce; add the peppers to the spaghetti. Rinse the spaghetti mixture in hot water and drain (to remove traces of the sauce).

Cover the bottom of 4 flat bowls with a few tablespoons of sauce. Arrange ¼ of the spaghetti in each bowl, leaving a hollow in the center. Place 2 quartered raw scallops in the center. Arrange 3 mussels on the edge of the plate; and, on the opposite side, place 3 artichokes. On each plate place 1 reserved uncut artichoke over the scallops. Spoon the remaining sauce over the scallops and mussels. Place 1 prawn in the center. If preparing in advance, cover with foil and set aside. To serve, heat in a 325° oven for 20 minutes.

Makes your day and 4 servings.

Clint Eastwood

Pennsylvania Pasta Sauce and Sausage

15 to 20 fresh plum tomatoes
2 tablespoons olive oil
3 cloves garlic, crushed
3 scallions, chopped
1¼ pounds fresh Italian sausage
½ cup chopped fresh parsley
1 tablespoon red pepper flakes (or to taste)
¼ cup chopped fresh oregano
2 bay leaves
Salt and pepper

Place the tomatoes in a large pot. Cover with water. Bring to a boil and continue to boil until the tomatoes start splitting (3 to 5 minutes). Remove the tomatoes from the water and allow to cool. Dispose of the water. Peel the skin off the tomatoes and quickly chop the tomatoes into small pieces. Add the olive oil, garlic, and scallions to the pot and fry until the garlic starts to turn brown. Add the sausages and lightly brown on all sides. Remove the sausages from the pot. Add tomatoes to the drippings and garlic mixture. Add the remaining herbs and spices. Bring the sauce to a boil. Add the sausage back into the pot. Reduce heat to low and let the sauce and sausage cook slowly. It is done as soon as the sausage is cooked through.

This is a very light tomato sauce. I hope everyone enjoys it as much as I do. You can adjust the spices or add other spices according to your taste.

Makes 4 servings.

Richard S. Shaffer
Chief of Police
Harrisburg, Pennsylvania

Randi Oakes starred as Officer Bonnie Clark, one of the female Chippies on *CHiPs* from 1979 to 1982.

still crisp. Cook the pasta according to the package directions. In a large frying pan, heat the olive oil and butter over low heat, making sure not to burn. Add the garlic and sauté for about 2 minutes. Add the pine nuts and slivered tomatoes, and continue cooking for another 2 minutes, stirring constantly, so it does not burn. The pine nuts can be browned, if you like. Remove from heat. Place the pasta and steamed broccoli in a large bowl; toss with the olive oil/pine nut mixture from the frying pan. Enjoy!

Makes 4 to 6 servings.

Randi Oakes Harrison

Lieutenant Diehl's Linguine and White Clam Sauce

12 ounces linguine
 3 cloves garlic, minced
 5 tablespoons olive oil
 3 tablespoons butter
 2 6½-ounce cans minced clams
 ⅓ cup white wine
 ½ teaspoon dried marjoram
 ¼ teaspoon dried thyme
 ¼ teaspoon dried basil
 ¼ teaspoon black pepper
 ¼ cup plus 1 teaspoon minced parsley
    Fresh grated Parmesan cheese
    Salt to taste

Cook the linguine. Meanwhile, sauté the garlic in the oil and butter over low heat for 1 to 2 minutes. Add the clam juice from cans (while pressing the lid down on the clams), wine, marjoram, thyme, basil, and pepper. Simmer, uncovered, over medium-low heat for 7 to 10 minutes. Stir in the clams and the ¼ cup of parsley. Simmer for 1 minute until heated through and then serve. Sprinkle with remaining parsley and freshly grated Parmesan cheese. Salt to taste.

Makes 4 servings.

Tom Atkins

Bonnie Clark's Penne with Broccoli

 1 head broccoli
16 ounces penne pasta
 8 tablespoons olive oil
 2 tablespoons butter
 4 cloves garlic, chopped
 ¾ cup pine nuts
 6 full slices sun-dried tomatoes (I prefer ones packed in oil), slivered

Clean and cut broccoli into florets and steam them until they are cooked, but

Pepper Anderson's Veggie-Pasta Casserole

16 ounces pasta (penne, macaroni, or corkscrew pasta—not spaghetti)
2 tablespoons vegetable oil
3 ribs celery, chopped
1 large onion, chopped
1 green bell pepper, chopped (optional)
½ small bunch broccoli, chopped (optional)
  Assorted other vegetables to taste (optional)
  Salt and pepper to taste
1 cup shredded cheddar cheese (optional)
1 10¾-ounce can cream of mushroom or cream of celery soup (optional)
¾ cup shredded tuna or chicken (optional)

Cook and drain the pasta according to the package instructions. (This can be done the day before if you like.)

Preheat the oven to 325°. In a skillet, sauté the chopped veggies in the oil and add salt and pepper to taste. (If you're really good on your fat intake, you can splurge and add a little butter to the oil as you sauté the vegetables.) You can add any vegetables you want to the sautéed mixture, but the celery and onion are, for me, the major veggies. Depending on your love for vegetables, adjust amount to taste. Stir the veggies into the pasta and pour into a round casserole dish. Bake for 20 minutes to blend the ingredients and their flavors. If you want to add cheese, you can add it to the top for the last 5 minutes of baking.

If you don't like quite such a bland casserole, you can add a can of condensed celery or mushroom soup. (I use cream of celery the most, because I love celery.)

As you see, this is a really easy home-made dish but wonderful. You can add or subtract and play with it. Sometimes I even add a can of corn. So have fun with it, but if you have a problem with it, don't call me.

Makes 6 to 8 servings.

Angie Dickinson

Angie Dickinson was sexy undercover cop Sgt. Suzanne "Pepper" Anderson for the Los Angeles Police Department on *Police Woman* from 1974 to 1978.

Oscar Goldman's Six-Million-Dollar Pasta

■ An Anderson favorite, this pasta is attractive and delicious. It is also extremely simple to prepare. All the ingredients are combined in one mixing bowl, and the sauce resembles a salsa since it is uncooked and tossed with the steaming hot noodles at the last minute.

2 to 3 pounds fresh Roma tomatoes
8 ounces fresh feta cheese
1 bunch fresh basil (20 to 30 leaves)
4 to 5 cloves garlic
25 Greek olives (marinated)
   Olive oil
   Balsamic vinegar
1 pound penne pasta

Richard Anderson starred as Chief George Unter-meyer on *Dan August* in 1970. He was also Oscar Goldman in *The Six Million Dollar Man* from 1974 to 1978 and in *The Bionic Woman* from 1976 to 1978.

In a large mixing bowl, wash the tomatoes and core them by cutting off the stems and removing the seeds (a grapefruit knife is handy for this procedure). Dice the tomatoes and put them into a larger mixing bowl. Crumble the cheese and add to the tomatoes. Clean the basil thoroughly and then tear into small pieces and add to the tomatoes and cheese. Chop the garlic and add to the bowl. Pit the olives and add to the bowl. Add about ¼ cup olive oil and mix gently but thoroughly. When each ingredient is coated with olive oil, add 1 or 2 splashes of balsamic vinegar and stir. Let the sauce sit at room temperature for 20 to 30 minutes.

Boil the pasta, drain it in a sieve, then immediately return the pasta to the cooking pot. Toss the fresh sauce into the steaming pasta, cover, and let sit for 3 to 5 minutes before serving.

Serving suggestion: This is delicious served with warm, fresh French bread or rolls. Serve and enjoy!

Makes 4 to 6 servings.

Richard Anderson

We Always Get Our Manicotti Shells

1 16-ounce box jumbo pasta shells
1 16-ounce carton nonfat cottage cheese
2 egg whites
1 teaspoon dried basil flakes
1 20-ounce jar spaghetti sauce
1 8-ounce package low-fat mozzarella cheese slices

Cook the pasta shells according to package instructions and drain. Preheat the oven to 325°. In a bowl, mix the cottage cheese, egg whites, and basil. Fill the shells with one tablespoon of the cottage cheese mixture. Grease a 9x13-inch baking dish with low-fat, nonstick spray (or coat with the sauce if you prefer). Place the shells in the pan and cover with the spaghetti sauce. Cover and bake until the sauce bubbles. Uncover and add the mozzarella cheese on top and bake until the cheese melts. Let stand for 5 minutes and then serve. (Ours never gets to stand that long because we can't wait.)

Makes about 6 servings.

Jim Taylor
Special Agent in Charge
Tennessee Bureau of Investigation

Pasta La Vista, Baby!

■ This recipe comes from my mother and grandmother, two of the best cooks in the world. It's simple, tasty, good for you, and was on the menu of Donati's Cafe, my grandparents' restaurant in Chicago.

3 **beefsteak tomatoes or 4 Roma tomatoes**
1 **bunch fresh basil leaves**
 Salt to taste
1 **pound pasta**
 Butter (optional)
 Really, all you need is fresh basil and tomatoes. I like to use Roma tomatoes and fresh basil leaves—not the kind in a jar.

Cut the tomatoes into small pieces and dice the basil into small pieces. Combine them in a bowl and sprinkle on salt to taste. Let stand for about 30 minutes. The combination will make its own sauce. It does not need refrigeration. While the sauce is sitting, boil the water for the pasta. You can use any kind of pasta that you like; we use rigatoni, but my grandmother just used spaghetti. Cook and strain the pasta and add butter if you like. Stir in the sauce and enjoy.

Makes 2 to 4 servings.

Dennis Farina

Before he starred as Lt. Mike Torello on NBC's *Crime Story* in 1987, Dennis Farina was a Chicago police detective for eighteen years.

CRIMINAL:	*"You made a mistake, and I'm not going to pay for it."*
SGT. JOE FRIDAY:	*"You going to use a credit card?"*

Lieutenant Hunter's Pesto Sauce

½ cup chopped fresh sweet basil
¼ cup chopped fresh parsley
¼ cup light olive oil
¼ cup grated Parmesan cheese
2 to 3 cloves garlic, chopped
   Lemon juice
¼ cup pine nuts

Turn on a blender and drop the basil and parsley through the small opening in the lid while the machine is running. Add the olive oil by slowly pouring in a thin stream. Add, one at a time, the Parmesan cheese, garlic, lemon juice, and pine nuts, blending after each addition. (This process can also be done in a food processor.)

Serving suggestion: This sauce can be used on noodles cooked al dente or, if slightly thinned with a few drops of oil, on salad as a dressing. It is also wonderful on steamed cauliflower.

It can also be used with large scallops. Slit and pipe large scallops (they must be large). Place the sauce in them. Broil for two minutes until crunchy.

Makes about 1½ cups.

James B. Sikking

James B. Sikking was one of the many stars of *Hill Street Blues*, in which he played Lt. Howard Hunter, the uncompromisingly militaristic leader of the precinct's SWAT team. One of the actor's hobbies is collecting caps, including those from police forces around the country.

Lieutenant Chapman's Favorite Fettuccine

8 ounces flat egg noodles
¼ pound or more baked ham, cut into
   bite-sized pieces
1 cup cooked green peas
1 stick butter, melted
½ cup freshly grated Parmesan cheese
½ cup cream
Coarse black pepper

In a large saucepan of boiling, salted water, cook the noodles according to package directions; drain and return to the pan. Add the ham and peas. Add the melted butter and lightly toss until well mixed. Add the cheese and toss. Stir in the cream and spoon onto plates. Pass additional cheese and coarse black pepper. This fettuccine is fabulous, but it must be served instantly—it is best if served hot.

Serving suggestion: Serve with a green salad and garlic bread. The recipe can be doubled for company. It's great, too, if you have leftover ham from a holiday meal.

Makes 2 servings.

James Luisi

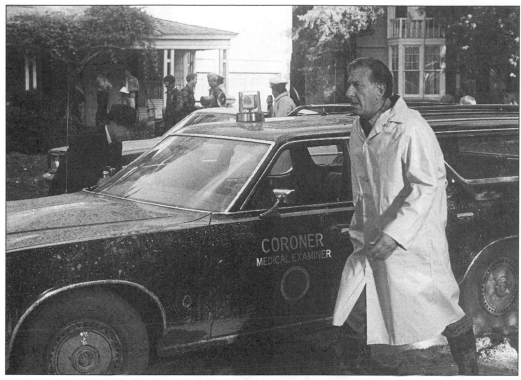

It began as an *NBC Sunday Night Mystery*, but Jack Klugman's *Quincy, M.E.* proved so popular that it became a regular series on NBC from 1976 to 1983. Quincy's knowledge of forensic medicine fit perfectly with his job as a medical examiner with the Los Angeles County Coroner's Office.

Quincy's Italian Sauce

DOA (Delicious On Arrival)

8 cloves fresh garlic, smashed
⅓ cup olive oil
1 small pork butt with bone
1½ pounds mixed sweet and hot Italian sausage
1 small cube of beef (to help cut the pork)
2 20-ounce cans crushed tomatoes
1 6-ounce can tomato paste
  Fresh basil
  Fresh oregano
  Fresh parsley
  Salt and pepper

In a skillet, brown the garlic in the oil. Then brown the meats. Put in the tomatoes and tomato paste and bring to a boil. Add the basil, oregano, parsley, and salt and pepper to taste. Simmer for 2 hours stirring often and adding more herbs to adjust the taste.

Makes about ½ gallon.

Jack Klugman

The Los Angeles County Coroner's office never had a medical examiner like Jack Klugman's Quincy, who was as much detective as pathologist.

McCloud's Taos Pesto Sauce

It's not from New York City!

2½ cups firmly packed fresh basil leaves, chopped
 2 large cloves garlic, pressed
 ½ cup chopped walnuts, almonds, or pine nuts
 ½ cup freshly grated Parmesan cheese
 ½ cup olive oil
    Salt to taste (use sparingly)

Mix the basil, garlic, nuts, and Parmesan cheese in a blender or food processor until well blended. Then add the olive oil in a slow, steady stream until a smooth paste is formed. Go easy on the oil. You might want to add a small amount of canola margarine to make the mixture a bit wetter. Mix to your own specifications. If you like, add additional fresh Parmesan. (We watch the fat we eat, so a sprinkle of Parmesan is about the only cheese we use.)

Pesto may be kept refrigerated for several weeks in an airtight jar. Cover the sauce with a thin layer of olive oil to prevent it from discoloring.

Makes about 4½ cups.

Dennis Weaver

Dennis Weaver was Deputy Marshal Sam McCloud, a Taos, New Mexico, lawman who found himself stuck on temporary assignment in Manhattan's Twenty-seventh Precinct. The show made a seven-year run, beginning in 1970, as an *NBC Mystery Movie.* "There you go."

Car 54 Fettuccine

■ Handed down through Grampa!

1 head garlic
3 tablespoons olive oil, divided
   Salt and pepper
½ pound spinach fettuccine
1 small onion, sliced thin
6 Roma tomatoes, seeded and
   chopped
1 6-ounce jar marinated artichoke hearts, drained and
   chopped
1 tablespoon fresh thyme,
   chopped
½ cup vegetable stock
   Grated Parmesan or Romano
   cheese
   Salt and pepper

Preheat the oven to 350°. Chop the tip off the garlic head to expose the cloves. Pull off the loose peel. Place on aluminum foil. Drizzle 1 tablespoon of the olive oil on garlic. Sprinkle with salt and pepper. Bake in foil for 45 minutes. Prepare the rest of the meal while the garlic bakes.

Add the fettuccine to a pot of boiling water. Cook according to package directions. Drain.

Add the remaining 2 table-spoons of olive oil to a large skillet and heat. Sauté the onion until wilted. Mix in the tomatoes, artichokes, and thyme. Sauté for 5 minutes more. Stir in the vegetable stock and bring to a boil. Add the pasta and heat through at high temperature for 2 minutes. Squeeze the garlic head to release the cloves and stir the cloves into the mixture. Season to taste and top with cheese. Grampa says if you eat this dish 3 times a week, you'll live to be 86.

Makes 4 servings.

Al Lewis

A favorite member of the Fifty-third Precinct on *Car 54, Where Are You?* is Al Lewis, who played Officer Leo Schnauser. At one time, Lewis owned a New York City restaurant called Grampa's.

"If you really want to study police methods, do what I do: watch television."

—Officer Gunther Toody
(*Car 54, Where Are You?*)

Well before he took on the guise of 007, Roger Moore was the suave and dashing, modern-day Robin Hood named Simon Templar, alias *The Saint*. Created by British novelist Leslie Charteris, *The Saint* made a slick and sophisticated run on television from 1963 to 1969. In 1976 Moore stepped into the shoes of another British sleuth of note in the film *Sherlock Holmes in New York*.

The Saint's Best-Ever Bolognese Sauce

They always want Moore.

1 tablespoon olive oil
2 medium onions, chopped
1 clove garlic, crushed
½ pound minced beef
1 16-ounce can crushed tomatoes
1½ cups water
½ cup dry white wine
2 tablespoons tomato paste
3 small beef stock cubes, crumbled
1 teaspoon dried oregano
½ teaspoon dried marjoram
½ teaspoon sugar
  Hot, cooked pasta
  Parmesan cheese

In a large saucepan, heat the oil. Add the onion and garlic, and sauté over low heat for about 15 minutes or until the onion is very soft. Add the beef and stir until well browned. Stir in the undrained crushed tomatoes, water, wine, tomato paste, stock cubes, herbs, and sugar. Bring to a boil and simmer, uncovered, stirring occasionally for about 2 hours or until the sauce is thickened. Serve with pasta and grated Parmesan cheese.

Makes 4 servings.

Roger Moore

Henry's Sunday Sauce

■ Dad made this for our family every Sunday.
                                    —*Monica Mancini*

1 small onion, chopped
2 cloves garlic, finely minced
4 tablespoons olive oil
1 teaspoon red pepper flakes (or ½ teaspoon if you can't take the heat)
2 20-ounce cans plum tomatoes, seeded and chopped

Award-winning musician Henry Mancini scored eighty movies and twenty television show themes, and he received four Academy Awards and twenty Grammy Awards. Among his best works were his scores for *Peter Gunn* and *The Pink Panther*.

In a large saucepan, sauté the onion and garlic in the olive oil. When the onion is soft, add the red pepper and then the tomatoes. Simmer for 30 minutes.

Makes enough sauce for 1 pound of pasta.

Henry Mancini
Submitted by daughter Monica Mancini

French Detective's Three-Helping Pasta Putanesca

3 cloves garlic, minced
2 tablespoons olive oil
1 tin anchovies
1 28-ounce can Italian tomatoes
1 heaping teaspoon ground basil
1 pinch oregano
1 pinch cayenne pepper
1 dozen green olives, pitted and halved
2 tablespoons capers

In a fairly good-sized pot, lightly brown the garlic in the olive oil. In a saucepan, heat the anchovies in their own juice until they break up and become paste, then add the garlic mixture. Add the tomatoes and the spices and cook for 20 minutes or so. Then add the olives and capers. Serve over your favorite pasta. It can be eaten immediately, then at 3 o'clock in the morning and then again for lunch the next day.

Makes 3 servings.

Alan Arkin

Alan Arkin starred as Inspector [Jacques] Clouseau in the film of the same name in 1968. He played a detective in *Little Murders* in 1971, and he was teamed with James Caan as a pair of San Francisco cops in 1974's *Freebie and the Bean*.

Rome Noodles Alfredo with Sour Cream

Wisconsin, that is.

■ This is not traditional Alfredo as it is prepared with low-fat sour cream instead of cream. Low-fat sour cream imparts a little more flavor and fewer calories.

½ **pound medium noodles, cooked**
   al dente and drained
½ **stick butter, melted**
¼ **cup low-fat sour cream**
¼ **cup toasted slivered almonds**

Toss the noodles in the melted butter and then into the sour cream. Toss to coat evenly. Transfer the noodles immediately to a serving dish, sprinkle with toasted almonds, and serve hot.
   Makes 6 servings.

Tom Skerritt

From 1992 to 1996, Tom Skerritt starred as Sheriff Jimmy Brock, the top lawman of Rome, Wisconsin, on *Picket Fences.*

Police Woman's Fettuccine à la Maki

4 **tablespoons butter**
4 **tablespoons all-purpose flour**
3 **cups milk**
2 **egg yolks**
1 **cup whipping cream**
1 **pound ricotta cheese**
1 **cup Parmesan cheese, grated**
½ **teaspoon salt**
8 **ounces fettuccine, cooked**
   Pimientos
   Parsley sprigs

Preheat the oven to 350°. In a saucepan, combine all of the ingredients except the fettuccini, pimientos, and parsley. Heat, stirring until thoroughly blended. Put the cooked noodles in a shallow baking dish and cover with the sauce. Bake for 1 hour and garnish with pimientos and parsley.
   Makes 2 servings.

Connie Maki
President
International Association of Women Police

Just the Ticket Tenderloin Pizziola

1 **pound boneless pork loin (beef may be**
   substituted)
½ **cup all-purpose flour**
½ **teaspoon salt**
½ **teaspoon black pepper**
2 **tablespoons olive oil, divided**
3 **cloves garlic, chopped**
2 **tablespoons chopped onion**
1 **teaspoon chopped shallots (optional)**
1 **teaspoon salted capers**
1 **small, sliced hot chili pepper (optional)**
½ **teaspoon oregano**
1 **cup whole peeled tomatoes**
1 **sprig rosemary**
1 **cup sliced red bell pepper**
1 **cup sliced mushrooms**
½ **cup dry red wine**

Cut the pork loin into 1-inch cubes. In a bowl, add the flour, salt, and black pepper. Coat the pork lightly in the flour mixture. Heat 1 tablespoon of the olive oil in a skillet over medium heat. Lightly brown the pork in the skillet. Remove the pork from the pan and set aside. Add the remaining olive oil, then sauté the garlic, onion, shallots, capers, chili pepper, and oregano for 1 minute. Add the tomatoes and rosemary and sauté for 5 minutes more. Add the red pepper, mushrooms, pork, and red wine. Reduce to low heat, cover, and simmer for 10 minutes.

Makes 2 servings.

Joseph F. Croughwell
Chief of Police
Hartford, Connecticut

Tony Rome's Pork Medallions Marsala

1½ pounds pork tenderloin
  2 tablespoons olive oil
  1 tablespoon margarine
  ½ cup all-purpose flour
  ½ teaspoon salt
  ½ teaspoon pepper
  1 12-ounce jar Frank Sinatra's Marsala
     Cooking Sauce
     Angel hair pasta

Cut the pork tenderloins into 24 medallions of equal size. Press the medallions lightly with the heel of your hand to flatten. In a large skillet, heat the olive oil and margarine over medium-high heat. Combine the flour, salt, and pepper. Dust the medallions with the seasoned flour. Sauté the medallions for 2 to 3 minutes per side. Reduce heat to medium. Add the Marsala Cooking Sauce. Cover the skillet and simmer for 5 minutes. Serve on a bed of angel hair or other pasta of your choice.

Serving suggestion: Accompany with steamed fresh broccoli seasoned with lemon butter.

Makes 6 servings.

Frank Sinatra

In addition to playing the classic private eye Tony Rome in films, Frank Sinatra also played a crimebuster in *The Detective* (1968) and a New York police inspector in 1977's *Contract on Cherry Street* (his first television movie). He also starred in 1980's *The First Deadly Sin.*

> *"All the laws in the world won't stop one man with a gun."*
> —Det. Lt. Mike Stone
> *(The Streets of San Francisco)*

Miss Marple's Pork Fillet

1½ pounds pork fillet
1   teaspoon crushed rosemary
    Salt and pepper
2   tablespoons vegetable oil
2   tablespoons brandy
2   ounces heavy cream
    Parsley

Take off any fat and cut the fillet into 1½-inch-thick medallions. Sprinkle these with rosemary and salt and pepper and allow to marinate for ½ hour or more. In a skillet, cook the medallions in the oil on high heat for 4 minutes on each side; then reduce heat and give them an additional 5 minutes per side. Transfer the medallions to a serving dish and keep warm. Put the brandy in the pan and scrape together the residues. Allow to bubble a little before adding the cream and stirring in. Simmer for 1 minute and pour over the medallions and garnish with parsley.

Makes 6 to 8 servings.

Dame Margaret Rutherford
Submitted by W. P. Davis

Dame Margaret Rutherford starred in four feature films as Agatha Christie's heroine Miss Marple, beginning with *Murder, She Said* in 1961.

Gumshoe's Ham

10 to 12 pounds fully cooked,
    bone-in ham
1   cup sliced onion
2   bay leaves
¼   cup firmly packed brown sugar
4   sprigs parsley
6   whole cloves
3   whole black peppercorns
1   pint beer

Glaze:

½   cup firmly packed brown sugar
¼   cup honey
    Whole cloves

Curried Fruit:

½   stick butter, melted
½   cup firmly packed light brown sugar
1   tablespoon curry powder
1   30-ounce can peach halves, drained
1   13¼-ounce can pineapple chunks,
    drained

Preheat the oven to 325°. Place the ham fat side up in a shallow roasting pan. Place the onion and bay leaves on the ham; sprinkle with sugar, parsley, cloves, and pepper. Insert a meat thermometer in the center of the thickest part away from the bone. Pour the beer into the pan around the ham. Cover the pan tightly with foil. Bake, basting (by removing the ham from the oven, removing the foil, basting with the beer, recovering with foil, and returning the pan to the oven) every 30 minutes for about 3 hours or until the meat thermometer registers 130°.

When the ham is done, remove it from the roasting pan and pour off all the fat and drippings. Reserve 2 tablespoons of drippings (but not the fat) and combine them with the brown sugar and honey to make the glaze. Return the ham to the roasting pan. Increase the oven temperature to 400°. With a sharp knife, carefully remove any skin. To score, make diagonal cuts in the fat about ¼-inch deep (being careful not to cut into the meat) and 1¼ inches apart (use a ruler to help you form a diamond pattern).

Stud the center of each diamond shape with a whole clove. To glaze the ham, brush the surface with half of the honey glaze. Return the ham to the oven and bake for 30 minutes longer, basting every 10 minutes with more of the glaze.

To make Curried Fruit, mix the butter, sugar, and curry powder. In a 1½-quart casserole, toss the fruit with the sugar mixture. Bake, uncovered, for 30 minutes in the same oven. Serve along with the ham.

For easier carving, cool the ham for 20 minutes. Place the ham so that the bone end is at the carver's right. From the thin side of the ham, cut 2 or 3 slices parallel to the length of the ham to make a flat surface. Turn the ham to rest on the cut surface. Cut a small, wedge-shaped piece from the shank end of the ham; remove. Holding a fork near the wedge-shaped cut to steady the ham, make thin horizontal slices down to the leg bone. Then run the knife horizontally along the bone to release the slices. For more servings, turn the ham back to the original position with the fat side up.

Makes 20 servings.

Philip Carey

In 1959 Philip Carey fit the bill as Raymond Chandler's Philip Marlowe, an independent loner detective. *Photograph courtesy of the Nashville Banner.*

Aloha Island Ribs

5 **pounds pork back ribs**
1 **teaspoon salt**
1 **cup sugar**
1 **cup catsup**
¾ **cup soy sauce**
⅓ **cup oyster sauce**
1 **large piece fresh ginger, peeled and mashed**
3 **cloves garlic**

In a saucepan, boil enough water to cover the ribs. Place the salt and ribs in the boiling water and simmer for 40 minutes. Drain and rinse the ribs well. In a large bowl, combine all the remaining ingredients for the marinade. Marinate the ribs for 3 to 4 hours. Broil or charcoal grill. Hint: Do not cut into single ribs. Broil whole and only until brown. Do not leave unattended because ingredients in the marinade will cause the ribs to burn easily.

Makes 4 servings.

Wayne G. Carvalho
Chief of Police
County of Hawaii, Hawaii

Michael Chiklis fit Commis. Tony Scali to a T on *The Commish* (1991–95). Said Scali in one episode, "Chases usually lead to friggin' injuries, but no one ever got hurt by a bowl of linguine." In real life, Chiklis was once a chef (while a struggling actor in New York City.)

potatoes. Pour the red wine into the pan with the roast. Preheat the oven to 350°.

Pour the corn syrup over the lamb to form a thin glaze over the roast and potatoes. (Be sure it's a very thin glaze.) The glaze will help the herbs and spices adhere to the roast and potatoes in addition to tenderizing and flavoring the meat. Sprinkle the parsley, oregano, salt, pepper, chopped garlic, and onion all over the roast. Cover and place in oven. Cook for 2½ to 3 hours, basting periodically. Uncover for the last 45 minutes to a hour to brown the roast. Remove and serve. Well, there you have it.

Serving Suggestion: By the way, a Greek salad and asparagus go particularly well with this robust holiday meal. A nice red table wine, dessert, and coffee are also in order.

Makes 4 to 6 servings.

*Be sure to choose a small leg of lamb as the larger ones are really mutton and are much gamier. A leg of lamb will usually serve four to six people. If this isn't enough, just cook two. Also be sure to have your butcher remove the glands before you bring the leg of lamb home.

Michael Chiklis

The Commish's Greek Lamb and Potatoes

1 leg of lamb*
2 cloves garlic, sliced
8 to 10 whole medium potatoes
¼ cup of red wine (any cabernet will do)
¼ cup corn syrup
　Fresh parsley
　Oregano
　Salt
　Fresh ground pepper
¼ clove garlic, finely chopped
1 white onion, finely chopped

Wash off the roast. Then, using a paring knife, insert slices of garlic about ¼- to ½-inch deep all over the roast, top and bottom. Peel the potatoes, slice them into quarters or halves, and place them in a roasting pan. Place the roast on top of the

Tige Andrews starred as Capt. Adam Greer, the man responsible for three young undercover police operatives on *The Mod Squad* from 1968 to 1973. He was also tough-talking, cigar-smoking Lt. John Russo on *The Detectives, Starring Robert Taylor*, from 1959 to 1962.

Captain Greer's Riz-Norma

1 eggplant
  Juice of ½ lemon
2 pounds beef or lamb, thinly sliced
2 tablespoons olive oil
1 or 2 cloves garlic, mashed
1 green pepper, cut up
6 ripe tomatoes, cut up
2 or 3 medium onions, sliced into strips
2 medium mushrooms, cut up
2 bay leaves
  Salt and pepper to taste
  Sage to taste
  Rosemary to taste
½ pound fresh green beans or asparagus
2 cups basmati rice, prepared according
  to package directions

Peel and slice the eggplant and squeeze lemon juice over it. Braise the beef or lamb strips in a skillet with the olive oil. Add the eggplant, stirring occasionally. Add the garlic. Add the green pepper, tomatoes, and onion and stir. Add the mushrooms and stir some more. Add the bay leaves and spices. Add the beans or asparagus. (For a juicier mixture, add a small can of peeled tomatoes and include the juice.) Cover the skillet and simmer until all the ingredients are heated through, continuing to stir occasionally. Serve over basmati rice.

Serving suggestion: Good with pita bread or crusty Italian bread.

Makes 6 servings.

Tige Andrews

Buford's Own Barbecue Sauce

1 8-ounce can crushed pineapple in
  heavy syrup
1 28-ounce bottle barbecue sauce
½ cup brown sugar
1 tablespoon sugar

Drain the pineapple and combine with the remaining ingredients. Let set for 20 minutes. This is great on chicken, pork chops, and ribs.

Makes about 4 cups.

Sheriff Buford Pusser

McNairy County Sheriff Buford Pusser was larger than life. The true story of the legendary Tennessee lawman, who was said to "walk softly and carry a big stick," was made into three *Walking Tall* feature films as well as a television movie and a series. A museum in Pusser's honor is located in his hometown of Adamsville, Tennessee.

From 1968 to 1979, James MacArthur was Det. Danny Williams, right-hand man to Jack Lord's Det. Steve McGarrett on *Hawaii Five-O*. Danno and his partners worked for the Hawaiian State Police.

Danno's Lamb Shanks

Cook 'em, Danno!

■ This recipe has been used in my family for years. (By the way, I am a chef at home and do a lot of the cooking as well as the cleaning up!)

2　**lamb shanks**
1　**onion, chopped**
1　**20-ounce can whole tomatoes**
1　**teaspoon oregano or more to taste**
　　Salt and pepper to taste

In a large pot, cover the lamb shanks with water and heat to a boil. Add the rest of the ingredients. Cover and keep at a rolling boil for 3 hours. Add water as needed. Serve with the rice of your choice and a vegetable of choice. Don't throw out the leftover broth. It's good too!

　　Makes 2 servings.

James MacArthur

Mannix's Hot Pot Lamb Chops

4 to 6 shoulder lamb chops
2 tablespoons all-purpose flour
2 teaspoons salt
½ teaspoon pepper
4 tablespoons butter, divided
1 7-ounce can sliced mushrooms
   Water
1 cube chicken bouillon
2 teaspoons A-1 steak sauce
1 pound onion, sliced
½ pound carrots, sliced
1¼ pounds potatoes, sliced

Preheat the oven to 350°. Trim excess fat off the chops. (If chops are large, cut them in half.) In a medium bowl, combine the flour, salt, and pepper. Dip the chops in the mixture and coat lightly. Save the seasoned flour.

In a skillet, brown the chops in 2 tablespoons butter. Remove the chops and stir the reserved flour mixture into the drippings in the skillet and form a smooth paste. Drain the mushrooms and add water to the mushroom liquid to measure three-fourths cup. Stir the liquid into the skillet along with the bouillon and the steak sauce. Reduce heat and simmer for 1 minute.

Put the chops in a baking dish and cover with the liquid, mushrooms, onion, carrots, and potatoes. Bake, covered, for at least 2 hours. (You can brush the potato slices with remaining melted butter and bake for 30 minutes longer.) If more sauce is desired, add a can of mushroom soup.

Makes 4 to 6 servings.

Mike Connors

Mike Connors was a private detective and an ace troubleshooter who was as good with his fists as he was with his wits in *Mannix* (1967–75). He reprised the role in Dick Van Dyke's *Diagnosis Murder* series in 1997. Connors also walked a fine line as an undercover agent named Nick on *Tightrope* in 1959.

Veal Cordon Blue

■ THE CASE OF THE RE-VEALED EVIDENCE

The sergeant looked at the pink flesh and knew that the death had been recent. His experience told him that the flat side of a large knife had been used to pound the flesh repeatedly. There were small shavings of a hip nearby, and he observed its European features with interest. Another object lay next to the hip; he noted its pale color as well as several holes the size a large-caliber handgun would inflict.

His training took hold. He instinctively knew how to handle the evidence. Deliberately , he placed the hip and the hole-ridden object on the tender pink flesh. The contrast was striking. He cautiously rolled the items together and secured them with a toothpick. "Sometimes the most common items are the best to use," he said to his assistant.

The messy part was yet to come; he would have to move quickly. Taking the parts as a whole, he gently rolled them in a powdered mixture until they appeared to be covered with fine sand. He looked around for a wetting agent, which he discovered in the nearby refrigerator. He expertly dipped the evidence in the slippery liquid and then applied a second coating. He stood over his work in silence. His years of training told him that the time had come. He reached for the skillet...

Veal cutlets
Swiss cheese, sliced

WHEN ONE WORD IS ENOUGH FOR A NAME

Match the crimebuster to the actor.

1. Baretta	A.	Robert Blake
2. Cannon	B.	Avery Brooks
3. Columbo	C.	William Conrad
4. Hawk	D.	Peter Falk
5. McCloud	E.	James Garner
6. Quincy	F.	Jack Klugman
7. Rockford	G.	James McEachin
8. Shaft	H.	Richard Roundtree
9. Spencer	I.	Robert Urich
10. Tenafly	J.	Dennis Weaver

SOLUTION

1. A, 2. C, 3. D, 4. B, 5. J, 6. F, 7. E, 8. H, 9. I. 10. G

Bavarian ham
Toothpicks
Salt and pepper
1 egg
Additional seasonings
Paprika
Breadcrumbs, seasoned
Vegetable shortening
Water

Gravy:

Flour
Kitchen Bouquet
Water

Take as many veal cutlets as necessary and pound them flat with a large knife blade. (Thinking of defense attorneys helps in this process.) Place a slice of Swiss cheese and Bavarian ham in the center and roll the cutlet up, securing it with a toothpick. Roll the cutlet into salt, pepper, and other seasonings you prefer. A touch of paprika is nice. Next, roll the veal in an egg you've assaulted with a whisk or fork, and then roll the veal in bread crumbs. (Seasoned, pre-packaged stuffing mix can also be used but then go easy on the salt and pepper spray.)

Brown the veal in a skillet with some shortening for about 5 minutes. Add some water to the skillet and let it simmer undercover for around 45 minutes. You can blow your cover toward the end to let the cutlets crisp up, or you can put them in the oven at 350° for 5 minutes.

To make skillet gravy, add a little flour to the pan drippings and stir. Add water as needed and add Kitchen Bouquet to taste.

Serving suggestion: Seasoned egg noodles make a good partner. Add a lemon wedge to each plate and you're done. Real cops don't need vegetables.

Case closed.

William K. Finney
Chief of Police, Saint Paul, Minnesota
Written and submitted by
Det. Sgt. Brook T. Schaub

David Suchet filled the bill perfectly as Agatha Christie's Belgian supersleuth Hercule Poirot, who pitted his famed little gray cells against murderers, kidnappers, embezzlers, and poisoners on PBS's *Mystery!*

Poirot's Favorite Leg of Lamb

4 or 5-pound leg of lamb
   Juice of 4 lemons
2 tablespoons wine vinegar
2 tablespoons olive oil
   Dijon mustard to taste
   Salt and pepper to taste
   Honey
   A few cloves garlic (optional)

With a sharp knife, make 7 or 8 slits in the meat. Combine the lemon juice, wine vinegar, olive oil, Dijon mustard, salt and pepper, and honey to taste. Smooth the sauce, which should not be too thin, all over the lamb, especially in the slits. (A few cloves of garlic may be placed in the slits, depending on the taste desired.) Place in a covered smoker over a very low heat for approximately 3 to 3½ hours, basting regularly with the remaining sauce.

Makes 4 servings. (For 2 people, make the same amount because they will always come back for more.)

David Suchet

Carolina Crock Pot Venison Roast

2 10¾-ounce cans cream of mushroom soup
1 3-to 4-pound venison roast
1 beef bouillon cube dissolved in 1 cup water
1 1-ounce envelope onion soup mix

Before leaving for work, put the cans of cream of mushroom soup into a slow cooker or Crock Pot. Place the venison roast on top of the soup. Add the beef bouillon and sprinkle the onion soup mix on top of the roast. Set on medium-low heat and cook for 8 or 9 hours.

Serving suggestion: The sauce in this dish can be served over rice or mashed potatoes.

Makes 4 to 6 servings.

Charles P. Austin Sr.
Chief of Police, Columbia, South Carolina
Submitted by Capt. J. R. Tate

Patrolman's Venison Potpie

3 tablespoons all-purpose flour
½ teaspoon salt
½ teaspoon pepper
1½ pounds boneless venison chuck or round steak (about ½-inch thick), cut into strips
3 tablespoons vegetable oil, divided
2 medium onions, thinly sliced
2 medium potatoes, peeled and cut into bite-sized chunks
1 medium carrot, sliced
1 cup beer
½ cup beef broth
2 tablespoons tomato paste
1 bay leaf
½ teaspoon dried thyme, crushed
1 recipe Single-Crust Pastry
¼ cup beer
1 tablespoon all-purpose flour
   Milk

In a shallow dish, combine the 3 tablespoons of flour, salt, and pepper (add more or less seasoning to taste). Coat the meat with the flour mixture. In a Dutch oven, brown the meat, a third at a time, in 1 tablespoon of hot oil. Remove the meat from the pan. Cook the onion in the drippings till tender. Drain off the fat.

Return the meat to the pan. Add the potatoes, carrot, the 1 cup of beer, broth, tomato paste, bay leaf, and thyme. Bring the mixture to boiling; reduce the heat. Cover and simmer for about 1 hour or until the meat is tender. Discard the bay leaf.

Meanwhile, prepare the Single-Crust Pastry; set aside. Stir together the ¼ cup of beer and the 1 tablespoon of flour. Add to the meat mixture. Cook and stir until thickened and bubbly. Turn the mixture into a 1½-quart casserole. Preheat the oven to 450°.

Place the pastry atop the casserole. Turn the pastry edge under; flute the pastry, pressing to the edges of the casserole. Cut several slits in the top to allow steam to escape. Brush the pastry top with milk. Place the casserole on a baking sheet. Bake for 15 to 20 minutes, or until brown.

Single-Crust Pastry

1¼ cups all-purpose flour
¼ teaspoon salt
⅓ cup vegetable shortening
   Water

In a medium mixing bowl, stir together the flour and salt. Cut in the shortening till the pieces are the size of peas. Sprinkle 1 tablespoon of water over part of the mixture, gently tossing with a fork. Push the dough to the side of the bowl. Repeat, using 1 tablespoon of water at a time, until all is moistened. Form the dough into a ball. On a lightly floured surface, flatten the dough. Roll the dough from the center to the edges until it is ⅛-inch thick and forms a circle 1 inch wider than a 1½-quart casserole dish.

Note: Venison should be cooked slowly over low heat as it has a tendency to dry out if overcooked or cooked too fast. Venison strips can also be marinated in advance to accent the flavor of the potpie.

Makes 6 servings.

Capt. Darrell E. Neas
Acting Chief of Police
Bismarck, North Dakota

Cleveland Venison and Noodles

2 **pounds venison, cubed**
  Bacon fat
1 **10¾-ounce can cream of mushroom soup**
1 **1-ounce package onion soup mix**
1 **16-ounce can whole tomatoes, diced**
  Cooked noodles

In a large saucepan, brown the venison in the bacon fat over medium heat. Add the mushroom soup, onion soup, and tomatoes. Cover and simmer for 2 hours. Serve over cooked noodles.

Makes 6 to 8 servings.

Rocco M. Pollutro
Chief of Police
Cleveland, Ohio

My Mother's Tried-and-True Tripe

■ Tripe is considered "Italian soul food." It's both a peasant's dish and a delicacy. (It can be purchased at your local supermarket or butcher.)

3 **pounds honeycomb tripe**
  Salt
5 **quarts cold water**
½ **cup olive oil**
1 **clove garlic, chopped**
½ **large onion, chopped**
1 **tablespoon dried red pepper flakes**
3 **bay leaves**
  Dash of Tabasco sauce
3 **ounces canned tomato paste**

1 **28-ounce can crushed tomatoes**
  Salt and pepper to taste
½ **cup freshly grated Parmesan cheese, plus more for serving**
  Freshly chopped parsley

Rinse the tripe under cold running water and scrub it with salt until it is white and clean. Place the tripe in a deep pot filled with about 5 quarts of cold water. Cover and let it come to a soft boil. Continue cooking for about 1 hour or until tender. Drain and rinse under cold water until it is cool enough to handle. Cut the tripe into pieces about 3 inches long and 1 inch wide. Reserve

Heat the oil in a large pot. Sauté the chopped garlic, onion, red pepper flakes, bay leaves, and Tabasco. Add the tomato paste and stir briskly. Add the can of tomatoes, salt, and pepper. Stir constantly until all the ingredients are blended and gently boiling. Add the tripe and simmer, covered, for about ½ hour. Now add the grated cheese and parsley. Simmer again for about 15 more minutes. Remove the bay leaves. Shut off the heat and wait about ½ hour before serving. Serve with plenty of grated cheese and additional salt and pepper.

Note: This can be prepared a day or two ahead of serving. It refrigerates well and can be frozen.

Makes 6 servings.

Col. Urbano Prignano Jr.
Chief of Police
Providence, Rhode Island

> *"Al Capone is dead. Eliot Ness is dead. But the struggle between the Capones and Nesses, witnessed by a pubic that is indifferent, goes on and on."*
>
> —Walter Winchell
> *(The Untouchables)*

than 35 minutes total). These times are for larger chicken breasts.

Richard Crenna

Inspector Clouseau's Poulet au Champagne

6 tablespoons butter, divided
4 shallots, chopped
   Salt and freshly ground pepper
4 chicken pieces
3 tablespoons brandy
2 tablespoons all-purpose flour
1 tablespoon tomato purée
¼ bottle champagne, divided
2 tablespoons lemon juice
   Pinch nutmeg
   Pinch cinnamon
   Pinch ginger
6 ounces button mushrooms
5 ounces cream

Melt 4 tablespoons butter in a large pan. Sauté the shallots until they are translucent. Remove and reserve the shallots but leave the butter in the pan. Season the chicken with salt and pepper and fry the chicken in the same butter over medium heat until golden brown. Pour warmed brandy over the chicken and ignite it. Remove the chicken from the pan. Add the flour and tomato purée to the pan juices and mix. Gradually add half of the champagne and all of the lemon juices and spices. Bring to a boil, and then return the chicken and shallots to the pan. Add the rest of the champagne. Cook, covered, for 45 minutes.

Meanwhile, sauté the mushrooms in the remaining butter, then add to the chicken. Cook for 10 minutes more. Remove the chicken, then stir the cream into the pan juices over gentle heat. Adjust the seasoning to taste. Bring to serving temperature and pour over the chicken.

Makes 4 servings.

Peter Sellers
Submitted by mother-in-law Iris Frederick

Richard Crenna has portrayed New York City police detective Frank Janek in a long-running series of television movies. He also played private eye and retired police officer Mitch O'Hannon on *Pros & Cons* in 1981.

Frank Janek's Barbecue Chicken

■ This recipe is very simple and a simply wonderful way to barbecue chicken. It has always been a family favorite.

   Chicken breasts
1 part lemon juice
3 parts barbecue sauce

Combine the lemon juice and the barbecue sauce.

When the coals are covered with white ash, place the chicken bone-side down on the grill for 10 minutes. Baste with sauce. Turn the chicken to skin-side down for 10 minutes. Baste. Turn for the final time. Baste. Close the grill hood and cook for an additional 15 minutes (and no more

Fletch's Chinese Barbecued Chicken

4 tablespoons peanut oil
2 tablespoons chopped fresh ginger root
¼ cup chopped scallions
2 cloves garlic, chopped
⅓ cup soy sauce
1 tablespoon sugar
1 tablespoon sesame oil
17 chicken thighs or 3 pounds chicken parts

In small skillet or saucepan, heat the peanut oil until hot. Add the ginger, scallions and garlic and stir-fry for 1 minute. Add the soy sauce and sugar and bring to a boil. Turn off heat and add the sesame oil. Marinate the chicken in this mixture for 1 or 2 hours. Remove the chicken from the marinade and barbecue or broil it until golden brown. Baste with the marinade; turn the pieces over and cook until done. The skin should be crispy.

Makes 8 servings.

Chevy Chase

Chevy Chase twice played author Gregory McDonald's Fletch, a Los Angeles investigative reporter who was a determined crime solver and master of disguises in *Fletch* (1985) and *Fletch Lives* (1989).

> *"It's a wilderness out there. And every so often a beast of prey comes sneaking in. Now, it's my job as a lawman to stalk him and run him out. That's my number one job—stalking, not fly-killing."*
>
> —Deputy Barney Fife
> *(The Andy Griffith Show)*

Jack Wagner, who was nominated for an Emmy, played Officer Frisco Jones on the day-time drama *General Hospital*.

Frisco's Baked Chicken

1 cut-up frying chicken
1 stick butter, melted
3 cups crushed toasted rice cereal
¼ cup garlic salt (adjust to taste)
    Pepper to taste

Preheat oven to 375°. Roll the chicken in the butter and then roll it in a mixture of the remaining ingredients. Bake in greased pan for 1 hour.
    Makes about 4 servings.

Jack Wagner

Cruiser Crock Pot Chicken and Rice

4 boneless chicken breast halves
1 cup white rice
1 onion, chopped
1 cup chopped celery (with leaves)
1 teaspoon thyme
½ teaspoon chopped garlic
2 cubes chicken bouillon
1 10¾-ounce can cream of mushroom soup
    Salt and pepper to taste
2 cups water

Mix all of the ingredients in a 4-quart (or larger) Crock Pot and make sure the liquid covers the rice and chicken. Cook, covered, on high for 3 to 4 hours or until the rice and chicken are tender.

Serving suggestion: Serve with salad and rolls.

Makes 4 servings.

Col. John R. Bailey
Director
Arkansas State Police

Marlowe's Crab-Stuffed Chicken

½ cup grated onion
½ cup chopped celery
3 tablespoons butter
1 7½-ounce can crab meat
½ cup herb-seasoned stuffing
6 chicken breasts
2 tablespoons all-purpose flour
¼ cup paprika
  Salt and pepper
2 tablespoons white wine (optional)
½ cup cream of chicken soup
½ cup sour cream

Preheat oven to 350°. Sauté the onion and celery in the butter. Remove from heat and add the crab meat and stuffing. Stir together. Cut a slit in each chicken breast and stuff each with the crab meat/stuffing mixture. Combine the flour, paprika, salt, and pepper and dust each breast. Place the chicken breasts in a large greased pan with wine and bake for 45 minutes.

Combine soup and sour cream. During the last 20 minutes of cooking, cover each breast with soup mixture.

Makes 6 servings.

Powers Boothe

During the 1980s Powers Boothe portrayed Raymond Chandler's classy Philip Marlowe in a series of five HBO movies set in 1930s Los Angeles. Marlowe's run-down office was on Hollywood Boulevard.

Nell Carter portrayed the sarcastic Sgt. Hildy Jones when Sheriff Elroy P. Lobo and his deputies joined a special Atlanta police task force on *Lobo* from 1980 to 1981.

Hildy's Favorite Chicken

1 pound mushrooms
4 tomatoes
6 scallions
2 garlic cloves
1 red onion
1 yellow onion
1 tablespoon margarine
   Lemon and pepper seasoning (or other
   seasoning to taste)
3 tablespoons vegetable oil
   Salt and pepper
1 whole chicken, cut up
   Parmesan cheese

Chop the mushrooms, tomatoes, scallions, garlic (I like to use bunches of garlic!), and onion and sauté them in the margarine in a saucepan or skillet. Season the vegetables only from the top. While they are sautéing, heat the oil with the salt and pepper in a shallow pan and cook the chicken, uncovered, over medium heat for 25 minutes. Pour the sautéed mixture over the cooked chicken, cover, and continue cooking for 20 more minutes. Sprinkle the chicken with Parmesan cheese (a lot if you like) and cook 10 minutes longer. Remove and eat.

Serving suggestion: Serve with rice or noodles; both are great. Enjoy!

Makes 4 servings.

Nell Carter

Top Gunn Quick Margarita Chicken

2 tablespoons corn oil
2 tablespoons lime juice
1 teaspoon honey
4 boneless, skinless chicken breast halves
1 cup finely crushed tortilla chips
1 14½-ounce can mild salsa
½ cup shredded Monterey Jack cheese
   Cilantro sprigs
   Lime wedges

One of the slickest private eyes in all of television history was Craig Stevens as Peter Gunn from 1958 to 1961. The show also had one of television's most memorable scores, which was composed by music master Henry Mancini.

Mix the first three ingredients together. Brush the chicken breasts with the mixture; then roll in the tortilla chips crumbs to coat. Arrange the chicken in a 9-inch microwave-proof baking dish. Microwave on HIGH for 8 to 10 minutes, rotating several times during cooking. Pour the salsa over the chicken, top with shredded cheese, and microwave on HIGH another 1 to 2 minutes or until the cheese is melted. Garnish with cilantro and lime wedges.

Makes 4 servings.

Craig Stevens

Hawaiian Eye Chicken in Wine Sauce

■ Mom gave us this recipe when we were first married, and it's still a favorite.
—*LaVelda (Mrs. Robert) Conrad*

3 **boneless chicken breasts, cut into strips**
Salt and pepper

All-purpose flour
4 **tablespoons olive oil**
1 **clove garlic, crushed**
½ **cup dry white wine**
3 **medium tomatoes, sliced**

Season the chicken with salt and pepper and then roll lightly in flour. In a medium skillet, heat the olive oil and garlic over medium heat. Add the chicken and fry on medium heat until lightly browned (7 to 10 minutes). Add the wine and cook for 2 minutes. Remove the chicken onto a platter.

Sauté the sliced tomatoes in the skillet until tender. Place the tomato slices over the chicken strips. Cover with pan drippings and serve immediately.

Note: For a little "Hawaiian" flavor, substitute pineapple slices for the tomatoes.

Makes 4 servings.

Robert Conrad

Working out of a poolside office at the Hawaiian Village Hotel in Honolulu were (back left to right) detectives Tom Lopaka (Robert Conrad), Tracy Steele (Anthony Eisley), and Greg MacKenzie (Grant Williams) on *Hawaiian Eye* (1959–63). Among their friends were singer Cricket Blake (Connie Stevens) and cabbie Kazuo Kim (Poncie Ponce).

Bob Hoskins tackled villainy in Toontown as gumshoe Eddie Valiant in *Who Framed Roger Rabbit?*

Gumshoe Chicken Valiant

Chicken pieces (vary number as needed)
Medium-sized potatoes, cut into thick chips
Garlic cloves, unpeeled
Fresh tomatoes
Pitted black olives
Fresh rosemary
2 tablespoons olive oil
Salt and pepper

Preheat the oven to 375°. Put all the ingredients into a large baking tray. Turn all the ingredients over in the pan with your hands so that everything is well coated with the olive oil. Bake for about 1 hour or until the chicken is done.

Makes 4 to 6 servings.

Bob Hoskins

Shaft's Paella Valencia

8 clams or mussels (adjust number according to preference)
1 cup chicken broth
1 medium artichoke
Salt
2 tablespoons olive oil
4 small chicken pieces (sliced)
4 hot Italian sausages or chorizo, sliced
4 slices pork tenderloin, cut ¼-inch thick
Salt and pepper
1 red pepper, cubed
1 green pepper, cubed
⅓ cup green beans
1 clove garlic, diced
2 20-ounce cans whole tomatoes, seeded and chopped
1 teaspoon paprika
1 large pinch saffron
1 cup rice
8 large shrimp, shelled and deveined
½ 10-ounce package frozen green peas
1 lemon, thinly sliced

Scrub the mussels and clams and set aside. In a deep pot, bring 1 inch of water to a boil. Add the clams and mussels. Cover and steam for 8 minutes or until the shells open. Remove the shellfish and pour 2 cups of the liquid from the pot into a measuring cup. If necessary, add chicken broth to make up any difference. Set aside.

Remove the heart from the artichoke and cut into 4 to 6 pieces. Bring a pot of salted water to a boil and then add the artichoke pieces. Cook for 15 minutes. Drain and set aside. Heat the oil in a paella pan or large shallow iron pan. Over medium heat, sauté the chicken and sausage for 5 minutes. Add the pork. Cook an additional 5 minutes. Cover and cook until all meat is tender. Salt and pepper to taste.

Add red and green peppers, green beans, and garlic to the cooked meat. Blend well with the oil in the pan. Stir in the tomatoes and paprika. Add the saffron to the rice and pour the rice into the pan. Increase the heat and add the reserved clam and chicken broth. Bring to a boil. Stir once, reduce heat, and simmer. Do not cover the pan or stir the rice again.

In about 10 minutes, add the shrimp and cook for an additional 5 minutes. Now add the clams and mussels in their shells along with the peas. Cook for 10 minutes or until the rice has absorbed all the liquid. (Note: if the rice is under-cooked, it will stick together.) When the cooking is completed, remove the pan from heat and let sit for 5 minutes. Garnish with lemon slices. Add additional salt and pepper to taste. Serve directly from the pan.

Makes 4 servings.

Richard Roundtree

Richard Roundtree scored big time as one of the coolest private eyes of all time when he took on the mantle of John Shaft in three feature films, beginning with *Shaft* in 1971. Roundtree also starred as the streetwise private eye from the Big Apple in the 1973 television series.

Hondo's Chicken Pilaf

■ As a kid in Texas, southern fried chicken was always my preference. I'd never heard of Greek chicken pilaf, but I hadn't met my wife, Cris, then either. She made me a believer when I first tasted this recipe, and I've never tired of it.

2 **fryer chickens, cut into serving pieces (or 5 whole, boned chicken breasts, skinned)**
   Salt and pepper
   Butter
2 **onions, finely chopped**
1 **garlic clove, minced**
1 **28-ounce can whole tomatoes, cut into small pieces**
1 **8-ounce can tomato sauce**
1 **teaspoon ground cinnamon**
½ **sherry wine**
   Water as needed
2 **cups chicken broth**
1 **cup water**
2 **cups uncooked rice**

Wipe the chicken dry and sprinkle with salt and pepper. Melt the butter in a Dutch oven and brown the chicken on all sides. Add the onion and garlic and sauté them until the onions are soft. Add the tomatoes, tomato sauce, and cinnamon. Add the wine. Add additional salt and pepper to taste. Add hot water as needed and simmer for 45 minutes or until the chicken is tender. Remove from heat and set aside.

In another pot, combine the chicken broth with the 1 cup of water and 1 cup of the sauce in which the chicken was cooked. Bring to a boil, add the rice, lightly salt, stir, cover, and simmer over low heat for 20 minutes or until the rice has absorbed the liquid and is cooked. (Do not uncover during cooking.)

When you're ready to serve, place the chicken on plates and pour some of the sauce over each serving along with a generous portion of the rice. Pour some of the remaining sauce into a gravy boat for optional use over the rice.

Serving Suggestion: An interesting garnish is plain yogurt, which can be served on each individual plate or in a separate serving dish placed on the table.

Makes 6 servings.

Steve Forrest

Steve Forrest (center) was head honcho as Lt. Dan "Hondo" Harrelson when he starred in *S.W.A.T.* in 1975. The initials stand for Special Weapons and Tactics. Also on the *S.W.A.T.* team were (from left to right) James Coleman as T. J. McCabe, Mark Shera as Dominic Luca, Rod Perry as Sgt. David "Deacon" Kay, and Robert Urich as Jim Street. For a time Forrest raised honeybees and sold the honey from their hives. He called his hobby and business "Honey from the Forrests."

Buffalo Chicken Breasts with Cream and Sun-Dried Tomatoes

■ We made this dish for the crew of *Cops* when they were in town.
　　　　　　—*Anna Lazlo (Mrs. Gil) Kerlikowske*

6　tablespoons butter
6　boneless, skinless chicken breast halves
¼　cup thinly sliced sun-dried tomatoes
½　cup white wine
½　cup heavy cream
6　to 8 sprigs fresh basil

Melt the butter in a large frying pan or saucepan. When the butter foams, add the chicken breasts 1 or 2 at a time. Sauté the chicken for 3 to 4 minutes on each side or until lightly golden brown and cooked. Remove to a warm serving dish. Add the sun-dried tomatoes to the pan and sauté slightly. Add the wine and boil rapidly until the sauce reduces and thickens slightly. Reduce the heat and pour in the cream. Add the basil. Reheat gently without boiling, season to taste, put the chicken back into the pan for another minute, and then serve immediately with rice or fettuccine. Remove basil sprigs if desired.
　　Makes 6 servings.

Gil Kerlikowske
Commissioner of Police
Buffalo, New York

Detective Harris's Bombay Chicken

10　to 16 pieces chicken (breasts, thighs, and legs)
1½　cups prunes
　1　3-ounce jar green Spanish olives, rinsed
½　cup olive oil
½　cup red wine vinegar
　1　4-ounce can capers, rinsed
　　Black pepper to taste

Among the many memorable *Barney Miller* (1975–82) characters from Manhattan's Twelfth Precinct station was the wisecracking detective Ron Harris, portrayed by Ron Glass.

¼　teaspoon cayenne pepper (use cautiously)
　6　cloves garlic, finely chopped
　　Basil
　　Oregano
　1　cup white wine

Place the chicken in a baking pan with the next 10 ingredients. Cover and marinate in the refrigerator overnight. Preheat the oven to 400°. Just prior to cooking, add the white wine. Bake, uncovered, for 1 hour or until done.
　　Serving suggestion: Serve with polenta or rice.
　　Makes 4 to 6 servings.

Ron Glass

Chris Noth, one of the acclaimed *Law & Order* boys, played Det. Mike Logan who worked shoulder to shoulder with Det. Lennie Briscoe to bring justice to the streets of New York City. Once the detectives had done their job, it was up to the city's attorneys to see that justice was served in the courts.

Mike Logan's Chinatown Chicken

■ I bombard this dish with every spice imaginable, but you can experiment.

1 medium onion, finely chopped
1 clove garlic, finely chopped
1 carrot, finely chopped
1 red bell pepper, finely chopped
   Small amount fresh ginger, finely chopped
2 tablespoons light olive oil
6 boneless, skinless chicken breasts
   Touch of powdered ginger
   Salt to taste
   Black pepper to taste
   Paprika to taste
1 cup vanilla or maple yogurt

Throw all the vegetables and the chopped ginger into a wok with the oil. While the mixture is sautéing, rub the chicken breasts with the powdered ginger, salt, pepper, and paprika. Slice the chicken and add to the wok. Before the chicken is done, add the yogurt and stir. Cover the wok and allow to simmer until the yogurt blends in. Serve over pasta or rice.

Makes 4 to 6 servings.

Chris Noth

Sergeant Billings's Spanish Rice and Chicken

■ Luis was my father's right-hand man and best friend for almost forty years. Luis was the real deal and could cook this kind of Spanish food with the best of 'em. My father was crazy about Luis and his cooking!   —*Greta Garner-Hewitt*

3 chicken breasts with skin and bone attached
½ teaspoon salt
½ teaspoon black pepper
3 bay leaves, divided
3 cups water
1 medium onion, chopped
¼ bell pepper, chopped

Luis Delgado is seen here with James Garner during a break in filming *My Fellow Americans* in 1996. Fans recognize Delgado as Officer Billings on *The Rockford Files.* For many years, Delgado was Garner's stand-in in filming, but he was also Garner's longtime assistant and friend.

2 cloves garlic, chopped
1 10-ounce can tomatoes
1 8-ounce can tomato juice
½ teaspoon saffron
1 cup long-grain white rice

In a 4-quart saucepan, boil the chicken, salt, pepper, and 1 bay leaf in 3 cups of water for 20 minutes. Set the chicken aside to cool, reserving the broth in a clean container to use later. Using the same saucepan, sauté the onion, bell pepper, and garlic until tender. Add the whole tomatoes, tomato juice, and 2 bay leaves. Reduce by a third until the sauce is medium thick. Preheat the oven to 350°. Separate the chicken from the skin and bones. Cut the meat into bite-sized pieces and mix into the sauce. Add 2 cups of the broth and simmer for 5 minutes. Add the saffron and stir well. Add the rice and stir. Cover and bake for 30 minutes or until the rice is cooked. Remove from the oven and stir. Put back into the oven and cook, uncovered, for 5 minutes longer. Remove the bay leaves. Serve and enjoy.

Makes 4 servings.

Luis Delgado
Submitted by Bobbie (Mrs. Luis) Delgado

Driving Captain Block crazy were Officers Gunther Toody (Joe E. Ross, left) and Francis Muldoon (Fred Gwynne, right) as they patrolled the Bronx's Fifty-third Precinct on *Car 54, Where Are You?* (1961–63).

Captain Block's On-Duty Fruity Chicken

Ooh, ooh—it's so good!

1 8-ounce bottle red Russian salad dressing
1 18-ounce jar apricot preserves
1 1-ounce package dry onion soup mix
8 boneless, skinless chicken breast halves

Preheat the oven to 350°. In a large bowl, mix together the dressing, preserves, and soup mix. Place the chicken in a lightly greased baking dish and cover with marinade. Cover with foil. Bake for 45 minutes. Remove the foil and cook 15 minutes longer. Serve with rice. Enjoy!

Makes 8 servings.

Paul Reed

Paul Reed played Capt. Martin Block, the unfortunate leader of New York's Fifty-third Precinct, home to Officers Toody and Muldoon of *Car 54, Where Are You?* comedic fame.

Walker's White Tornado Enchiladas

1 pint half & half
1 20-ounce can stewed tomatoes
4 cups shredded Monterey Jack cheese
   (you may want more), divided
1 4-ounce can jalapeño peppers, diced
   Vegetable oil
2 dozen corn tortillas

In a saucepan, combine the half & half, stewed tomatoes, 1 cup of the shredded cheese, and the peppers (or to desired taste). Stir constantly over low heat until the ingredients are hot and mixed well, like a thick cream.

In a frying pan, heat the vegetable oil. Fry each tortilla until lightly crisp and then dip each one through the cheese mixture. In a baking dish, layer the tortillas, generously sprinkling shredded cheese between the layers. Top with any remaining shredded cheese. Heat in the oven just until the cheese on top has melted.

Makes 6 servings.

Chuck Norris

The star of *Lone Wolf McQuade* and other films, former karate champion Chuck Norris has been one of television's most popular stars of the 1990s in *Walker, Texas Ranger.*

Checkpoint Chicken Enchiladas

6 cans all-white chicken breast meat
2 ¼-ounce cans chopped black olives
1 cup chopped bell pepper
1 cup chopped onion
   Salt and pepper to taste
6 to 8 10¾-ounce cans cream of
   chicken soup, divided
16 ounces sour cream
24 soft flour tortillas
3 cups grated cheddar cheese

Preheat the oven to 350°. Mix the chicken, olives, bell pepper, and onion together. Add salt and pepper to taste. Add 1 can of the soup and ½ cup of the sour cream. Mix all together.

Pour 1 can of soup into a large baking dish and spread over the bottom. Spoon two tablespoons of the chicken mixture into a tortilla, roll it up like an enchilada, and place it in the baking dish. Continue to layer the dish with rolled up enchiladas. Mix the remaining cans of soup and the sour cream together and pour over the enchiladas. Cover the top with grated cheese. Bake, uncovered, for 30 to 45 minutes. Serve hot.

Makes 6 servings.

Frank Latham
Chief of Police
Hewitt, Texas

American Detective Sesame Chicken

3 to 4 pounds chicken breasts
¼ cup sesame seed
3 tablespoons vegetable oil
¼ cup soy sauce
2 tablespoons brown sugar
¾ teaspoon ground ginger
¼ teaspoon black pepper
2 cloves garlic, pressed
4 whole green onions, sliced, divided

Cut the chicken into 1-inch chunks. Combine the sesame seed and oil in a pan. Cook over medium-low heat until seed turns golden. Let cool. Stir in the next five ingredients and half of the green onions. Mix in the chicken, cover, and chill for 2 to 3 hours. Arrange the chicken in a single layer to allow the marinade to cover pieces. Preheat broiler. Broil 6 inches from heat for about 10 minutes. Turn and broil 5 minutes more until done. Garnish with the remaining green onions.

Makes 4 to 6 servings.

Det. John Bunnell

Lt. John Bunnell hosts television's popular *American Detective* series.

Scooby Doo's Turkey Enchiladoos

■ This is a favorite dish prepared by my cook, Kathy McCaskey.

	Vegetable oil
12	corn tortillas
1	28-ounce can Las Palmas red chili sauce
16	ounces sour cream
3	cups cooked and shredded turkey
1	pound Monterey Jack cheese, cut into finger-sized strips
1	4-ounce can green chili peppers, cut into strips
¼	pound cheddar cheese, grated
4	scallions, sliced

In an 8- to 10-inch skillet, pour oil ¼-inch deep and heat over medium-high heat. Soften the tortillas one at a time by placing in the hot oil for a few seconds on each side (use tongs). Drain the tortillas on paper towels. Preheat the oven to 325°.

Dip each tortilla, one at a time, in the chili sauce. Place 1 to 2 teaspoons of sour cream down the center of each tortilla along with ¼ cup of turkey, 1 strip of Monterey Jack cheese, and 1 or 2 chili strips. Roll the tortillas and place them seam-side down in a 9x13x2-inch casserole dish. Pour the remaining sauce over them and sprinkle the grated cheese and scallions on top. Bake, uncovered, for about 30 minutes.

Makes 12 servings.

Don Messick, the voice of Scooby Doo

Motor City Chicken Fajitas and Rice

■ This grilled chicken main dish is one of my favorites—especially when cooked outdoors on the barbecue. The chicken breasts can be served individually with your choice of side dishes or sliced and rolled up into a tortilla. Either way, the marinade makes them special.

½ cup vegetable oil
⅓ cup lime juice
2 cloves garlic, minced
½ teaspoon pepper
½ teaspoon salt
¼ cup wine vinegar
¼ medium onion, grated
1 teaspoon sugar
1 teaspoon oregano
¼ teaspoon cumin
6 boned and skinless chicken breasts

SCENE OF THE CRIME

Match the locale with the television series.

1. *Barney Miller*
2. *Bourbon Street Beat*
3. *Big Shamus, Little Shamus*
4. *Carter Country*
5. *Colonel March of Scotland Yard*
6. *Dan August*
7. *Homicide*
8. *In the Heat of the Night*
9. *Inspector Morse*
10. *Harbourmaster*
11. *Hec Ramsey*
12. *Kodiak*
13. *Magnum, P.I.*
14. *Miss Marple*
15. *Murder, She Wrote*
16. *Spenser: For Hire*
17. *Surfside Six*
18. *Toma*
19. *The Untouchables*
20. *Walker, Texas Ranger*

A. Alaska
B. Atlantic City, NJ
C. Baltimore, MD
D. Boston, MA
E. Cabot Cove, ME
F. Chicago, IL
G. Clinton Corners, GA
H. Dallas, TX
I. Greenwich Village, NY
J. London, England
K. Miami, FL
L. Newark, NJ
M. New Orleans, MA
N. New Prospect, OK
O. Oahu, HI
P. Oxford, Eng.
Q. Santa Luisa, CA
R. St. Mary Mead, Eng.
S. Scott Island, Cape Ann, MA
T. Sparta, MI

SOLUTION

1. I, 2. M, 3. B, 4. G, 5. J, 6. Q, 7. C, 8. T, 9. P, 10. S, 11. N, 12. A, 13. O, 14. R. 15. E, 16. D, 17. K. 18. L, 19. F, 20. H

24 soft flour tortillas
Salsa and Rice (recipe follows)
Condiments of your choice

Combine all of the ingredients, except the chicken and tortillas, and Salsa and Rice, to make a marinade. Pour the marinade over the chicken breasts in a plastic bag or glass bowl and refrigerate overnight.

Grill the meat for 8 minutes on the first side; turn and grill for 5 to 7 minutes on the second side. Immediately slice into strips and serve in warm tortillas with your favorite condiments, such as tomatoes, cheese, green onions, black olives, salsa, sour cream, and guacamole.

Serving suggestion: These fajitas go well with Salsa and Rice.

Salsa and Rice

2 tablespoons vegetable oil
1½ cups rice
½ cup chopped green pepper
½ cup chopped onion
1 large clove garlic, minced
2¾ cups chicken broth
⅓ cup salsa (mild or hot)

In a large frying pan, heat the oil and brown the rice, green pepper, onion, and garlic. Add the broth and salsa and stir. Cover the pan and simmer for 20 minutes until the broth is absorbed.

Makes 4 to 6 servings.

Isaiah McKinnon
Chief of Police
Detroit, Michigan

Classified Chicken

We'll give you this recipe, but then we'll have to kill you.

4 6-ounce packages chipped beef, diced
4 whole chicken breasts, cut in half, boned, and skinned
1 10¾-ounce can undiluted cream of mushroom (or celery) soup
½ pint sour cream

Preheat the oven to 275°. Cover the bottom of a flat, greased baking pan with chipped beef. Place the chicken breasts on top. Mix the soup and sour cream and pour over all. (It can be refrigerated at this point.) Bake, uncovered, for 3 hours.

Makes 8 servings.

David D. Whipple
Executive Director
Association of Former Intelligence Officers

Country Cop's Poached Chicken with Peach Chutney

1 **chicken bouillon cube**
2 **boneless chicken breasts**
1 **large onion**
2 **ripe peaches**
2 **tablespoons raisins**
2 **teaspoons vegetable oil**
2 **teaspoons curry powder (or to taste)**
1 **teaspoon brown sugar**
   Dash of red wine vinegar
½ **cup instant or quick rice**
½ **teaspoon coarsely ground black pepper (optional)**

Craig Stevens as Peter Gunn.

Dissolve the bouillon in about 2 inches of water and poach the chicken breasts at a low temperature until tender. While the chicken is cooking, chop the onion and peaches into small cubes. When the chicken is done, sauté the peaches, onion, and raisins together in the vegetable oil. As the onion becomes soft and translucent, add the curry powder, brown sugar, and vinegar and mix the ingredients thoroughly. Put the chicken breasts on a bed of rice and spoon on the peach chutney mix while it is hot. Sprinkle on pepper if desired.

Makes 2 servings.

David Hunter

COP·POP

Match the television or movie theme with the artist who had a radio hit with the tune. Dum-de-dum-dum.

1. "Axel F" (*Beverly Hills Cop*)	A. Harold Faltermeyer, No. 3, 1985
2. "Bad Boys" (*Cops Theme*)	B. Jan Hammer, No. 1, 1985
3. "Believe It or Not" (*The Greatest American Hero*)	C. Issac Hayes, No. 1, 1971
4. "Dragnet"	D. Inner Circle, No. 8, 1993
5. "Hawaii Five-O"	E. Mike Post,
6. "Hill Street Blues"	Pete Carpenter,
7. "Keep Your Eye on the Sparrow" (*Baretta*)	No. 10, 1975
	F. Mike Post, No. 10, 1981
8. "Miami Vice"	G. Ray Anthony Orchestra,
9. "Peter Gunn"	No. 3, 1953
10. "The Rockford Files"	H. Ray Anthony Orchestra,
11. "S.W.A.T."	No. 8, 1959
12. "Theme from *Shaft*"	I. Rhythm Heritage, No. 1, 1975
	J. Rhythm Heritage, No. 20, 1976
	K. Joey Scarbury, No. 2, 1981
	L. The Ventures, No. 4, 1969

SOLUTION
1. A, 2. D, 3. K, 4. G, 5. L, 6. F, 7. J, 8. B, 9. H, 10. E, 11. I, 12. C

From 1958 to 1964, the coolest private eyes on Hollywood's Sunset Strip were Roger Smith (left) and Efrem Zimbalist Jr. as Jeff Spencer and Stuart Bailey respectively. That's *77 Sunset Strip* to be exact.

Efrem Zimbalist Jr. graduated from *77 Sunset Strip* to become Inspector Lewis Erskine on *The FBI* from 1965 to 1974. Daughter Stephanie Zimbalist followed in his crime-solving shoes in the 1980s to star in *Remington Steele*.

Inspector Erskine's Lemon Chicken on Spinach Leaves

■ This is a recipe that my wife often uses, and it is my favorite.

> 3 large whole chicken breasts, halved
> 1 cup chicken broth
> ½ cup sugar
> ½ cup lemon juice
> 2 tablespoons water
> 1 tablespoon dry sherry
> 1½ teaspoons soy sauce
> 2 tablespoons cornstarch
> 1 10-ounce bag spinach
> 1 teaspoon salt
> ½ cup cornstarch
> ½ cup vegetable oil

Working with 1 breast half at a time, place it skin up. With the tip of a sharp knife, starting parallel and close to the large end of a rib bone, cut and scrape the meat away from the bone and rib cage, gently pulling back the meat in one piece as you cut. Discard the bones. Remove the skin and white tendons.

In a 1-quart saucepan, mix well the chicken broth, sugar, lemon juice, water, sherry, soy sauce, and cornstarch. Cook over medium heat, stirring constantly, until the sauce is smooth and thickened. Keep warm.

Shred the spinach coarsely and arrange on a platter. Sprinkle the chicken with salt. Coat the chicken with about ½ cup cornstarch. In a 12-inch skillet, over medium-high heat in hot oil, cook the chicken until lightly browned and fork tender (about 10 minutes). Arrange the chicken on the spinach and pour some sauce over the chicken. Pour the remaining sauce into a gravy boat and pass separately.

Makes 6 servings.

Efrem Zimbalist Jr.

Charleston Baked Chicken

½ stick butter
1 broiler-fryer chicken (about 3 pounds),
   cut up
   Paprika
1 small head green cabbage (about ½
   pound), cored and cut into ½-inch
   thick slices
   Salt and pepper
2 red cooking apples, cored and sliced
1 medium onion, thinly sliced
1 tablespoon grated lemon rind
2 teaspoons caraway seed
1 teaspoon sugar
1½ cups shredded Swiss cheese

Melt the butter in a large skillet with a cover. Dust the chicken lightly with paprika. Place chicken in skillet and brown on both sides over medium heat. Cover and reduce heat. Cook for 30 minutes.

Preheat the oven to 375°. Place cabbage slices on the bottom of a buttered 9x13-inch baking dish. Sprinkle with salt and pepper. Cover the dish with aluminum foil. Bake, covered, for 20 minutes or until the cabbage is almost tender. Remove the cabbage from the oven. Uncover and arrange the apples and onion over the cabbage. Sprinkle with lemon rind, caraway seed, and sugar. Place the chicken pieces over top. Cover with foil and continue baking 25 to 30 minutes longer or until the cabbage and chicken are tender. Remove from the oven; uncover. Sprinkle with cheese. Return to the oven just until the cheese is melted, about 5 minutes.

Makes 4 to 6 servings

Frederick L. Marshall
Chief of Police
Charleston, West Virginia

Green Mountain Chicken Parmesan

4 chicken breast halves, skinned and
   boned
2 16-ounce cans Italian-style stewed
   tomatoes
2 tablespoons cornstarch
½ teaspoon oregano or basil, crushed
¼ teaspoon hot pepper sauce (optional)
¼ cup grated Parmesan cheese
   Fresh parsley sprigs

Preheat the oven to 425°. Place the chicken in a baking dish. Bake, covered, for 15 minutes. Drain the chicken. In a saucepan, combine the tomatoes, cornstarch, oregano, and pepper sauce, and then cook, stirring constantly, until the sauce is thickened. Pour the heated sauce over the chicken; top with the cheese. Bake, uncovered, for 5 minutes more. Garnish with parsley.

Variation: To make this chicken mozzarella, I pour the sauce over cooked pasta and top with mozzarella cheese and bake until the cheese is melted. This makes a great main dish with a salad. I have also used uncooked chicken tenders or chicken strips instead of breast halves.

Makes 4 servings.

Col. A. James Walton Jr.
Commissioner
Vermont State Police

> *"Swallow what's bitter in the cup and move on."*
> —Lt. Howard Hunter
> *(Hill Street Blues)*

Emmy-winning writer and producer Stephen J. Cannell has been the creative source behind many of television's finest detective and police series, including *The Rockford Files, Tenspeed and Brownshoe, Wiseguy*, and *The Commish.* Cannell himself played a cop as Lt. Donald Dutch Dixon on *Renegade* and hosted the anthology series *Scene of the Crime.* He has recently taken up his lifelong dream of writing novels and has penned the best-selling thrillers *The Plan* and *Final Victim.*

Write 'em Up Barbecue Chicken

Chicken breasts, thighs, and legs (on the bone)
Seasoned salt
1 stick melted butter
Juice of 5 lemons
2 tablespoons Worcestershire sauce
Dash of garlic juice

Lightly sprinkle the chicken parts with seasoned salt. Make a sauce by combining the butter, lemon juice, Worcestershire, and garlic juice. Put chicken on the grill and baste with the sauce. Cook until brown and juices run clear when tested with a fork. Turn the chicken frequently, basting each time.

Stephen J. Cannell

Rockford Salsa Chicken Preserves

2 pounds boneless, skinless chicken thighs or breasts, cut into ¾-inch slices
2 tablespoons taco seasoning mix (homemade or packaged)
4 teaspoons olive oil
1 16-ounce bottle mild or hot chunky salsa
⅔ cup peach preserves or other preserves

Coat the chicken pieces with taco seasoning. Heat the oil in a large skillet over medium-high heat. Add the chicken and cook until browned, stirring occasionally. Add the salsa and preserves to the pan and lower the heat. Cover and simmer for 15 minutes. Serve over hot rice.

Serves 6 hungry police family members.

Bill Fitzpatrick
Chief of Police
Rockford, Illinois

Sergeant Howard's Stuffed Chicken with Tapenade

It's O.K. with Kay!

■ This recipe is from a good friend, Kevin McGowan, who also happens to be an ex-NYPD officer and now is a chef. This recipe goes well with Interrogation Room Garlic Mashed Potatoes (page 87).

1 cup black Calamata olives, pitted
1 tablespoon fresh basil
1 tablespoon fresh rosemary
1 tablespoon fresh thyme
2 anchovy fillets
2 tablespoons capers
1 teaspoon coarse black pepper
2 tablespoons extra virgin olive oil

4 boneless chicken breasts, pounded
¼-inch thick
2 large eggs, beaten
½ cup seasoned bread crumbs
3 tablespoons vegetable oil

In a food processor, make the tapenade by combining the olives, herbs, anchovies, capers, pepper, and olive oil. Pulse until chopped but not puréed (very important). Set aside. Make sure the chicken breasts are pounded to ¼-inch thickness. Place 2 to 3 tablespoons of the tapenade onto each chicken breast. Form into a log shape by tightly rolling the breasts around the tapenade and tucking in the sides. Dip the breasts in the eggs, covering completely. Roll the breasts in the seasoned bread crumbs until covered. Preheat the oven to 400°.

Heat the 3 tablespoons of oil in an ovenproof sauté pan. Place the breasts in the pan and sauté until browned on one side. Turn the breasts over and bake for about 8 minutes.

Makes 4 servings.

Melissa Leo

Rod Steiger (right) won an Oscar for best actor for his role as Sheriff Gillespie in the 1967 movie *In the Heat of the Night.* The film, which copped five Academy Awards, also starred Sidney Poitier (left) as Det. Virgil Tibbs and was adapted into a television series of the same name in 1988.

Catch a Crook Chicken Cacciatore

¼ cup olive oil
9 chicken thighs
1 large onion, chopped
½ pound mushrooms, sliced
1 6-ounce jar artichoke hearts
½ cup dry white wine
3 cloves garlic, minced
1 tablespoon tomato paste
2 cups canned tomatoes, chopped
½ teaspoon allspice
Ground pepper to taste
2 bay leaves
⅓ teaspoon dried thyme
Salt to taste

Heat the olive oil in a large skillet. Cook the chicken until lightly browned on all sides. Preheat the oven to 350°. Add the onion, mushrooms, and artichokes and sauté for 1 or 2 minutes. Splash in the wine and bring to a boil. Reduce heat and add the remaining ingredients. Simmer for about 5 minutes. Transfer the mixture to a large ovenproof casserole. Cover and bake at 350° for 50 to 60 minutes. Remove the bay leaves and adjust the seasoning.

Makes 4 servings.

Rod Steiger

Michael Warren was one of the regulars to answer the roll call as Officer Bobby Hill on *Hill Street Blues* from 1981 to 1987.

Cop's Cornish Game Hens

2 Cornish game hens
1½ sticks margarine
1 medium onion
3 cloves garlic
   Lawry's seasoning salt
   Garlic salt
   Pepper

Preheat the oven to 350°. Clean the hens and cut off the neck and bottom (save the gizzards and prepare the same as hens). Melt the margarine in the microwave or a saucepan. Cut the onion into slices and then into halves. Cut up the garlic into small pieces (don't mince). Put the hens into a glass baking dish. Pour the melted margarine over the hens on both sides. Place the onion in the pan with the chicken. Rub the garlic on the chicken and drop into the pan. Season to taste with Lawry's salt, garlic salt, and pepper (do not season the insides of the hens). Bake for 40 minutes. Turn the hens over and cook for another 40 minutes. Increase the temperature to 450° and cook for approximately 10 minutes more per side or until golden brown.

Makes 4 servings.

Michael Warren

Peace Officer's Pheasant Cock-a-Leekie

■ Here is one of our favorite recipes. It's easy and delicious.

- 3 **pounds leeks**
- 1 **large pheasant, cleaned**
- 2½ **quarts chicken stock**
- 1 **generous handful barley**
  Salt and pepper to taste

Wash and trim the leeks well and slice them. Place all the ingredients in a large pot and simmer until the pheasant is tender and the barley is soft (40 minutes or more). Remove the pheasant, slice off and chop up the meat, discard the bones, and return the meat to the pot. Adjust the seasoning and serve.

Makes 4 servings.

Darleen Carr-Parker and Jameson Parker

Jameson Parker (left) and Gerald McRaney starred as brothers A. J. (Andrew Jackson) and Rick Simon respectively in *Simon & Simon* (1981–88) on which the two opposite personalities operated a small detective agency on a shoestring in San Diego.

Darleen Carr-Parker, wife of Jameson Parker, played the daughter of two famous television detectives. She was Cindy Smith, daughter of Henry Fonda and Janet Blair (and sister to Ron Howard and Michael-James Wixted) on *The Smith Family* in 1971; and she was the daughter of Karl Malden's Mike Stone on *The Streets of San Francisco* in the early 1970s.

Richard X. Slattery played countless cops in film and on television, including Barney Fife's superior, Captain Dewhurst, in Raleigh on *The Andy Griffith Show*, Lieutenant Modeer in *Switch*, and a police captain in the daytime drama *The Verdict Is Yours*. Furthermore, Slattery was a real-life New York City cop for twelve years, and his father was a career policeman in New York City before him. In fact, Slattery started acting by performing in police department training films when he was an instructor at the police academy.

Captain Dewhurst's Turkey and Broccoli Divan

1 pound broccoli, cut into spears, cooked, and drained
1½ cups cubed, cooked turkey or chicken
1 10¾-ounce can cream of chicken soup
⅓ cup milk
½ cup shredded cheddar cheese
2 tablespoons dry bread crumbs
1 tablespoon butter or margarine, melted

Preheat the oven to 450°. In a 9-inch shallow baking dish, arrange the broccoli and turkey. In a small bowl, mix the soup and milk and pour over the broccoli and turkey. Sprinkle the cheese over the soup mixture. Mix the bread crumbs and margarine and sprinkle over the cheese. Bake for 20 minutes.

Makes 4 servings.

Richard X. Slattery

Long Island Duck à l'Orange

■ This recipe originated in France. The original recipe called for all fresh ingredients. As time passed, modifications were made to the original recipe that allowed for the use of prepared foods commonly found in our country.

1 Long Island duckling, cut into pieces, with giblets
1½ cups water
1 cup all-purpose flour
1 teaspoon salt
1 medium onion, halved and sliced
1 6-ounce can frozen orange juice, thawed
1 4-ounce jar sliced mushrooms
2 tablespoons currant jelly
2 tablespoons Kitchen Bouquet
Wild rice, cooked according to package directions (optional)

Preheat the oven to 500°. Put the giblets and water into a saucepan, bring to a boil, and then simmer. In a medium bowl, mix the flour and salt. Pierce the skin of the duck pieces and then coat with flour. Place the duck on a rack in a roasting pan. Bake about ½ hour or until well browned.

Remove the duck and set aside. Drain the fat from the pan, reserving 1 tablespoon. Brown the onion in a Dutch oven with the reserved duck fat, and add the duck pieces, orange juice concentrate, mushrooms with liquid, currant jelly, and Kitchen Bouquet. Cover and simmer for 1½ hours. Serve with wild rice.

Makes 4 servings.

Joseph L. Monteith
Chief of Police
Suffolk County, New York

Richie Brockelman's Moosh

The thing of it is, is it's delicious.

1   chicken, cooked
2   4-ounce packages wild or plain rice
1   small handful fresh parsley
1   orange bell pepper
1   yellow bell pepper
¼   onion
    Assorted olives
2   jalapeño peppers or more for *mas calor*
1   handful raisins
    Tortillas
    Chutney
    Salsa

Cook the chicken yourself or buy a cooked chicken. Cook the rice according to the package directions. Chop the parsley, peppers, onion, olives, and jalapeño peppers. Open the raisin box and grab a handful. Tear the meat off the chicken bones and discard the bones. (I also get rid of the skin to avoid getting even fatter than I already am.) Combine all the ingredients in a big bowl and moosh them together. Heat the tortillas on the stove, ladle on some chutney and/or salsa, roll up the tortilla, and eat.

Dennis Dugan was the star of 1978's *Richie Brockelman, Private Eye*, a *Rockford Files* spin-off. Barbara Bosson was his secretary, Sharon.

This goes well with a cerveza, chablis, margaritas, or even Sprite or water.

Makes 4 servings.

Dennis Dugan

Fighting crime in Los Angeles schools in the late 1980s on *21 Jump Street* were (from left to right) Holly Robinson, Dustin Nguyen, Peter DeLuise, Steven Williams, and Johnny Depp.

Jump Street Jumbo Scampi

They'll jump for this!

4   tablespoons olive oil
4   tablespoons melted butter
¼   cup lemon juice
    Pepper to taste
3   tablespoons finely minced shallots
3   cloves garlic, finely minced
2   pounds jumbo shrimp or prawns, shelled and deveined
    Lemon slices and parsley to garnish
    Grated cheese of choice (optional)

Combine the olive oil, butter, lemon juice, pepper, shallots, and garlic in a shallow baking dish. Add the shrimp and turn several times to coat thoroughly. Place shrimp in a preheated broiler about 4 inches from the heat for about 2 minutes, and then turn and broil the other side for about 1 minute longer. Don't overcook. Arrange on a serving platter and pour the remaining sauce over the shrimp. Garnish with lemon and sprinkle with parsley.

Variation: Serve hot on cooked pasta. Add cheese if desired.

Makes 6 to 8 servings.

Peter DeLuise
Submitted by father Dom DeLuise

Annapolis Seafood Casserole

4 tablespoons butter
4 tablespoons all-purpose flour
1½ cups half & half
4 tablespoons sherry
  Salt and white pepper to taste
1 pound medium shrimp, deveined and partially cooked
1 pound ocean scallops, partially cooked
1 pound mushrooms, cleaned and partially cooked
2 14-ounce cans artichoke hearts, drained
1½ cups grated Parmesan cheese

Melt the butter in a saucepan. Add the flour and blend in. Slowly add half & half, stirring continuously. Add salt and pepper. Cook until creamy and smooth. Remove from heat and add sherry. Preheat the oven to 350°. Scatter the shrimp, scallops, mushrooms, and artichoke hearts in a baking dish. Cover with white sherry sauce. Sprinkle generously with Parmesan cheese. Bake for about 30 minutes or until the sauce bubbles.
  Makes 6 servings.

Joseph S. Johnson
Chief of Police
Annapolis, Maryland

Roberta's Delaware Ranch Crab Cakes

1 large egg
8 saltine crackers, crushed
2 teaspoons Louisiana seasoning (Zatarain's or Old Bay), divided
¾ teaspoon Worcestershire sauce
6 drops or so Tabasco sauce
⅛ teaspoon freshly ground pepper
6 tablespoons mayonnaise, divided
1 pound lump crabmeat, drained
  Louisiana seasoning, to taste

Preheat the oven to 350°. Combine the egg, crackers, 1 teaspoon Louisiana sea-

soning, the Worcestershire sauce, Tabasco, pepper, and 3 tablespoons mayonnaise. Stir in the crabmeat. Shape crabmeat mixture into 6 3-inch patties. Place on a lightly greased baking sheet. Combine the remaining 3 tablespoons mayonnaise and the remaining teaspoon of Louisiana seasoning and spread lightly and evenly on the crabcakes. Sprinkle a little more seasoning on top if desired. Bake for 20 minutes or until lightly golden (do not overbake). Serve with tartar sauce and/or lemons. Enjoy!
  Makes 6 servings.

J. Richard Smith
Chief of Police
Dover, Delaware

Helen's Meritorious Maryland Crab Cakes

1 pound crab meat
8 saltine crackers, finely crumbled
1 tablespoon mayonnaise
1 teaspoon prepared mustard
1 egg yolk
  Pinch of parsley
  Salt and pepper to taste
  Butter or margarine

Pick through the crab meat thoroughly to remove all shells. Place the crab in a mixing bowl. Add the saltines. Add the remaining ingredients and mix together. Pat the meat together firmly into cakes about 3 inches round and a little flattened. Place the cakes on a plate and refrigerate for a while before cooking. (Chilled cakes stay together better while cooking.) You can either bake the cakes in the oven at 350° until brown on top or pan-fry them in butter or margarine (I think the latter is the best way).
  Makes 6 servings.

Terrence B. Sheridan
Chief of Police
Baltimore County, Maryland

ATF Marinated Shrimp Kabob

■ This recipe is dedicated to my friends whose names are engraved on the walls honoring our fallen officers.

1 pound large, unpeeled fresh shrimp
1 15¼-ounce can pineapple chunks, undrained
1 8-ounce can tomato sauce
2 tablespoons brown sugar
1 teaspoon prepared mustard
1 medium green pepper, cut into 1-inch cubes
Rice, cooked according to package directions, kept warm

Peel and devein the shrimp and set aside. Drain the pineapple chunks, reserving ¼ cup of the juice. Set the pineapple aside. Combine the reserved pineapple juice and the tomato sauce, brown sugar, mustard, and green pepper. Add the shrimp and toss gently to coat. Cover and marinate for 2 hours in the refrigerator, stirring occasionally. Remove the shrimp from the marinade and reserve the marinade. Alternate the shrimp, pineapple, and green pepper on 4 skewers. Grill over medium hot coals for 3 to 4 minutes on each side or until done; baste with marinade. Serve over rice with some of the marinade.

Makes 4 servings.

Richard L. Garner
Special Agent in Charge, Field Division
U.S. Treasury Department
Bureau of Alcohol, Tobacco, & Firearms

In her role as Margo Hughes, actress Ellen Dolan helps law and order keep the upper hand on the long-running daytime drama *As the World Turns.*

Baked Trout à la Margo

1 whole trout
2 tablespoons olive oil
8 or 10 small red potatoes
3 or 4 tablespoons butter, divided
Salt and pepper
2 or 3 cloves garlic, coarsely chopped
1 lemon
Thyme
Parsley
White wine

Preheat the oven to 350°. Brush a large (big enough to accommodate the whole trout) piece of aluminum foil with the olive oil. Slice the potatoes to form a bed. Put 2 or 3 tablespoons of the butter on the potatoes and season with salt and pepper to taste. Sprinkle half of the chopped garlic on the potatoes.

Place the trout on the bed of potatoes and salt and pepper the cavity. Slice the lemon into 8 pieces. Place the remaining garlic and five pieces of the lemon in the cavity. Place the thyme and parsley in the cavity (to taste, but at least a handful). Place the remaining butter and lemon pieces, along with more thyme and parsley, on top of the fish. Create a pouch by folding the top and sides of the foil. Preheat the oven to 350°.

Place the foil pouch containing your dish on a cookie sheet. Bake for 15 minutes. After 15 minutes, open the pouch, prick the skin of the fish, and pour white wine over it. The fish is fully cooked when a milky, white fluid results from pricking the skin.

Serving suggestion: This is excellent with steamed kale as a side dish and a Stag's Leap Sauvignon Blanc (good luck finding it) as your wine.

Makes 1 to 2 servings.

Ellen Dolan

Sea Hunt Zesty Grilled Swordfish

■ If you want to be healthy, eat as much fish as you can afford. To keep these seafood meals from becoming monotonous, you'll appreciate innovative recipes like this one.

1 **pound swordfish fillets, boned and cut into 1-inch pieces**
2 **tablespoons soy sauce**
2 **tablespoons orange juice**
1 **tablespoon vegetable oil**
1 **tablespoon catsup**
1 **tablespoon chopped fresh parsley**
1 **small clove garlic, chopped**
½ **teaspoon fresh lemon juice**
¼ **teaspoon dried oregano**
¼ **teaspoon freshly ground pepper**
  Freshly cooked rice

Arrange the swordfish in a single layer in a shallow baking dish. Combine all the

Lloyd Bridges can do it all, from playing a cowboy to a crime-solving frogman (*Sea Hunt*); but he was just a regular cop on the beat as the star of *Joe Forrester* in 1975.

remaining ingredients, except the rice, in a small bowl and mix well. Pour over the fish, turning to coat well. Let stand at room temperature, turning once, for 30 minutes.

Preheat the broiler or prepare the barbecue grill. Broil or grill the fish 4 inches from the heat source for 8 minutes. Baste with the sauce, turn the fish, and continue cooking until the fish flakes apart easily with a fork (about 7 to 10 minutes). Serve over rice.

Makes 4 servings.

Lloyd Bridges

Simon & Simon's Shrimp New Orleans

2 pounds fresh jumbo shrimp in the shell
Black pepper
White pepper
Red pepper
Gumbo filé powder
3 bell peppers (any color), sliced
2 Vidalia onions sliced
5 ribs celery, chopped into ¼-inch pieces
2 tablespoons Worcestershire sauce
1½ sticks butter, sliced into pats
2 lemons, sliced

Preheat the oven to 350°. Toss the shrimp into a 3-inch deep baking tin. Coat with black pepper. Dust with white pepper, red pepper, and a touch of gumbo filé. Layer on the slices of green pepper and onion. Place the celery over the onion and splash on the Worcestershire sauce. Lay the pats of butter and lemon slices over the top. Bake for 10 to 15 minutes. Remove from the oven and stir thoroughly. Return to the oven and cook for 15 minutes longer. (Reduce cooking time for smaller shrimp.)

Serving suggestion: Serve with a lot of French bread and white wine.

Makes 4 servings.

Gerald McRaney

Gerald McRaney portrayed Rick Simon, the laid-back (well, okay, the lazy and loafing) half of the brother/detective duo on *Simon & Simon*. Rick's more professional younger brother was A. J., played by Jameson Parker. (One can only speculate that maybe Rick might have been more disciplined if he had served in the marines.)

One of Miss Marple's (Joan Hickson) favored pastimes—when not solving an Agatha Christie crime—is watching gardens grow.

Miss Marple's Cider Cod

 1 pound cod fillets
12 ounces tomatoes, halved
 4 ounces mushrooms
10 fingers dry cider (10 ounces)
 1 tablespoon butter
 1 tablespoon all-purpose flour
 3 ounces grated cheddar cheese
   Salt and pepper

Preheat the oven to 350°. Put four portions of cod into a greased, ovenproof dish. Top the cod with tomatoes and mushrooms. Pour the cider over this and bake for 15 minutes. Drain the liquid into a jug and cover the dish with foil. Melt the butter in a saucepan. Over low heat, add the flour to the saucepan and let sit for 2 minutes. Remove the pan from the heat and stir in the cider liquor. Season. Place the pan over medium heat and simmer, stirring for 2 minutes. Pour the sauce over the fish and sprinkle the cheese over this. Broil for 5 minutes. Salt and pepper to taste and serve.

Makes 4 servings.

Joan Hickson

Woody Paris's Chilean Sea Bass

10 Maui onions, sliced
 1 stick unsalted butter
12 Roma tomatoes, seeded and chopped
   (or the canned and drained equivalent)
 5 chopped shallots
 3 cloves garlic, minced
 3 basil leaves, chopped
 1 tablespoon extra virgin olive oil
 ½ cup chicken broth (if necessary)
12 pieces Chilean sea bass, each 2 inches
   wide and 2½ inches long
   Salt and pepper to taste

In a skillet, cook the onion in the butter on low heat until caramelized (between 1 and 2 hours). Purée the tomatoes, shallots, garlic, and basil. Heat the olive oil in a saucepan and then add the puréed ingredients and cook on low for 30 minutes. Add chicken broth as necessary to maintain the liquid. Preheat the oven to 425°. Season the bass with salt and pepper to taste and place in a shallow baking dish. Cover the bass with the onions. Bake for 10 to 12 minutes. Use 2 pieces of bass per serving and serve over a proportionate amount of sauce.

Makes 6 servings.

James Earl Jones

James Earl Jones (bottom) starred as Woody Paris, a police captain who taught criminology at a college, while Hank Garrett (top) was his immediate superior, the deputy chief of police, on *Paris* in 1979. Jones returned to crime solving in 1990 as Gabriel Bird in *Gabriel's Fire* and promptly won an Emmy.

NOBLE Grilled Glazed Halibut

1 small onion, minced
1 small green bell pepper, minced
⅓ cup dry sherry
1 tablespoon peeled ginger root, minced
1 tablespoon low-sodium soy sauce
1 tablespoon honey
1 clove garlic, minced
1 pound halibut, cut into 4 pieces

In a saucepan, sauté the onion and green pepper. Combine with the sherry, ginger, soy sauce, honey, and garlic and place in a 1-cup measuring glass. Microwave on high for one minute, or until the mixture boils.

Cool the mixture slightly and then place the halibut in an 11x7x1½-inch baking dish. Pour the marinade over the halibut. Cover and chill for 2 hours. Remove the halibut from the marinade and reserve the marinade. Preheat a 10-inch microwavable browning skillet on high heat for 8 minutes. Arrange the halibut on the skillet with the thickest portion toward the outside of the skillet. Microwave, uncovered, on HIGH for 2 minutes. Turn the halibut over and baste with the marinade. Microwave on HIGH for 1½ to 2 minutes; let stand, covered, for 2 minutes. Serve immediately with warm marinade.

Note: You can also use tuna, salmon, shark, or swordfish.

Makes 4 servings.

Ira Harris
National Organization of Black Law Enforcement Executives

Barricaded Barbecued Salmon Fillet

Hickory chips for barbecuing
Fresh salmon (any size that will fit on the grill)
Walla Walla onion, thinly sliced
Fresh lemon, sliced
Fresh garlic, sliced
Lemon pepper
Butter cubes, sliced

Soak 1 cup of hickory chips in water for about 30 minutes prior to barbecuing. Turn the barbecue to the lowest setting. Place the hickory chips in an empty tuna can and rest the can on the coals. Make a foil pan to set the fillet in. The pan should have edges (do not use an aluminum pan). Do not cover the fillet with the foil. Cover the top of the fillet with the onion, lemon, garlic, lemon pepper, and butter. Place the foil pan with the salmon on the grill rack. Periodically baste the salmon with the melted butter mixture from the foil pan. Cooking time is approximately 30 minutes but will depend on the thickness of the fillet. (It is done when the color is light pink all the way through.)

Serving suggestion: This is excellent served with steamed baby red potatoes that are lightly sprinkled with fresh rosemary.

Annette M. Sandberg
Chief
Washington State Patrol

The Detective's Gumshoe Sole in White Wine Sauce

2 tablespoons butter
½ cup sliced mushrooms
    Juice of ½ lemon
    Salt and white pepper to taste
6 fillets of sole
½ cup white wine
½ pound bay shrimp
1½ cups White Wine Sauce
    (recipe follows)

Melt the butter in a skillet. Add the mushrooms, lemon juice, and a little salt. Brown the mushrooms lightly and set aside. Salt and pepper the fish and fold each fillet in half. Arrange the fillets in the skillet and cover with the wine. Poach gently until the fish flakes (about 10 minutes). Reduce broth to one-third and add the mushrooms and shrimp to the White Wine sauce; heat and pour over the fillets.

White Wine Sauce

3 tablespoons butter
2 shallots, minced
2 tablespoons all-purpose flour
½ cup white wine
½ cup milk
½ cup heavy cream
    Salt and pepper

Melt the butter, add shallots, and cook until lightly browned. Stir in the flour; add the wine, milk, and cream. Stir until thickened, add salt and pepper to taste, and simmer for 10 minutes.

Makes 6 servings.

Kirk Douglas

Kirk Douglas (second from left) played a tough, bitter New York City police detective in the 1951 film *Detective Story*. William Bendix, left, co-starred as one of his colleagues.

Karl Malden's television beat from 1972 to 1977 was on *The Streets of San Francisco* as Det. Lt. Mike Stone (left) with partner Steve Keller played by Michael Douglas. The characters in the series were based on the Carolyn Weston novel *Poor, Poor Ophelia*.

Mike Stone's Salmon Fillets with Apricot Sauce

15 ounces apricot preserves
 1 tablespoon horseradish
     Onion juice to taste
 ¼ teaspoon nutmeg
 ¼ teaspoon cinnamon

 1 tablespoon vinegar
 6 to 8 salmon fillets

Preheat the oven to 325°. Stir the first 6 ingredients together to make a sauce. Place the fillets in a shallow, lightly greased baking pan. Pour the sauce over top. Bake for 30 to 45 minutes.

Makes 6 to 8 servings.

Karl Malden

Tennessee River Fried Catfish and Fries

No red herrings here.

4 to 6 fresh catfish fillets, weighing about
   ½ pound each
   Salt and pepper
3 or 4 cups yellow cornmeal
1 or 2 quarts vegetable oil

Wash the fish thoroughly and pat dry. Generously salt and pepper. Put the cornmeal in a medium-sized paper bag (you need a bag that you can roll the sides down to seal the meal and fish. Drop the fish into the bag one at a time and shake several times to coat the fish.

Put the vegetable oil in a 4- or 5-quart cast-iron skillet or flat-bottomed kettle. Heat the oil to a rolling boil. Test the temperature by dropping a small piece of fish into it. The oil should roll up around it. Make sure the oil is hot enough before you put any more fish in. Leave enough room for the fish to float to the top as they cook.

Note: You need to have your kettle of oil ready to start cooking as you are salting and mealing your fish.

Makes 4 to 6 servings.

Thomas Ward
Sheriff of Perry County
Linden, Tennessee

Detective Sipowicz's Tuna Casserole

Sorry, Charlie, it's too late to "lawyer up"!

2 6½-ounce cans tuna
1 16-ounce bag frozen peas
2 10¾-ounce cans cream of mushroom
   soup
2 cups chopped fresh mushrooms
2 .8-ounce cans French-fried onion rings

Preheat the oven to 350°. Drain the tuna and put into a flat casserole dish. Add the peas, soup, mushrooms and 1 of the cans of onion rings. Mix well. Sprinkle the remaining onion rings on top of the casserole. Bake for 35 minutes.

Makes 6 to 8 servings.

Dennis Franz

Dennis Franz won an Emmy for his role as Det. Andy Sipowicz on *NYPD Blue*, but he also tackled crime on the streets as Lt. Norman Buntz on *Hill Street Blues*.

Thomas Magnum's Crunchy Tuna Melt

For when that little voice inside you is hungry.

■ I have made this recipe for Tom since he was a little boy.   —*Martha Selleck, Tom's mother*

2   6½-ounce cans water-packed tuna, drained and flaked
1   cup finely chopped celery
¼   cup finely chopped green pepper
¼   cup finely chopped onion
¼   cup mayonnaise
1   tablespoon lemon juice
    Dash of black pepper
6   slices Roman Meal bread or other favorite bread, toasted
6   slices cheddar or Monterey Jack cheese

Combine the first 7 ingredients. Using an ice cream scoop or large spoon, mound the tuna mixture onto each toast slice. Top each with one slice of cheese. Place the sandwiches on a baking sheet and broil for 2 or 3 minutes until the cheese is bubbly.
    Makes 6 servings.

Tom Selleck

On-the-Beat Eggs DelBuono

■ This recipe comes from a lovable old Italian lady named Millie DelBuono, who brought it to America from the "Old Country."

4   small zucchini, each about 5 inches long
2   tablespoons olive oil
2   cloves garlic, chopped
8   eggs
4   tablespoons grated Locatelli cheese
    Salt and pepper to taste
1   loaf Italian bread

One of the hottest private eyes of the 1980s was Tom Selleck's Thomas Magnum on *Magnum, P.I.* Before he was Magnum, Selleck's perfect private investigator Lance White annoyed Jim Rockford on *The Rockford Files.*

Peel and quarter the zucchini and then cut the quarters into 2-inch lengths. Heat a 10-inch frying pan to medium-low heat. Add the olive oil, garlic, and zucchini. Cook for 25 minutes or until the zucchini is soft. In a medium bowl, scramble the eggs and add the grated cheese. Pour the mixture over the zucchini in the frying pan. Add salt and pepper to taste and stir until the eggs have cooked. Serve immediately with sliced Italian bread.

Makes 4 servings.

John C. Gallagher
Police Commissioner
Suffolk County, New York

Mississippi Red Beans and Rice

2 cups dried red beans
6 cups water
¼ pound bacon
1 medium onion, chopped
1 large green pepper, chopped
2 cloves garlic, minced
2 bay leaves
¼ cup parsley, chopped
1 teaspoon salt
1 teaspoon black pepper
¼ teaspoon oregano
    Dash or so of cayenne or crushed
    red pepper
1 tablespoon Worcestershire sauce
4 cups cooked rice

Wash the beans and soak them in a large saucepan of water overnight. Drain; add the 6 cups of water. (An alternative to soaking overnight is to cover the beans with 6 cups water and bring to a boil and to continue boiling for 2 minutes. Remove from heat, cover the pan, and let stand for 1 hour.)

In a medium skillet, sauté the bacon until crisp. Remove the bacon from the skillet and drain on paper towels; crumble the bacon into small pieces. Add the onion, green pepper, and garlic to the bacon fat in the skillet and sauté until tender. Add the crumbled bacon, onion mixture, bay leaves, parsley, salt, pepper, oregano, red pepper, and Worcestershire sauce to the beans. Bring to a boil; reduce the heat and simmer, covered, for 2 hours. The thickness may be varied, if desired, by adding more water. Serve over cooked rice.

Makes 8 to 10 servings.

Robert L. Johnson
Chief of Police
Jackson, Mississippi

Mort's Chilies Rellenos Casserole

2 cups half & half
2 eggs
⅓ cup all-purpose flour
3 4-ounce cans whole green chilies
4 cups grated Monterey Jack cheese
2 cups grated sharp cheddar cheese
1 8-ounce can tomato sauce

Preheat the oven to 375°. Beat the half & half, eggs, and flour until smooth. Split the chilies open with your thumbs, empty out the seeds, and dry the chilies on paper towels. Place a layer of chilies in the bottom of the greased casserole dish. Cover with a layer of the cheeses. Add another layer of chilies. Pour the egg mixture over top and sprinkle the rest of the cheese on top. Bake for 1 hour or until the cheese is golden brown.

Makes 4 servings.

Ron Masak

> *"Time has little to do with infinity and jelly doughnuts."*
> —Thomas Magnum
> *(Magnum, P.I.)*

Crime-Solver Chili Corn Casserole

1 16-ounce can creamed corn
1 16-ounce can whole-kernel corn, undrained
2 tablespoons melted butter
8 ounces sour cream
1 teaspoon salt
½ cup cornmeal
½ pound cubed Monterey Jack cheese
2 eggs, beaten
1 4-ounce can chopped green chilies

Preheat the oven to 350°. Mix all the ingredients in a 2-quart casserole dish. Bake for 1 hour. This is great with a cold beer.
   Makes 4 servings.

Det. John Bunnell

Clint Walker was one of television's biggest policemen when he portrayed Cal "Kodiak" McKay, a member of the Alaska State Police Patrol on *Kodiak* in 1974. Eskimo locals nicknamed him Kodiak after a great bear that roamed the area.

Kodiak's Garlic-Braised Tofu with Stir-Fry Vegetables

■ Use any or all of these vegetables (organic if possible):

2 or 3 ribs celery, cut into large pieces
1 large red onion, cut into large pieces
1 handful broccoli florets or asparagus, in season, cut 1 inch long
   A few thin slices red cabbage
2 or 3 baby bok choy, cut into large pieces
1 bunch green onions, cut into small lengths
1 or 2 leeks, sliced thick
4 or 5 shiitake (or other) mushrooms, sliced thin
1 8-ounce can water chestnuts, rinsed
2 large handfuls bean sprouts
1½ tablespoons olive oil
3 large cloves garlic, minced
1 block extra-firm tofu, sliced into bite-sized rectangles
1 to 2 teaspoons sesame oil
2 handfuls pine nuts or raw cashews
   Soy sauce (low sodium preferred)
   Dr. Bronner's protein-balanced seasoning (optional)
   Cornstarch (optional)

Wash and cut all the vegetables first so they are prepared when you start to braise the tofu. Heat the olive oil in a skillet and then add the minced garlic. Braise the tofu until golden brown; then turn and brown the other side and set aside.
   Sprinkle sesame oil in a large wok or skillet and stir-fry vegetables. Keeping the heat high, add the vegetables quickly. (This only takes a couple of minutes). Start adding the celery, onion, broccoli, and cabbage first, stirring or tossing constantly. Add the next five ingredients. Add the bean sprouts last. Remove from heat while the vegetables are still crisp. Add the braised garlic/tofu and mix together well. Use soy sauce and Dr. Bronner's seasoning to season to taste. (A little cornstarch mixed with water may be added to thicken the mixture if desired.)
   Makes 2 to 3 servings.

Clint Walker

B.O. PLENTY'S
CHUCK WAGON CASSEROLE

1½ lbs. GROUND BEEF
1 CUP CHOPPED CELERY
1 GREEN PEPPER CHOPPED
1 MEDIUM ONION, FINELY CHOPPED
1 CAN TOMATO SAUCE
1 TBSP. CHILI POWDER
1 TSP. EACH SALT, PAPRIKA
1 SMALL CAN PORK & BEANS
1 CAN REFRIDGERATED BISCUITS
10 HALF INCH CUBES CHEESE

BROWN MEAT. POUR OFF DRIPPINGS.
ADD CELERY, GREEN PEPPER, ONIONS,
TOMATO SAUCE AND SEASONINGS.
SIMMER FOR 20 MINUTES. ADD PORK &
BEANS. TURN INTO 2½ qt. CASSEROLE.
PLACE A CUBE OF
CHEESE ON EACH
BISCUIT; FOLD IN
HALF. PLACE ON
MEAT MIXTURE.
BAKE 400°
FOR 15
MINUTES.

AN' WATCH WHERE YOU SPIT!

PTOO

DICK LOCHER
CHICAGO TRIBUNE

Rod Steiger as Chief Bill Gillespie in *In The Heat of the Night*.

Dispatchers

BREAKFAST DISHES

Inspector Henderson's Eggs Florentine

■ Bob enjoyed entertaining at brunch on Sundays around the pool—with Bloody Marys, fresh orange juice, and coffee to start. He would toss a delicious mixed green salad with lots of mushrooms and veggies and purple onions, accompanied by fresh sourdough garlic bread toasted on the barbecue. Cooking was one of his hobbies, but cleaning up was not!
—*Bette (Mrs. Robert) Shayne*

2 **pounds fresh spinach (cooked, drained, and chopped)**
2 **tablespoons lemon juice**
½ **cup grated Parmesan or cheddar cheese**
½ **cup chopped onion**
2 **cloves garlic, minced and sautéed in a small amount of olive oil**
6 **eggs**

Preheat the oven to 350°. Season the spinach with the lemon juice, and then put the spinach into oiled individual ramekins. Sprinkle cheese over the spinach and, using the back of a spoon, make a 1-inch-deep well in each. Crack and drop one raw egg into each well and bake until the eggs are set, about 8 minutes.
    Makes 6 servings.

Robert Shayne
Submitted by Elizabeth (Mrs. Robert) Shayne

Robert Shayne played Inspector Bill Henderson of the Metropolis Police Department on *The Adventures of Superman* from 1952 to 1957. George Reeves was the Man of Steel.

One of the top hard-boiled mystery writers of all time is Mickey Spillane, creator of Mike Hammer. More than 200 million copies of Spillane's books are in print, and his Big Apple private eye has been the star of numerous films and three television series.

Hammered Potatoes and Eggs

■ This is great for a late-night snack when you're hungry but don't want to go gourmet. It's even good the next day. Or two. Now I'm hungry!

    Vegetable oil
    White potatoes, sliced thinly
    Onion, sliced into rings
    Green pepper, sliced
6 **eggs, or more, according to the**
    number served

Heat vegetable oil in 2 frying pans. In one, fry up a mess of raw white potatoes—nicely sliced, of course. Not too thick. In the other pan, do the same with a batch of onion circles and green pepper. Since these two will be mixed together, don't overload the pans.

While they're cooking and being turned at regular intervals, beat up enough eggs to suit yourself. I always use at least 6. When the spuds are nicely browned, and the peppers and onions likewise, mix together in one of the skillets—maybe pouring off some of the cooking oil, if necessary. Let them be joined like man and wife. Then pour the eggs over the vegetables and savor the smell. You can keep it loose or let it set like an omelet.

Use condiments as you like.

Mickey Spillane

One Riot, One Ranger Red-Eye Dish

Always gets its man.

Butter
1 5-ounce package herb croutons
1 pound sausage or bacon
6 eggs, beaten
1 cup milk
1 medium onion, chopped
1 large jalapeño pepper, chopped
½ to 1 cup Pace picante sauce (optional:
   for extra hot version)
1 10¾-ounce can cream of chicken soup
1 10¾-ounce can cream of mushroom
   soup
   Salt and pepper to taste
8 ounces Monterey Jack cheese, sliced

Butter the bottom of a 9x13-inch oven-proof glass casserole dish. Sprinkle the croutons on the bottom of the dish. Brown the meat, drain the fat off, and spread the meat over the croutons. In a mixing bowl, mix the eggs, milk, onion, jalapeño pepper, picante sauce, soups, salt, and pepper. Pour over the meat and top with cheese. Cover the dish tightly with foil. Refrigerate overnight. The next morning preheat the oven to 350°. Bake for 45 to 50 minutes or until set.

Makes 6 to 8 servings.

Sr. Ranger Capt. Bruce Casteel
Texas Rangers

Protect-and-Serve Soufflé

1 pound mild or hot sausage
6 eggs
2 cups milk
1 teaspoon salt (optional)
   Pepper to taste
1 teaspoon dried mustard
2 slices white bread, cubed
1 firmly packed cup grated sharp
   cheddar cheese

Brown the sausage, drain well, and set aside. In a bowl, beat the eggs. Add the milk, salt, pepper, and mustard. Add the cubed bread and stir. Add the cheese and sausage. Put into a 9x13-inch baking dish and refrigerate overnight. Preheat the oven to 375°. Bake for 45 minutes. Let stand a few minutes before serving.

Makes 12 servings.

Robert G. Allen
Acting Chief of Police
Indianapolis, Indiana

SAMPLE TEN-CODES

10-1	Receiving poorly
10-2	Receiving well
10-3	Administrative/special assignment
10-4	Acknowledgment/O.K.
10-7	Out of service
10-8	In service
10-9	Repeat transmission
10-13	Consider suspects very dangerous
10-16	Prisoner transport
10-20	Your location
10-28	Check full registration/stolens only
10-30	Check for warrants/record information
10-40	Suspicious person
10-45	Vehicle accident-property damage
10-46	Vehicle accident-personal injury
10-47	Ambulance requested
10-53	Holdup/robbery
10-58	Prowler
10-61	Fire
10-70	Burglary-residence
10-71	Burglary-nonresidence
10-72	Item/vehicle is stolen
10-82	Send backup
10-83	Shots fired
10-93	Traffic violation
10-95	Meal break
10-97	On the scene

Sergeant Joe Getraer's Blueberry Pancakes

■ This is a recipe that I have been feeding my family for Sunday breakfast for years. With thick, lean bacon and warm maple syrup, these are the best. This is a pretty simple recipe, and the results are so much better than packaged or mix pancakes.

1 cup all-purpose flour
1 teaspoon baking powder
½ teaspoon salt
1 egg
1 tablespoon sour cream
1 tablespoon molasses
1 cup buttermilk
½ cup blueberries, fresh, in season, or frozen (optional)

Combine the flour, baking powder, and salt and mix. Add the egg, sour cream, molasses, and buttermilk and stir into a slightly lumpy batter. Fold in the blueberries. You're ready to go. Depending on how many mouths there are to feed (and the expanse of the appetites), you can double or triple this recipe.

Makes 6 to 8 pancakes.

Robert Pine

Robert Pine (center) was Sergeant Getraer, the superior officer to motorcycle patrolmen Jon Baker (Larry Wilcox, left) and Francis Poncherello (Erik Estrada, right) on *CHiPs* (1977–83). In 1976 Pine starred as Inspector Larry Johnson on *Bert D'Angelo/Superstar*.

Washington State Swedish Pancakes

10 eggs
 4 cups milk
 ⅓ cup sugar
 1 stick butter, melted
 4 cups all-purpose flour
    Butter
    Confectioners' sugar
    Fruit purée or jam
    Whipped cream (optional)

Beat the eggs, milk, sugar, and melted butter with an electric mixer until blended. On low speed, slowly mix in the flour. Heat the griddle or stove to about 350° and pour a thin layer of batter—preferably onto a round griddle or pan. Once the crêpes are cooked, lightly butter and sprinkle with sugar and confectioners' sugar and your favorite fruit purée. Roll the crêpe and add either confectioners' sugar or whipped cream to the top and serve.
    Makes 22 pancakes.

Annette M. Sandberg
Chief of Police
Washington State Patrol

Amy Carlson and Tim Gibbs team up as Officer Josie Watts and Lt. Gary Sinclair, an on-again, off-again couple on NBC's popular daytime drama *Another World.*

Flak Jacket Flapjacks

It's Watts for breakfast.

 3 eggs, well beaten
1½ cups all-purpose flour
 3 cups milk
 6 tablespoons vegetable oil
1½ teaspoons salt
 1 teaspoon sugar

Combine all ingredients until well blended. Pour ¼ cup of the mixture at a time into a nonstick skillet that's hot enough to make a drop of water jump. These are perfect when served with fresh berries and syrup and dusted with confectioners' sugar. Try your own special creation!
    Makes 6 to 8 pancakes.

Amy Carlson

> *"...Dr. Richard Kimble, an innocent victim of blind justice, falsely convicted of the murder of his wife, reprieved by fate when a train wreck freed him en route to the death house; freed him to hide in lonely desperation, to change his identity, to toil at many jobs; freed him to search for a one-armed man he saw leave the scene of the crime; freed him to run before the relentless pursuit of the police lieutenant obsessed with his capture."*
>
> —Narrator William Conrad
> from *The Fugitive*

One of the coolest big-screen cops of all time was Steve McQueen's Bullitt in 1968; the movie co-starred Jacqueline Bisset. Bullitt's famous car chase up and down the streets of San Francisco is considered one of the best in silver-screen history.

Bullitt's French Toast

1 egg per slice of bread
   Splash of milk
1 teaspoon vanilla extract
6 to 8 slices thickly sliced sandwich
   bread (Texas toast)
   Confectioners' sugar
   Maple syrup

Whip and mix together the eggs, milk, and vanilla extract. Dip the bread slices into the mixture and place into a non-stick skillet over medium heat. Fry the bread until the bottom side is golden brown, and flip over to brown the other side. Slice the toast into triangular halves; sprinkle with confectioners' sugar.

Serving Suggestion: Serve with maple syrup and slices of crisp bacon on the side.

Makes 2 servings.

Steve McQueen
Submitted by daughter Terry McQueen

Captain Janet Hamilton's Neon Jungle Doughnut Recipe

The perfect cop-out, and a real who doughnut.

■ I have not done anything involving cooking for fifteen years, so in order to bring a certain truth to the characters I play, I usually make them women who don't cook either. So here's what my cop characters do:

Go to the Yellow Pages.
Find the listing for doughnut shops.
Indulge.

Suzanne Pleshette

Suzanne Pleshette has starred in numerous films and television shows. Among them was the 1987 television movie *Neon Jungle* in which Pleshette played a police captain assigned to a tough precinct.

Cold Cop's Hot Coffee Cake

Top of the morning from the world's top cop.

■ I asked one of my officers, Scott Deal, and his wife, Mary, for this recipe because it is so good. When Mary sends a piece of this cake to work with Scott to give to my wife, Jan, and me, it never gets home. I do tell my wife that Mary sent cake for both of us, but Mary understands why it never makes it home because she likes it too. I thought you might enjoy it as well.

1 package yellow cake mix
1 3-ounce package instant vanilla pudding
1 3-ounce package instant butterscotch pudding
1 cup water
½ cup vegetable oil
4 eggs
1 teaspoon vanilla extract

Topping:

½ cup packed brown sugar
½ cup chopped nuts
1 teaspoon ground cinnamon

Preheat the oven to 350°. In a large bowl, mix the cake mix and puddings while dry. Mix the water, oil, eggs, and vanilla, and combine with the dry ingredients. Mix well. In a separate bowl, combine the topping ingredients. Pour about half of the batter into a greased bundt pan and then sprinkle with half of the topping mixture. Pour the remaining batter into the pan and sprinkle with the remaining topping. Bake for 45 minutes or until a toothpick inserted in center comes out clean. After it's done, let it cool and then pop the cake out onto a plate with the top up.

Makes about 12 servings.

Gerald Ownby
Chief of Police
The North Pole, Alaska

Joan Hickson stars as Agatha Christie's sleuth Miss Marple on PBS's *Mystery!* In 1961 Hickson shared several scenes with Dame Margaret Rutherford, who played Miss Marple in the feature film *Murder, She Said.*

Miss Marple's Marmalade

2 pounds Seville oranges
2 large lemons
4 pounds sugar
3½ pints water, divided

Scrub the fruit. Slice off the tops and bottoms and boil until tender in 2½ pints of water. Strain off the water and reserve. When the fruit is cool enough, halve the oranges and lemons and scoop out the pips and pith. Boil the fruit in 1 pint of water for 20 minutes then strain it into the reserved water. Slice the peel evenly and put into the reserved water. Add the sugar over low heat and stir until dissolved then bring to a brisk boil until the mixture becomes set (about 20 minutes). Let stand for 15 to 20 minutes and then put into jars and seal.

Makes about 12 pints.

Joan Hickson

Abe Vigoda starred as Det. Phil Fish on *Barney Miller* from 1975 to 1977 before starring in the spin-off, *Fish*. Ironically, Vigoda's best-known previous role was as a Mafia leader in *The Godfather*.

Fish's Breakfast Dish

■ My favorite recipe that I cook is hot oatmeal. Here is how I make it.

1 **cup water**
   Pinch salt
½ **cup oatmeal**
   Low-calorie sweetener or sugar
   Cream, milk, or non-dairy creamer

In an ovenproof glass bowl, put 1 cup of water and a pinch of salt. Add ½ cup of oatmeal. Stir. Place into the microwave for 2½ minutes. Take the glass bowl out and pour the oatmeal into a regular bowl. Add low calorie sweetener or sugar. Add cream, milk, or nondairy creamer. Enjoy!

   Makes 1 serving.

Abe Vigoda

Sharon Gless and Tyne Daly played New York City police officers Chris Cagney and Mary Beth Lacey who were best buddies on *Cagney & Lacey* (1982–88). In the 1976 feature film *The Enforcer*, Daly shared the beat in San Francisco with Clint Eastwood's Harry Callahan.

Sweet Justice

DESSERTS

Enos's Non-Hazzard-ous Nut Snackers

1 egg white
¾ cup firmly packed brown sugar
2 tablespoons all-purpose flour
½ teaspoon vanilla extract
2 cups pecan halves

Preheat the oven to 250°. Beat the egg white until it stands in soft peaks. Mix in the brown sugar, flour, and vanilla. Fold in the pecans until they are well coated with the mixture. Place the coated pecans about 1 inch apart on a cookie sheet. (I cover the cookie sheet with aluminum foil and lightly apply nonstick vegetable spray. You can use baking paper.) Bake for 30 minutes. Turn the oven off and leave the snackers in the oven for 30 minutes more. Store in an airtight container. They also freeze well.

Makes 2 cups.

Sonny Shroyer

Sonny Shroyer has been beloved by folks far and wide ever since 1979, when he took on the role of Deputy Enos Strate on *The Dukes of Hazzard*.

Rocky Road Candy

It's Rio Grande!

■ This is one of my favorite recipes. I especially enjoy this treat during the holidays!

1 12-ounce package chocolate chips
1 stick butter or margarine
1 14-ounce can sweetened condensed milk
1 10½-ounce package miniature marshmallows
3 cups coarsely chopped pecans

Combine the chocolate chips, butter, and sweetened condensed milk in a large microwave-safe mixing bowl. Place in the microwave oven on high for 3 minutes. Remove from the microwave and stir. Add the marshmallows and pecans and mix well. Pour the mixture into a 9x13-inch greased pan and spread evenly. Cool and cut into squares.

For a tasty Christmas gift, this candy may be placed in decorative tins or glass containers and wrapped with a beautiful bow.

Note: If the candy is to be stacked, waxed paper may be placed between each layer to prevent sticking.

Makes about 2 dozen.

Russ Leach
Chief of Police
El Paso, Texas

> *"A man confined to prison is a man who has given up his liberty, his pursuit of happiness. No more carefree hours, no more doing whatever you want, whenever you want. No more peanut butter and jelly sandwiches."*
>
> —Deputy Barney Fife
> *(The Andy Griffith Show)*

Here Comes the Judge's Peanut Brittle

■ This recipe really comes from FBI family member Frankie Stuart, but my wife and I adopted it as our own!

1 cup raw unsalted peanuts
1 cup sugar
½ cup light corn syrup
⅛ teaspoon salt
1 teaspoon butter
1 teaspoon vanilla extract
1 teaspoon baking soda

Mix together the peanuts, sugar, corn syrup, and salt. Cook on high in the microwave for 4 minutes. Stir. Cook another 4 minutes. Add the butter and vanilla, and cook for 1 or 2 minutes until the peanuts are lightly browned. Add the baking soda and stir in gently. Pour the mixture onto waxed paper or a Teflon-coated cookie sheet. Spread thinly very quickly. Cool for 30 minutes to 1 hour. Break into small pieces and enjoy!

Makes about 1 pound.

Judge William Webster
Former Director
Federal Bureau of Investigation

American Fork Fingerprints

■ They're great served with a gallon of very cold milk!

¾ cup peanut butter
1½ sticks butter
¾ cup sugar
¾ cup firmly packed brown sugar
2 eggs
1 teaspoon vanilla extract
1½ cups all-purpose flour
¾ teaspoon baking soda
½ teaspoon salt
1½ cups oatmeal
1 24-ounce package semisweet or milk chocolate chips

Preheat the oven to 325°. In a large mixing bowl, cream together the peanut butter, butter, and sugars. Add the eggs and vanilla; beat until smooth. Stir together the flour, baking soda, and salt. Add to the creamed mixture and then add the oatmeal. Press the mixture into a jelly roll pan. Bake for 12 to 15 minutes (no longer) or until the mixture begins to turn brown around the edges. Remove the mixture from the oven and immediately pour on the chocolate chips and let melt. When the chips are melted, spread the mixture with a spatula and allow to completely cool. When the chocolate has hardened, spread on the Frosting (recipe follows).

Frosting:

1 cup confectioners' sugar
¾ cup peanut butter
1½ sticks butter
⅛ cup or less milk
1 teaspoon vanilla extract

In a mixing bowl, combine the confectioners' sugar, peanut butter, butter, and milk. Beat until smooth. Add the vanilla and mix in.
  Makes 2 to 3 dozen.

John D. Durrant
Chief of Police
American Fork, Utah

City of Angels Chocolate Chip-Oatmeal Badges

■ My husband is a police officer in Los Angeles. I make these often for all the guys he works with. They love them and always request more.

2 sticks butter, softened
½ cup sugar
1 cup firmly packed brown sugar
2 eggs
1 teaspoon vanilla extract
1½ cups all-purpose flour
1 teaspoon baking soda
1 teaspoon ground cinnamon
½ teaspoon salt (optional)
2½ cups Quaker oats, uncooked
1½ cups semisweet chocolate chips

Preheat the oven to 350°. In a large bowl, mix together the butter and both sugars. Add the eggs and vanilla and mix well. In a separate bowl, mix the flour, baking soda, cinnamon, and salt. Add the flour mixture to the butter mixture and mix well. Stir in the oatmeal and chocolate chips.
  Drop the batter by the spoonful onto a thick, ungreased cookie sheet. Bake until the cookies are nice and brown (about 10 minutes). Do not overbake. Enjoy!
  Makes about 3 dozen.

Marlee Matlin

Marlee Matlin starred as attorney and detective Tess Kaufman in the police drama *Reasonable Doubts* from 1991 to 1993. In real life, Matlin is married to a Los Angeles police officer, Jack Grabowski.

After-Tour Whiskey Balls

2 sticks butter
⅓ cup sugar
4 teaspoons Jameson's Irish Whiskey
    (or to taste)
2 teaspoons vanilla extract
2 cups all-purpose flour
    Chocolate confectioners' sugar

Preheat the oven to 325°. Cream the butter and sugar. Add the whiskey and vanilla and mix. Add the flour and mix. Chill for 4 hours in the refrigerator. Remove and shape into balls. Bake on an ungreased cookie sheet for 20 minutes. Cool slightly and roll in chocolate confectioners' sugar.
   Makes about 3 dozen.

Lt. Patrick F. O'Brien
President
Police Emerald Society

Traffic Court Date and Nut Cookies

■ This recipe is from my grandmother, one of the best cooks in the country.

1 cup sugar
2½ cups all-purpose flour
1 cup nuts (she used pecans)
1 teaspoon baking soda
1½ sticks butter or margarine
2 eggs, lightly beaten
1 pound dates, cut up

Preheat the oven to 350°. Mix all the ingredients together and pinch off small pieces of dough. Pat flat, place on cookie sheet, and bake for 12 to 15 minutes.
   Makes about 4 dozen.

James A. Rhinebarger
Chairman
National Troopers Coalition

Big Sky Country Chocolate Chip-Banana Cookies

■ This is the original Helena Police Department cookie, and we can't get enough of 'em!

2¼ cups all-purpose flour
2 teaspoons baking powder
¼ teaspoon baking soda
½ teaspoon salt
⅔ cup mashed bananas (about
    2 medium-sized bananas)
⅓ cup evaporated milk
1 teaspoon vanilla extract
⅔ cup shortening
⅔ cup sugar
2 eggs
1 12-ounce package chocolate chips
1 cup nuts

Preheat the oven to 400°. Sift together the flour, baking powder, baking soda, and salt. In a separate bowl, mix together the bananas, evaporated milk, and vanilla. In a large bowl, combine the shortening and sugar; beat until fluffy. Stir in the eggs. Next, stir in about a third of the flour mixture. When smooth, stir in half of the milk/ banana mixture. Repeat until all is used. Stir in the chocolate chips and nuts. Drop the batter by the spoonful onto a cookie sheet and bake for 10 minutes. They're very soft.
   Makes about 4 dozen cookies.

William J. Ware
Chief of Police
Helena, Montana

> **"Of course, I'll have to notify the police. This is a case for Homicide."**
> —Dr. MacDonald in *D.O.A.* (1950)

Cheryl Ladd (center) joined the crew of *Charlie's Angels* from 1977 to 1981 as Kris Munroe. Here she joins Jaclyn Smith (left), who played Kelly Garrett, and Kate Jackson, who played Sabrina Duncan. In 1994 Ladd played a top-notch Honolulu forensics expert, Dr. Dawn Holli Holliday, in *One West Waikiki*.

Kris Munroe's Angel Sugar Cookies

1 cup sugar
1 cup confectioners' sugar
2 sticks margarine, softened
½ cup vegetable oil
2 eggs
½ teaspoon salt
2 teaspoons vanilla extract
1 teaspoon baking soda
1 teaspoon cream of tartar
4 cups all-purpose flour

Preheat the oven to 350°. Mix all the ingredients well and cool for 1 hour. Roll the dough into 1½-inch balls. Place on non-stick cookie sheet. Press flat with a fork dipped in sugar. Bake for 10 to 12 minutes.

Makes about 3 dozen.

Cheryl Ladd

Law and order in Hazzard County was maintained by James Best's Sheriff Rosco P. Coltrane (left), seen here with Sorrell Booke, who played Mayor Jefferson Davis "Boss" Hogg. *The Dukes of Hazzard* ran from 1979 to 1985 on CBS, and in 1997 the gang returned to television for a reunion movie. *Courtesy of Steve Cox Collection.*

Rosco P. Coltrane's Marble Squares

They're the best!

    8 ounces cream cheese, softened
 2⅓ cups sugar, divided
    3 eggs, divided
    1 stick margarine
   ¼ cup water
1½ ounces unsweetened chocolate
    2 cups all-purpose flour
   ½ cup sour cream
    1 teaspoon baking soda
    1 teaspoon salt
    6 ounces chocolate chips

Grease an 11x16-inch pan. In a large bowl, combine the cream cheese, ⅓ cup of sugar, and 1 egg. Mix well and set aside. In a saucepan, combine the margarine, water, and unsweetened chocolate; bring to a boil. Remove from heat. Preheat the oven to 375°. In a separate bowl, combine the flour and remaining 2 cups of sugar. Stir in the chocolate mixture. Add the 2 remaining eggs, sour cream, baking soda, and salt. Mix well. Pour into the prepared pan. Spoon the cheese mixture over the batter. Cut through with a knife to give a marbled effect. Sprinkle with chocolate chips. Bake for 25 to 30 minutes. Prepare and spread Topping (recipe follows) over baked dough. Cut into squares.

Topping:

2 cups sugar
1 stick margarine
½ cup milk
2 cups unsweetened chocolate chips

In a saucepan, combine the sugar, margarine, and milk. Bring the mixture to a boil. Remove from heat and add the chocolate chips. Stir until the mixture starts to thicken.
   Makes 12 servings.

James Best

Topeka 10-4 Chocolate Chip Cookies

It's hard not Topeka at these while they're baking!

1 16-ounce package refrigerated chocolate chip cookie dough
8 ounces cream cheese, softened
⅓ cup sugar
1 pint half & half
1 4-ounce package instant chocolate pudding
¼ cup chopped nuts

Preheat the oven to 375°. Gather the cookie dough into a ball and flatten. (You may need to flour the cookie dough and rolling pin in order to flatten it.) Roll out the dough onto a round baking sheet. Bake for 12 to 15 minutes or until browned. Combine the cream cheese and sugar and refrigerate. Combine the half & half and instant pudding with a whisk. Let sit until firm (about 5 minutes).
   When the cookie is taken out of the oven, let it cool for 10 minutes. Run a knife or spatula under the cookie to loosen it from the pan. Once the cookie has completely cooled, spread the cream cheese mixture on top. Layer the pudding mixture over the cream cheese. Sprinkle the chopped nuts over all. Chill until served. Cut with a pizza cutter.

Dean Forster
Chief of Police
Topeka, Kansas

Bulletproof Butter Cookies

1½ sticks butter
 1 cup sugar
 2 eggs, lightly beaten
 1 teaspoon vanilla extract
 1 teaspoon lemon extract (or substitute an extra teaspoon of vanilla)
2½ cups all-purpose flour

Preheat the oven to 375°. Cream the butter and sugar thoroughly. Add the eggs and extract. Sift the flour and add to the above mixture. Mix well. With a cookie press, make long-ridged ribbons across an ungreased cookie sheet. Bake for 8 to 10 minutes or until the edges turn golden. Cut the ribbons into 3-inch pieces while still hot.
   Makes about 5 dozen.

Donald F. Kane
Police Commissioner
Nassau County, New York

> *"People are being cheated, robbed, murdered, raped. And that goes on twenty-four hours a day, every day in the year. And that's not exceptional, that's usual. It's the same in every city in the modern world. But suppose we had no police force, good or bad. Suppose we had...just silence. Nobody to listen, nobody to answer. That battle's finished. The jungle wins. The predatory beasts take over."*
>
> —John McIntire as Police Commissioner Hardy in *The Asphalt Jungle* (1950)

Vicky's Vice Iced Oatmeal-Raisin Cookies

2 sticks real butter
3 cups all-purpose flour
1 tablespoon baking soda
1 teaspoon salt
2 tablespoons cinnamon
1 16-ounce box dark brown sugar
½ cup sugar
2 eggs
1 tablespoon vanilla extract
3 cups oatmeal
1 cup baking raisins
½ cup almonds, pecans, or walnuts
   (optional)

Preheat the oven to 350°. In a large bowl, melt the butter in the microwave. While you're waiting for this, mix the flour, baking soda, salt, and cinnamon, and set aside. Add the sugars to the melted butter and beat for a couple of minutes. Beat the eggs in a separate bowl. Add the eggs and vanilla to the sugar/butter mixture. Gradually add the flour mixture, beating slowly as you add it. When all the flour is wet, stir in the oatmeal and raisins (and nuts). Drop by the tablespoonful onto a cookie sheet. Bake for about 9 to 13 minutes (depending on your oven).

Icing:

1 stick real butter
1 16-ounce box confectioners' sugar
1 teaspoon vanilla extract
¼ cup (or less) milk

Melt the butter in the microwave. Add the sugar and vanilla. Beat well. Add the milk by the tablespoonful until the mixture reaches the consistency you desire. Brush the mixture on the cookies when they're just a little warm so that the icing will melt into the cracks. Cool on waxed paper or cookie racks. Store in an airtight container when cooled.
   Makes about 3 dozen.

Jerome G. Boles II
Chief of Police
Lansing, Michigan

Copcakes Forrester

¾ cup sugar
1¼ cups plus 2 tablespoons Bisquick
2 tablespoons butter
1 egg, beaten
½ to ⅔ cup milk
½ teaspoon grated orange rind

Preheat the oven to 375°. Stir the sugar into the Bisquick. Cut in the butter until very fine. Add the egg, milk, and rind. Beat well until smooth. Pour into greased and floured muffin tins, or tins lined with muffin papers. Bake for 20 minutes. When the cupcakes are cool, top with Icing.

Icing:

   Confectioners' sugar
½ teaspoon grated orange rind
   Orange juice

Combine a quantity of confectioners' sugar with the peel and enough orange juice to be spreadable. It does not require much orange juice.
   Makes about 4 dozen.

Lloyd Bridges

Chris Ballard's Kiefels

■ Kiefels have been a traditional holiday treat in my wife's family for generations. My mother-in-law passed down this recipe to my wife. A kiefel is a delicious morsel that falls somewhere between a cookie and a miniature pie. They go great with coffee, eggnog, and (my favorite combo) cold milk.

Dough:

3 cups all-purpose flour
3 egg yolks, slightly beaten
2 sticks butter, melted
1 package all-natural yeast (in just enough lukewarm water to dissolve)
¼ cup half & half (just enough to moisten the dough and have it stick together)
   Confectioners' sugar

Filling:

Prune or apricot preserves

Preheat the oven to 375°. Sift the flour into a bowl. Make a well in the flour and add the egg yolks and butter. Stir together by hand. Add the dissolved yeast and mix thoroughly. Add enough half & half to make a pie dough consistency. Roll out the dough onto a board covered with confectioners' sugar. Cut into small squares and fill with preserves. Bake for 8 minutes or until lightly brown.

Note: For the best results, use an air-filled cookie sheet so that the kiefels will not burn on the bottom.

Makes about 3 dozen.

Mark Goddard

Mark Goddard co-starred as big-city plainclothes Det. Sgt. Chris Ballard, who played a detective in *The Detectives, Starring Robert Taylor. Photograph courtesy of the* Nashville Banner.

China's Snowballs

■ This recipe is named after my eight-year-old daughter, China. It is a delicious, simple, buttery, nutty, festive cookie, although it is a little time-consuming. We usually make them at holidays and even give them as gifts in decorative containers. Making them is part of the fun.

2 sticks butter
¼ cup confectioners' sugar
2 teaspoons vanilla extract
1 tablespoon water
2 cups all-purpose flour
1 cup finely chopped walnuts, pecans, or a combination
   Approximately 1½ cups additional confectioners' sugar for rolling

Preheat the oven to 250°. In a mixing bowl, cream together the butter and the ¼ cup of confectioners' sugar. Then add the vanilla and water. Next gradually blend in the flour and nuts. The mixture will be dry but should hold together. Roll the dough into small balls (about 1½ inches in diameter) and then place them about 2 inches apart on an ungreased cookie sheet; place the cookie sheet into the oven. Bake for 20 to 30 minutes.

The cookies are done when the bottoms are a light golden brown. Do not overcook. If the tops should begin to crack, remove from the oven and immediately roll the cookies in confectioners' sugar. The cookies will be somewhat fragile when they are first removed from the oven, and they must be immediately rolled in the confectioners' sugar and placed on a cookie-cooling rack.

After you have rolled all the cookies in the confectioners' sugar once, repeat so that the cookies are rolled in the sugar at least 3 times. The confectioners' sugar seals the cookies and forms an icing as it creates layers and "melts" around the cookie.

It takes quick, "ginger" fingers to do the first rolling, and it may be a bit too hot for children to join in. But we have found the subsequent rolling of the snowballs (as well as the making of the dough balls) to be great fun for children to do, or so China says!

Serving suggestion: These are delicious for adults with coffee or an after-dinner liqueur, or for children with milk or hot chocolate.

Makes 3 to 4 dozen.

David Soul

Capital Coconut Cake

■ My son loves this cake!   —*Ruth Thompson*

½ cup vegetable shortening
1¼ cups sugar
2 cups sifted cake flour
2½ teaspoons baking powder
¼ teaspoon salt
1 cup milk
1 teaspoon vanilla extract
3 egg whites
   Coconut milk

Preheat the oven to 350°. Cream the shortening and sugar until fluffy. Sift the flour, baking powder, and salt together 3 times. In a mixing bowl combine dry ingredients and milk alternately, adding a small amount of each and beating after each addition until smooth. Add the vanilla. Beat the egg whites until they peak and stir into the batter. Bake in 2 greased and floured 8- or 9-inch cake pans for 30 minutes or until done. Let cool and then dribble coconut milk over the cake before frosting.

> *"When a man carries a gun all the time, the respect he thinks he's getting might really be fear. So I don't carry a gun because I don't want the people of Mayberry to fear a gun; I'd rather they would respect me."*
>
> —Sheriff Andy Taylor
> (*The Andy Griffith Show*)

Fred Dalton Thompson plays many roles. As an attorney, he was the legal counsel for the Senate Judiciary Committee investigating Watergate during the early 1970s. As an actor, he played Clint Eastwood's Secret Service boss in the 1993 film *In the Line of Fire*. In 1994 he was elected to the U.S. Senate by Tennesseans.

Frosting:

1⅔ **cups sugar**
½ **cup water**
¼ **teaspoon cream of tartar**
½ **cup egg whites (3 eggs)**
2 **cups flaked coconut**

Combine the sugar, water, and cream of tartar. Stir over low heat until the sugar is dissolved. Then boil the mixture without stirring until the syrup threads from a spoon. Beat the egg whites until stiff. Gradually add the syrup to the egg whites, beating constantly until the frosting is cool enough to spread. Frost the tips and sides of the cake. Then sprinkle coconut on the top and sides.

Makes 10 to 12 servings.

U.S. Senator Fred Thompson

FBI Cake

■ I made this recipe for my husband, Bill, the first time I cooked a meal for him when we were dating. He was FBI director at the time, and the recipe came from a cookbook called *Maida Heatter's Book of Great Chocolate Desserts.* The author said in her book that the recipe was called FBI Cake because it was served to J. Edgar Hoover by the author's mother. Hoover liked it so much that he threatened an FBI investigation if he didn't get the recipe. Bill must have liked it. He eventually married me!   —*Lynda Webster*

1¾ cups sifted all-purpose flour
½ teaspoon baking soda
1 teaspoon baking powder
¼ teaspoon salt
½ cup unsweetened cocoa powder
½ stick sweet butter, softened
1 teaspoon vanilla extract
1¾ cups sugar
4 eggs, separated
1¼ cups milk

Preheat the oven to 325°. Butter and dust two 8- or 9-inch cake pans with flour. Sift together the flour, baking soda, baking powder, salt, and cocoa; set aside. Cream the butter. Add the vanilla and sugar and mix well. Add the yolks. Add the dry ingredients and milk, alternating as you go. In a small bowl, beat the egg whites until they form peaks but are not dry or stiff. Add the whites to the chocolate mixture and fold together only until blended. Bake for 45 minutes or until the cake pulls way from the sides of the pan.

Frosting:

2 cups whipping cream, whipped
1 teaspoon vanilla extract
¼ cup sifted confectioners' sugar
1 cup chopped almonds

Mix together all of the ingredients until they form a spreadable mixture. Spread onto the cooled cake.

    Makes 10 servings.

William Webster
Former Director
Federal Bureau of Investigation

Lexington Chocolate-Chocolate Cake

8 ounces cream cheese, softened
1 cup sour cream
½ cup water or coffee-flavored liqueur
2 eggs
1 package (2-layer size) chocolate cake mix
1 package (4-serving size) instant chocolate pudding and pie filling
1 cup semisweet chocolate chips
   Confectioners' sugar

Preheat the oven to 325°. Mix the cream cheese, sour cream, liqueur (or water), and eggs with an electric mixer on medium speed until well blended. Add the cake mix and pudding mix; beat until well blended. Fold in the chocolate chips. The batter will be stiff. Pour into a greased and floured 12-cup fluted tube pan. Bake for 1 hour to 1 hour and 5 minutes or until a

Efrem Zimbalist Jr. starred as Inspector Lewis Erskine in *The FBI.*

toothpick inserted near the center comes out clean. Cool for 5 minutes. Remove from the pan. Cool completely on a wire rack. Sprinkle with confectioners' sugar before serving. Garnish, if desired.

Makes 10 servings.

L. E. Walsh
Chief of Lexington-Fayette
Urban County Division of Police
Lexington, Kentucky

Carol's Killer Chocolate Cake

1 package devil's food cake mix
1 6-ounce package instant chocolate pudding mix
1¾ cups milk
2 eggs
12 ounces semisweet chocolate bits

Preheat the oven to 350°. Mix the first 4 ingredients by hand using about 50 strokes. Fold in the chocolate bits. Grease and flour a bundt pan. Pour the batter into the pan. Bake for approximately 55 minutes or until a toothpick inserted into the center comes out clean.

Makes 10 servings.

Howard Safir
Commissioner of Police
New York, New York

Rocky Mountain Chocolate Dream Cake

1 package chocolate or devil's food cake mix
½ cup mayonnaise
½ pint whipping cream
⅓ cup confectioners' sugar
1 teaspoon instant coffee
1 teaspoon cocoa
1 16-ounce can chocolate cake frosting

Follow the mixing directions on the cake mix package but substitute the mayonnaise for oil. Bake according to the pack-

age directions in three 8-inch pans. Cool the layers completely on a wire rack.

Whip the cream until soft peaks form. Add the confectioners' sugar, instant coffee, and cocoa. Whip until firm. Spread the whipped cream mixture between the layers and frost with prepared chocolate frosting. Refrigerate for at least 3 hours before serving. Refrigerate any leftovers.

Makes 10 servings.

David L. Michaud
Chief of Police
Denver, Colorado

Winchester Double-Barreled Triple Fudge Cake

■ Many years ago, I was the Shenandoah Apple Blossom Festival Queen, and I must say that the Winchester Police Department took very good care of me. —*Greta Garner-Hewitt*

1 4-ounce package chocolate pudding and pie filling mix
2 cups milk
1 package chocolate cake mix
½ cup semisweet chocolate pieces
½ cup chopped nuts
Whipped cream (optional)

Preheat the oven to 350°. Mix and cook the pudding according to its package directions; blend the dry cake mix directly into the pudding while it is still warm. Pour into a greased 9x13x2-inch baking pan. Sprinkle the chocolate pieces and nuts on top. Bake for 30 minutes. Serve warm with whipped cream if you like.

Makes 12 servings.

Col. Allen Barley
Chief of Police
Winchester, Virginia

James Garner tried on Raymond Chandler's memorable gumshoe and found Philip Marlowe a pretty good fit in the 1969 feature film *Philip Marlowe.*

Marlowe's Low-Cholesterol Lemon Cake

■ This is our family's favorite cake, which was given to us by our friend Shawna Trabert. It's made for every birthday and holiday, and it's always gone by morning—eaten by thieves in the night!

    Nonstick cooking spray
    All-purpose flour
1 package white cake mix
⅓ cup vegetable oil
1¼ cups water
3 egg whites
1 teaspoon vanilla extract
1 3-ounce package sugar-free lemon
    gelatin

Preheat the oven to 350°. Grease a bundt pan with the cooking spray and then coat it with flour. In a mixing bowl, mix well by hand the remaining ingredients. Pour the batter into the prepared pan and bake for 40 to 50 minutes. Cool on a rack for 10 minutes. Remove from the pan and let cool for about 1 hour before applying Glaze.

Glaze:

1 egg white
3 cups confectioners' sugar
    Juice of 1 lemon

Mix all the ingredients well and drizzle over the cake. Don't forget to glaze inside the tube area too.
    Makes 10 servings.

James Garner

Officer's Log

Cake:

Vegetable spray
6 eggs, separated
1 cup sugar, divided
1 teaspoon baking powder
1 teaspoon vanilla extract
1 cup chopped walnuts

Preheat the oven to 350°. Heavily coat a 10x15-inch jelly roll pan with vegetable spray. In a mixing bowl, beat the egg yolks well with ½ cup of the sugar until light and creamy. Set aside. In a separate bowl, beat the egg whites with the remaining ½ cup of sugar until frothy but not stiff or dry. Mix in the baking powder and the vanilla. Fold in the nuts. Fold the 2 mixtures together.

Put the mixture in the baking pan. Evenly spread out the walnuts in the pan with a spatula. Bake for 15 minutes or until cake is golden. Immediately loosen the cake edges with a rubber spatula, cover with a terry-cloth towel and place on cooling rack; invert. Roll the cake in the terry-cloth towel from the long side; then flatten the cake out again and remove the towel. Refrigerate on a rack for 1 to 2 hours.

Filling/Frosting:

1 pint heavy cream
6 tablespoons sugar
2 teaspoons vanilla extract
1 package hot cocoa mix

Whip the cream with the sugar and vanilla. Divide the mixture in half. Spread half over the cooled cake. Roll the cake to form a log. Cut off a fourth of the log at about a 45° angle and place the remaining three-fourths-length piece on a serving dish. Lay the quarter-length next to the larger piece to look like a branch coming off a tree. Mix the cocoa together with the remaining whipped cream mixture and then spread this mixture over top of the log and branch. (Cut the baking edges off for appearance.)

Optional: Decorate with halved maraschino cherries, pine branches, or walnut halves.

Makes 6 to 8 servings.

Donald F. Kane
Police Commissioner
Nassau County, New York

North Pole Chocolate Applesauce Raisin Cake

■ This one came from my grandmother to my mother and then to me. I love it and could it eat it all day long!

½ cup vegetable shortening
1 cup sugar
1 egg
1 cup raisins (or more if you like lots of raisins)
1¾ cups sifted all-purpose flour
1 teaspoon baking soda
¼ teaspoon salt
1 teaspoon ground cinnamon
2 tablespoons cocoa powder
1 cup applesauce

Preheat the oven to 350°. Cream together the shortening, sugar, egg, and raisins. Add the dry ingredients and then the applesauce. Pour the batter into a greased and floured 5x7-inch loaf pan and bake for 45 minutes or until a toothpick inserted in center comes out clean. (This is a moist cake).

Variation: Nuts can be added, and 1 cup of apple pie filling can be substituted for the applesauce. (Just make sure to mix in those ingredients by hand at the end to preserve their consistency.)

Makes 6 to 8 servings.

Gerald Ownby
Chief of Police
The North Pole, Alaska

Ruth's Windy City Raisin Cake

They don't call it Cook County for nothing!

2 eggs
1 cup vegetable oil
1½ cups sugar
1 cup strong coffee
1 teaspoon ground nutmeg
1 teaspoon ground cinnamon
1 teaspoon ground cloves
3½ cups all-purpose flour
1 teaspoon baking soda
1 15-ounce box raisins

Preheat the oven to 375°. Mix the eggs, oil, sugar, coffee, nutmeg, cinnamon, and cloves. Add the flour and baking soda. Mix well. Add the raisins and stir. Pour the mixture into a greased and floured tube pan. Bake for 1 hour or until a toothpick inserted in center comes out clean. Enjoy!

Makes 10 servings.

Matt L. Rodriguez
Superintendent of Police
Chicago, Illinois

Topeka Top Cop Cake

1 20-ounce can cherry pie filling
1 20-ounce can crushed pineapple, undrained
1 package yellow cake mix
1 cup chopped nuts
1 stick butter (use real butter)

Preheat the oven to 350°. Grease a 9x13-inch pan. Pour in the cherry pie filling and spread around, then layer the pineapple on top. Sprinkle on a layer of the dry cake mix, followed by a layer of nuts. Cut the butter into small pieces and layer over the top. Bake for 30 to 35 minutes.

Makes about 12 servings.

Dean Forster
Chief of Police
Topeka, Kansas

Mrs. G.'s Criminal Justice Cinnamon Cake

3 eggs
1½ cups sugar
2 cups sifted all-purpose flour
2 teaspoons baking powder
¾ cup milk
4 tablespoons melted butter
4 additional tablespoons melted butter
½ cup sugar
2 teaspoons ground cinnamon

Preheat the oven to 400°. Beat the eggs until light and foamy; slowly add sugar. Fold in the dry ingredients, alternating with the milk. Mix in the butter. Place the batter in a greased 9x13-inch pan. Pour the 4 additional tablespoons melted butter over the top of the batter, then sprinkle on the sugar and cinnamon to make a topping. Bake for 25 minutes.

Makes about 12 servings.

Terrence B. Sheridan
Chief of Police
Baltimore County, Maryland

"Okay, Jimbo...Dennis. I know you're in there. And I know you know it's ticket season again—Policeman's Ball and all that. So come to the door when I knock this time. I know you're in there."

—Message from Dennis Becker
on Jim Rockford's Answering Machine

Incredible Iowa Oatmeal Cake

1 cup oatmeal
½ cup boiling water
1 stick butter
1 cup sugar
1 cup firmly packed brown sugar
1 egg
1½ cups all-purpose flour
1 teaspoon baking soda
½ teaspoon salt
2 teaspoons baking powder
1 teaspoon vanilla extract

Combine the oatmeal, boiling water, and butter and let stand for 30 minutes. Preheat the oven to 350°. Add the sugars and egg. Beat in the remaining ingredients. Bake in a greased and floured bundt pan for 30 to 35 minutes. While warm, turn out onto a large cake plate.

Walnut Topping:

1 cup firmly packed brown sugar
1 stick butter
¼ cup evaporated milk
1 cup chopped walnuts
  Dash vanilla extract

Cook the first 4 ingredients in a saucepan over medium heat. When thickened, stir in the vanilla and pour mixture over the warm cake.
  Makes 10 servings.

William H. Moulder
Chief of Police
Des Moines, Iowa

As Jim Rockford (James Garner, right) takes care of the chips and dip, Officer Al Mazurski (Bucklind Beery) carries the cake celebrating the promotion of Dennis Becker (Joe Santos, left) to the rank of lieutenant in an episode of *The Rockford Files*. Buck Beery is the son of actor Noah Beery Jr., who played Jim Rockford's lovable dad, Joseph "Rocky" Rockford.

Stafford Repp played Gotham City's own Police Chief O'Hara on *Batman* from 1966 to 1968, and in 1957 he was Lieutenant Raines on *The Thin Man.*

Chief O'Hara's Bourbon Whiskey Cake

■ This recipe was one of Stafford's favorites at Christmastime. He so enjoyed it, and I always made extras for friends and family.

1   package Duncan Hines butter cake mix
1   6-ounce box instant vanilla pudding
1   cup milk
4   eggs
½   cup vegetable oil
1   shot glass whiskey
1   cup chopped walnuts

Preheat the oven to 350°. In a mixing bowl, combine all the ingredients except the nuts. Beat for 5 minutes and then add the nuts. Pour into a greased bundt pan and bake for 50 to 55 minutes.

Sauce:

½   cup whiskey
¾   cup sugar
1   stick butter, melted

Heat the ingredients and let boil for a few minutes. Remove the cake from the oven and spoon ½ the Sauce over the hot cake. Let stand in the pan for 10 minutes. Turn out the cake and spoon the rest of the Sauce over the cake. Let it sit in the refrigerator overnight.

Makes 10 servings.

Stafford Repp
Submitted by Theresa (Mrs. Stafford) Repp

Walking Tall Cherry Jubilee Cake

1 package Duncan Hines Cherry
  Supreme Cake Mix
1 cup pear nectar or apricot nectar
½ cup vegetable oil
½ cup sugar
½ teaspoon cherry flavoring or 1 teaspoon juice of maraschino cherries
3 drops red food coloring
1 whole egg

Preheat the oven to 350°. In a large bowl, mix all the ingredients except the egg. Beat at medium speed for 1 minute. Add the egg and beat. Spread the batter in a greased and floured 10-inch tube pan. Bake at 350° for 45 minutes until a toothpick inserted in center comes out clean. Cool right-side up for 15 minutes; remove from the pan.

Topping:

1 cup confectioners' sugar
6 maraschino cherries, finely chopped
2 tablespoons juice from cherries

Mix all the topping ingredients together and pour on the warm cake.
  Makes 10 servings.

Buford Pusser
Submitted by Pauline (Mrs. Buford) Pusser

Squad Car Sour Cream Pound Cake

■ This is my very favorite recipe.

3 cups cake flour
¼ teaspoon salt
½ teaspoon baking soda
2¾ cups sugar
6 eggs, separated
2 sticks margarine, softened
8 ounces sour cream
1 tablespoon vanilla flavoring
1 teaspoon lemon flavoring

In a bowl, combine the flour, salt, and baking soda. Cream the sugar, egg yolks, and margarine; add the flour mixture alternately with the sour cream and flavorings. Pour the batter into a greased, fluted cake pan. Place cake in a cold oven and bake at 325° for one hour or until a toothpick inserted in center comes out clean or the cake springs back when touched.
  Makes 10 servings.

Johnnie Johnson
Chief of Police
Birmingham, Alabama

Law and Oregon Cheesecake

■ I got this recipe from Nancy Taber in our Internal Affairs Division.

1½ pounds cream cheese, softened
 5 eggs
 ⅔ cup sugar
 1 teaspoon almond extract

Preheat the oven to 325°. Mix all the ingredients and pour into a greased 10-inch springform pan. Bake for 25 to 30 minutes. Cool for 10 minutes. Add the topping.

Topping:

1 cup sour cream
1 teaspoon vanilla extract
3 tablespoons sugar

Mix the Topping ingredients until smooth. Pour over the cheesecake and bake for an additional 10 minutes. Cool and refrigerate for several hours.
  Variation: This cheesecake has no crust. A graham cracker crust may be added if desired.
  Serving suggestion: Serve with fresh Oregon marionberries, strawberries, raspberries, blueberries, peaches, or any fruit of choice.
  Makes 8 to 10 servings.

Charles A. Moose, Ph.D.
Chief of Police
Portland, Oregon

The Chief's Mother-in-Law's Mud Cake

Having to do with another kind of "law and order."

1 cup all-purpose flour
¾ cup sugar
½ teaspoon baking soda
⅓ teaspoon salt
½ teaspoon vanilla extract
½ cup sour cream
¼ cup vegetable shortening
1 ounce chocolate
1 egg
1¼ cups hot water, divided
½ cup pecans
½ cup firmly packed brown sugar
2 teaspoons cocoa powder

Preheat the oven to 350°. Grease the bottom of a 1½-quart casserole dish. Combine the flour, sugar, baking soda, salt, vanilla, sour cream, vegetable shortening, chocolate, egg, and ¼ cup of the hot water in the casserole dish. Beat for 1½ minutes with a wooden spoon. Sprinkle pecans over the batter and cover with brown sugar and cocoa. Pour the remaining 1 cup of hot water over the sugar mixture. Bake for 50 to 55 minutes. Turn the cake upside down when cooled.

Makes 8 to 10 servings.

Al A. Philippus
Chief of Police
San Antonio, Texas

Lieutenant Crowley's Cream Cheese Cake

Crust:

1½ cups graham cracker crumbs
¼ cup sugar
1 stick margarine, melted

Preheat the oven to 350°. Mix the crumbs and sugar in a bowl and then mix in the melted margarine. Mold this to the bottom and sides of a greased springform pan (one whose sides spring away from the bottom). Bake for 10 minutes and cool.

Cake:

2 8-ounce packages cream cheese, softened
1½ cups sugar
4 eggs
⅛ teaspoon salt
1 teaspoon vanilla extract

Preheat the oven to 350°. Beat the cream cheese with an electric mixer while adding the sugar until the mixture is smooth. Add the eggs one at a time, beating well after each addition. Beat in the salt and vanilla. Pour onto the cooled crust. Bake for 55 minutes. Cool for 15 minutes.

Note: It's a good idea to place some foil or a cookie sheet on the oven shelf

---

Our heroes read the morning papers:

NICK: *"I'm a hero; I was shot twice in the* **Tribune.***"*
NORA: *"I read you were shot five times in the tabloids."*
NICK: *"It's not true. He didn't come anywhere near my tabloids."*

—William Powell and Myrna Loy as
Nick and Nora Charles in *The Thin Man* (1934)

Angie Dickinson starred as Sgt. Suzanne "Pepper" Anderson, and Earl Holliman was Lt. Bill Crowley from 1974 to 1978 on *Police Woman*. Holliman also starred in the 1990s television series *P.S. I Luv U,* in which he played detective agency boss Matthew Durning.

below the one on which the cake is cooking to catch any drippings from the springform pan.

Topping:

16 ounces sour cream
¼ cup sugar
2 teaspoons vanilla extract

Preheat the oven to 450°. Combine sour cream, sugar, and vanilla. Pour over the cake. Return the cake to the oven and bake for 10 minutes. Cool for a few minutes and refrigerate.

Note: The cake seems to be better if prepared the day before serving.

Makes 10 servings.

Earl Holliman

Dick's Modus Operandi Chocolate Mousse Pie

1 **envelope unflavored gelatin**
⅓ **cup orange juice**
6 **ounces semisweet chocolate chips**
1 **teaspoon vanilla extract**
2 **large eggs**
¼ **cup sugar**
1 **pint heavy cream with sugar and vanilla added to taste, whipped to stiff peaks and well chilled**
1 **Dick's Special Pie Crust (recipe follows) Whipped cream topping Shaved chocolate**

In a medium saucepan, sprinkle gelatin over the orange juice and let stand for 1 minute. Stir constantly over medium heat until the mixture is translucent and no granules are visible. Reduce heat to medium low and slowly stir in the chocolate chips until completely melted.

Remove the pan from heat, stir in vanilla, and set aside to cool at room temperature.

In a mixing bowl, beat the eggs on medium-high until thick and light yellow in color. Slowly beat in the sugar until the mixture is lemon colored and very thick. (You can write in it and it will not disappear right away.) Gradually and gently mix the room-temperature chocolate mixture with the egg mixture until it just reaches the point of being completely blended. Fold the whipped cream into the above mixture, making sure that the bowl and utensils are chilled. Gently pour the mixture into the pie crust and chill overnight (it also freezes well). Garnish with whipped-cream topping (I usually pipe on about ¾ pint using a large star tip) and chocolate shavings.

Dick's Special Pie Crust:

8 **to 12 soft Dutch chocolate cookies**
2 **to 3 tablespoons butter or margarine, softened**
½ **cup finely chopped nuts (your choice, but walnuts work really well)**

Preheat the oven to 300°. In a food processor, reduce the cookies to medium-sized crumbs. Add the butter or margarine. Mix in the nuts. Gently press into a 10-inch pie plate, making sure to build up the sides as far as possible. Don't press hard because this makes the crust very hard. Place in oven, turn off the heat, and leave in the oven for 8 to 10 minutes. Cool the crust at room temperature and chill very well before adding the mousse.

    Preparation time: 1 to 2 hours
    Calories: 1 gazillion
    Cholesterol: 1 year's supply
    Fat: Lie to yourself and say "absolutely none"
    Makes 8 servings.

David G. Walchak
Chief of Police
Concord, New Hampshire
Submitted by Lt. Richard Bertolami

1950s MYSTERIES

Match the actors to the television series.

1. *City Detective*
2. *Crime Photographer*
3. *Jimmie Hughes, Rookie Cop*
4. *Mark Saber Mystery Theater*
5. *Mr. Lucky*
6. *Mr. and Mrs. North*
7. *Naked City*
8. *The Plainclothesman*
9. *Police Woman Decoy*
10. *Racket Squad*
11. *Rocky King: Inside Detective*
12. *Staccato*
13. *The Telltale Clue*
14. *The Thin Man*
15. *Treasury Men in Action*

A. Rod Cameron
B. John Cassavetes
C. Tim Conway
D. Richard Denning and Barbara Britton
E. James Franciscus
F. Beverly Garland
G. Walter Greaza
H. Reed Hadley
I. Roscoe Karns
J. Peter Lawford and Phyllis Kirk
K. Ken Lynch
L. Darren McGavin
M. William Redfield
N. Anthony Ross
O. John Vivyan

SOLUTION

1. A, 2. L, 3. M, 4. C, 5. O, 6. D, 7. E, 8. K, 9. F, 10. H, 11. I, 12. B, 13. N, 14. J, 15. G

Crime-Free Chess Pie

■ Sheriff Ward has received national attention for having his residence attached to his well-run jailhouse, an act that has drawn comparisons to Sheriff Andy Taylor in fictional Mayberry. Here's a pie that Aunt Bee herself would be proud of!

1   **stick margarine**
1½ **cups sugar**
3   **eggs**
1   **tablespoon cornmeal**
1   **teaspoon vinegar**
1   **teaspoon vanilla extract**
1   **pastry shell, unbaked**

Preheat the oven to 350°. Melt the margarine. Mix the sugar, eggs, cornmeal, vinegar, and vanilla just enough to combine. Add the margarine. Pour into the unbaked pastry shell. Bake for 1 hour.
    Makes 8 servings.

Thomas Ward
Sheriff of Perry County
Linden, Tennessee

Mickey Spillane actually became his famous, fictional character Mike Hammer in the 1963 film *The Girl Hunters.*

WHAT A CHARACTER!

Match the crime-solving character with the actors who portrayed them.

1. Boston Blackie   9. Perry Mason
2. Charlie Chan   10. Ellery Queen
3. The Falcon   11. The Saint
4. Mike Hammer   12. Sam Spade
5. Martin Kane   13. Dick Tracy
6. The Lone Wolf   14. Philo Vance
7. Philip Marlowe   15. Mr. Wong
8. Miss Marple

A. William Gargan, Lloyd Nolan, Lee Tracy, and Mark Stevens

B. Richard Hart, Lee Bowman, Hugh Marlowe, George Nader, Lee Phillips, Peter Lawford, and Jim Hutton

C. George Sanders, Tom Conway, John Calvert, and Chuck McGraw

D. E. L. Park, Warner Oland, Sidney Toler, Roland Winters, Ross Martin, Peter Sellers, Peter Ustinov, and J. Carrol Naish

E. Warren William, Ricardo Cortez, Donald Wood, Raymond Burr, and Monte Markham

F. George Sanders, Louis Hayward, Hugh Sinclair, Roger Moore, Ian Ogilvy, and Simon Dutton

G. Humphrey Bogart, Robert Mitchum, Philip Carey, Howard Duff, James Garner, Dick Powell, and Robert Montgomery

H. Boris Karloff and Keye Luke

I. Humphrey Bogart, Howard Duff, and Ricardo Cortez

J. Ralph Meeker, Mickey Spillane, Darren McGavin, Armand Assante, and Stacy Keach

K. William Powell, Basil Rathbone, Warren William, Paul Lukas, Edmund Lowe, Wilfrid Hyde-White, Grant Richards, James Stephenson, William Wright, and Alan Curtis

L. Gracie Fields, Dame Margaret Rutherford, Joan Hickson, Helen Hayes, and Angela Lansbury

M. Ralph Byrd, Morgan Conway, and Warren Beatty

N. Bert Lytell, Lionel Barrymore, David Powell, William Russell, Forrest Stanley, Raymond Glenn, Chester Morris, and Kent Taylor

O. Henry B. Walthall, Jack Holt, Bert Lytell, Melvyn Douglas, Frances Lederer, Warren William, Gerald Mohr, Ron Randall, and Louis Hayward

SOLUTION
1. N, 2. D, 3. C, 4. J, 5. A, 6. O, 7. G, 8. L, 9. E, 10. B, 11. F, 12. I, 13. M, 14. K, 15. H

Cookeville Chocolate Pie

¾ cup sugar
3 level tablespoons all-purpose flour
⅓ cup cocoa
1½ cups milk
3 eggs, separated
1 teaspoon vanilla extract
1 tablespoon butter
1 cooked pastry shell
⅓ cup sugar

In a medium saucepan, mix together the ¾ cup of sugar, flour, and cocoa. Stir in the milk and heat until warm. Add the egg yolks gradually and cook until thickened. Add the vanilla and butter. Spoon into the pastry shell. Preheat the oven to 350°. Beat the egg whites until soft peaks form. Blend in the ⅓ cup of sugar. Spoon over the filling mixture. Bake until lightly browned.
   Makes 8 servings.

William Benson
Chief of Police
Cookeville, Tennessee

District Cop Pie

8 ounces nondairy whipped topping
¼ cup lemon juice
8 ounces crushed pineapple, drained
1 14-ounce can sweetened condensed milk
2 ounces pecans, finely chopped
1 deep-dish graham cracker piecrust

> *"I'm not sure I agree with you a hundred percent on your police work, there, Lou."*
> —Frances McDormand as Marge Gunderson in *Fargo* (1996)

Mix the first 5 ingredients together and pour into the piecrust. Let stand for 4 hours in the refrigerator.
   Makes 8 servings.

Larry Soulsby
Chief of Police
Washington, D.C.
Submitted by Tracie Dean

Southern Pecan Pie from the North

3 eggs, well beaten
1 cup light corn syrup
½ cup sugar
1 cup chopped pecans
2 tablespoons butter, melted
1 teaspoon vanilla extract
¼ teaspoon salt
1 9-inch piecrust, unbaked

Preheat the oven to 350°. Combine the first 7 ingredients and place in the piecrust. Bake for 45 minutes.
   Note: I also cover the pie with aluminum foil for the first 30 minutes to keep from burning the crust.
   Makes 8 servings.

Col. A. James Walton Jr.
Commissioner
Vermont State Police

Southern Pecan Pie from the South

3 tablespoons butter
¾ cup sugar
3 eggs
⅛ teaspoon salt
¾ cup light corn syrup
¼ cup honey
1 teaspoon vanilla extract
1½ cups chopped pecans
1 9-inch pastry shell, unbaked
½ cup pecan halves (optional)

Preheat the oven to 350°. In a mixing bowl, cream the butter and sugar together.

Add the eggs and salt and beat well. Add the corn syrup and honey and beat well. Stir in the vanilla and chopped pecans. Pour the filling into the pastry shell and place the pecan halves on top (if desired). Bake for 50 to 55 minutes. Cool before slicing.

Makes 6 to 8 servings.

Robert L. Johnson
Chief of Police
Jackson, Mississippi

Crime Stoppers Sweet Potato Pie

■ The Crime Stoppers program was established in 1976 by Albuquerque police detective Greg MacAleese.

3 **eggs**
½ **cup sugar**
½ **stick butter, softened**
⅓ **cup milk**
1 **teaspoon ground nutmeg**
½ **teaspoon salt**
1 **teaspoon vanilla extract**
1 **teaspoon ground cinnamon**
1 **heaping cup mashed sweet potatoes**
2 **tablespoons lemon juice**
1 **9-inch pastry shell, unbaked**

Preheat the oven to 425°. Beat the eggs and sugar. Add the butter, milk, nutmeg, salt, vanilla, and cinnamon and mix well. Blend in the potatoes and lemon juice. Pour into the unbaked pastry shell. Bake for 10 to 15 minutes. Reduce heat to 350° and continue to bake for 40 to 45 minutes longer.

Makes 6 to 8 servings.

Joseph M. Polisar
Chief of Police
Albuquerque, New Mexico

Robert Forster is seen here as a Native-American deputy sheriff in *Nakia* in 1974, but he also played a cartoon detective named Gumshoe in *Once a Hero* in 1987.

Montana Marshal's Pumpkin Pie

■ This is my mom's recipe. I'll eat this any month of the year. You'll need more than three forks!

2 eggs, beaten
1 16-ounce can pumpkin
½ cup sugar
½ cup firmly packed brown sugar
1½ tablespoons pumpkin pie spice
1 tablespoon all-purpose flour
½ teaspoon salt
1 13-ounce can evaporated milk
1 9-inch pastry shell, unbaked

Preheat the oven to 425°. Combine the eggs and pumpkin. Blend in the sugars, spice, flour, and salt. Mix well. Add the evaporated milk and mix well. Pour the mixture into the pastry shell. Bake for 15 minutes. Reduce heat to 350° and continue to bake for 35 to 40 minutes or until a tester inserted near the center comes out clean. Cool and store in the refrigerator.

Makes 6 to 8 servings.

Keith King
Marshal
Three Forks, Montana

Tough Guise Peach Pie

It's champion!

Coconut-Almond Pie Crust:

1 cup blanched almonds
1 cup moist-style flaked coconut
¼ cup sugar
½ stick butter or margarine

Preheat the oven to 375°. Grind the almonds until medium fine. Mix with the coconut. Work the sugar and butter together with your fingers or a spoon. Add the almond mixture to the butter mixture to form a crumbly mixture. Press evenly into the bottom and sides of a 9-inch glass pie plate. (Reserve 3 tablespoons of the crumbly mixture for topping the filling later.) Bake for 10 to 12 minutes or until light golden brown. If the edges begin to get too brown, cover them with aluminum foil but leave the center uncovered. Place the remaining crumbly mixture in a shallow pan and toast in the oven at the same time as the pie shell. (This should take only 5 minutes.)

Filling:

1 cup sour cream
   Dash salt
6 tablespoons confectioners' sugar, divided
1 teaspoon orange juice
1 teaspoon shredded orange rind
1 teaspoon vanilla extract
3 cups sliced fresh peaches
½ cup whipping cream
1 Coconut-Almond Pie Crust

Beat the sour cream. Add the salt, 4 tablespoons of the confectioners' sugar, orange juice, orange rind, and vanilla. Spread on the bottom and sides of the crust. Place peaches in the crust. Whip the cream and fold in the remaining 2 tablespoons of confectioners' sugar. Cover the peaches with the whipped cream. Sprinkle top with remaining coconut-almond mixture. Chill.

Makes 8 servings.

Kirk Douglas

Lockup Key Lime Pie

■ This is not only the best pie recipe but the easiest! You won't want to escape from this!

1 **14-ounce can sweetened condensed milk**
½ **cup fresh key lime juice (it helps to roll the limes on a countertop before cutting to squeeze)**
3 **egg yolks**
1 **9-inch graham cracker crust Whipped cream**

Blend the first 3 ingredients together well with an egg beater. Pour the mixture into the graham cracker crust and top with whipped cream. Chill for 2 hours and keep refrigerated.

Variation: You may substitute lemon juice and the recipe then becomes Lemon Icebox Pie.

Makes 6 to 8 servings.

Jessica Walter

Jessica Walter starred as a chief of detectives in *Amy Prentiss*, an *NBC Mystery Movie* during the early 1970s. Her daughter, Jill, was played by Helen Hunt.

Tyne Daly as Det. Mary Beth Lacey.

Lacey's Key Lime Pie

3 egg yolks
1 14-ounce can sweetened condensed milk
¾ cup lime juice
1 9-inch baked and cooled pie shell
   (or chilled crumb crust)
1 cup heavy cream

In a large bowl, whip the egg yolks and sweetened condensed milk. Gradually beat in the lime juice. Pour into the pie shell and chill for 6 hours. Whip the heavy cream and spread over the pie.

Alternate Meringue Topping:

3 egg whites
6 tablespoons sugar

Whip the egg whites until they form stiff peaks. Whip in the sugar 1 tablespoon at a time. Pile on top of the pie. Brown for 3 to 4 minutes in a 425° oven. Let cool.

Makes 8 servings.

Tyne Daly

Prosecutor's Coconut Cream Pie

You'll plea-bargain for more.

1 cup sugar
2 heaping tablespoons cornstarch
2 cups milk
1 teaspoon vanilla extract
2 egg yolks
1½ ounces flaked coconut
1 9-inch pastry shell, baked

Combine the sugar, cornstarch, milk, and vanilla. Beat the egg yolks until pale yellow and add to the mixture. Cook the mixture on medium heat, stirring constantly, until it thickens. Add the coconut and pour into the pastry shell.

Meringue:

2 egg whites
¼ cup sugar
½ teaspoon cream of tartar
½ teaspoon vanilla extract
1½ ounces flaked coconut

Beat the egg whites until stiff. Add the sugar, cream of tartar, and vanilla and beat until the mixture peaks. Spread the meringue over the pie and sprinkle with flaked coconut. Return the pie to the oven to lightly brown the meringue and coconut.

Makes 6 to 8 servings.

U.S. Senator Fred Thompson

Chain of Evidence Cherry-Apple Pie

A sweet Diehl!

1 cup sugar
2 tablespoons all-purpose flour
1 teaspoon ground cinnamon
¼ teaspoon ground nutmeg
3 cups Granny Smith apples peeled, cored, and sliced
2 cups pitted tart cherries
1 9-inch double-crust pastry shell, unbaked
2 tablespoons butter
1 tablespoon milk
½ teaspoon sugar
   Additional dash ground cinnamon

Preheat the oven to 375°. Stir together the sugar, flour, cinnamon, and nutmeg and set aside. In a large bowl, combine the apples and cherries. Add the sugar mixture and toss to coat. Put all in a crust-lined, 9-inch pie plate. Dot the fruit with the 2 tablespoons butter. Place the top crust on and pinch the edges to seal. Cut slits in the top crust. Brush the top of the crust with milk. Combine the ½ teaspoon of sugar and the dash of cinnamon and sprinkle over the top. Cover the edge of the pie with aluminum foil to prevent the crust from burning. Bake for 25 minutes. Remove the foil. Bake for 20 to 25 minutes longer or until the top is golden brown.

Makes 8 servings.

Tom Atkins

No Alibi Apple Crisp

Guilty only of being delicious!

6 to 8 medium Jonathan apples, cored, peeled, and sliced
1 tablespoon lemon juice
1½ teaspoons ground cinnamon
1 stick butter, softened
1½ cups firmly packed brown sugar
3 heaping tablespoons all-purpose flour
1 cup oats

Preheat the oven to 350°. Arrange the apple slices in the bottom of an ungreased, 9-inch square pan. Sprinkle with lemon juice and dust the top with cinnamon. Cream together the butter and sugar. Cut in the flour and oats to form a dough. Add additional butter or dry ingredients as needed to create a dough the consistency of modeling clay. Form thin patties of dough and lay over the apples. Overlap the dough and press down to form a flat surface that completely covers the apples. Bake for 45 minutes or until the pastry is a deep brown. Serve warm with milk or cream.

Makes 6 servings.

Tom Casady
Chief of Police
Lincoln, Nebraska

Beverly's Peace Officers' Peach Cobbler

2 sticks butter or margarine
2 cups self-rising flour
2 cups sugar
2 cups whole milk
2 29-ounce cans sliced peaches in heavy syrup (Drain 1; reserve the syrup in the other.)

Preheat the oven to 350°. Melt the butter in a 9x13-inch glass baking dish. Mix the flour, sugar, milk, and the syrup from 1 can of the peaches until well blended. (The mixture will be very soupy and slightly lumpy.) Pour the mixture into the baking pan. Evenly distribute the sliced peaches over the mixture. Bake in the lower third of oven for about 1 hour or until golden brown.

Note: Any fruit, fresh or canned, can be used. If using fresh fruit, add sugar to taste and allow the fruit to stand for a day to form juice.

Makes 12 servings.

Beverly J. Harvard
Chief of Police
Atlanta, Georgia

Lord Peter Wimsey's Gingery Sherry Log

■ This may sound extraordinary, but it's delicious and so simple that even I can make it.

10 ounces whipping cream
1 generous glass or so medium to dry sherry
16 ginger nuts (biscuits or cookies)
Flaked chocolate

Whip the cream until it forms stiff peaks. Pour the sherry into a shallow dish. Dip two ginger biscuits into the sherry just long enough for them to absorb a little liquid but not long enough to become soggy—10 seconds is quite long enough. Sandwich them together with a generous dollop of whipped cream and then stand them up sideways in the middle of a large sheet of very lightly oiled aluminum foil. This is the beginning of your log.

Continue the log with alternating layers of whipped cream and soaked biscuits, adding more sherry to the soaking dish as necessary. When all the biscuits are used up, coat the whole log in a layer of the remaining whipped cream. Crush the chocolate flakes over the log to decorate.

Wrap the log in the foil and place carefully in the refrigerator to chill for an hour or so before serving. Don't let it freeze, however.

This should serve 4 people, but you can vary the quantities to suit yourself.

Ian Carmichael

Ian Carmichael is the dapper, unflappable supersleuth Lord Peter Wimsey on *Mystery!*

Jonathan Hart's Crime Brûlée

1 quart heavy cream
2 tablespoons sugar
8 egg yolks, well beaten
2 teaspoons vanilla extract
  Light brown sugar

Preheat the oven to 275°. Heat the cream in a double boiler until hot but not scalding. Take off heat and add the sugar, stirring until dissolved. Add the egg yolks and vanilla. Mix well. Pour into a shallow baking dish. Place the dish in hot water. Bake for 35 to 40 minutes or until set. Cool and place in the refrigerator overnight. Sift the brown sugar over top and place under a well-heated broiler. Brown and place back in the refrigerator until ready to serve.

Makes 6 servings.

Robert Wagner

Bonnie's Crime-Fighting Crème Caramel

■ This is my favorite dessert.

¾ cup sugar, divided
3 tablespoons water
5 cups milk
1 egg
2 egg yolks
1 tablespoon vanilla extract

In a heavy saucepan, boil ¼ cup of the sugar with the water until the sugar caramelizes and is amber brown. Set aside to cool.

Scald the milk, allow it to cool slightly, and pour it into the pan with the caramelized sugar. Stir over low heat until the caramel is dissolved in the milk. Beat the egg with the yolks and add the remaining sugar and the vanilla. Slowly

As cunning cat burglar Alexander Mundy, Robert Wagner reluctantly became a good guy after a pardon from prison in *It Takes a Thief* from 1968 to 1969. He returned as millionaire supersleuth Jonathan Hart with Stefanie Powers as his wife and partner on *Hart to Hart* from 1979 to 1984.

pour in the caramelized milk, stirring slowly to mix. Preheat the oven to 325°.

Pour the custard into individual cups. Place in a shallow pan filled with boiling water and bake for 30 to 40 minutes or until set. Test by inserting a knife into the custard. If the knife comes out clean, the custard is set. Serve warm or chilled.

Makes 6 servings.

Richard S. Shaffer
Chief of Police
Harrisburg, Pennsylvania

NIELSEN'S TOP TEN COP/DETECTIVE/ CRIME-FIGHTING SHOWS

This is a listing of which cop shows have finished in A.C. Nielsen's top ten for a season. The year indicates when the television season began.

NUMBER 1
  The Andy Griffith Show (1967)

NUMBER 2
  Dragnet (1953)

NUMBER 3
  Dragnet (1954)
  The Andy Griffith Show (1966)
  Hawaii Five-O (1972)
  Magnum, P.I. (1982)
  Murder, She Wrote (1985)

NUMBER 4
  The Andy Griffith Show (1960, 1964)
  Ironside (1970)
  Charlie's Angels (1977)
  Murder, She Wrote (1986)

NUMBER 5
  The Andy Griffith Show (1963)
  The Fugitive (1964)
  Batman (1965)
  The NBC Sunday Night Mystery Movie (1972)
  Hawaii Five-O (1973)
  Charlie's Angels (1976)
  Simon & Simon (1983)
  Murder, She Wrote (1992)

NUMBER 6
  77 Sunset Strip (1959)
  The Andy Griffith Show (1962, 1965)
  Magnum, P.I. (1983)

NUMBER 7
  The Andy Griffith Show (1962)
  Hawaii Five-O (1970)
  Mannix (1971)
  Kojak (1973)
  Simon & Simon (1982, 1984)

NUMBER 8
  Gangbusters (1952)
  Dragnet (1955)
  The Untouchables (1960)
  Adam 12 (1971)
  Baretta (1976)
  Murder, She Wrote (1984, 1988, 1991)

NUMBER 9
  Cannon (1973)
  Murder, She Wrote (1987)
  Miami Vice (1985)
  Moonlighting (1986)

NUMBER 10
  Ironside (1972)
  Hawaii Five-O (1974)
  The FBI (1970)
  Cagney & Lacey (1983)
  NYPD Blue (1995)

Sergeant Billings's Spanish Flan

15 tablespoons sugar, divided
 6 eggs
1½ cups milk
 1 teaspoon vanilla extract
    (or other flavor)

Caramelize 8 tablespoons of the sugar in the top part of a double boiler. Once the sugar is caramelized, coat the pan sides and bottom with the melted sugar. Set the caramel by turning the pan upside down under cold running water until the caramel stops cracking and is cool. Set aside.

Heat the water in the bottom pan of the double boiler until boiling. While the water is heating, mix the flan by separating the six eggs, putting the whites into a large bowl and the yolks in a small bowl. Beat the egg whites with a mixer until very stiff peaks form. Add the 6 yolks and mix well again. Add the remaining 7 tablespoons of sugar and beat well for 7 to 10 minutes. Add the milk and mix well again. Add the extract and mix well.

Pour the mixture into the coated pan in the top of the double boiler. (Have the water level just touching the bottom of the top pan.) Cover and simmer for about 45 minutes or until the custard is firm all the way into the middle. A toothpick inserted into the center should come out clean. Take a large platter (bigger than the circumference of the flan pan) and place it upside down over the pan. Hold securely and quickly invert the pan, being careful of the caramel, which is now melted around the flan. Serve hot or cold like pie. Enjoy!

Makes 6 to 8 servings.

Luis Delgado
Submitted by Bobbie (Mrs. Luis) Delgado

MODUS OPERANDI

Match the vehicle to the show or character.

 1. *Bronk*
 2. Amos Burke
 3. Andy Taylor
 4. Columbo
 5. Sonny Crockett
 6. Green Hornet
 7. Michael Knight
 8. Magnum
 9. *Mod Squad*
10. Inspector Morse
11. Ellery Queen
12. Jim Rockford
13. Scooby Doo
14. Spenser
15. J. J. Starbuck
16. Starsky
17. Dan Tanna
18. Toody and Muldoon

A. Black Beauty
   (1966 Chrysler Imperial)
B. 1955 Cadillac
C. Car 54
D. Dusenberg
E. Ferrari
F. Ferrari Spider/Testarossa
G. 1974 Ford Torino
H. Jaguar
I. KITT
   (black Pontiac Trans-Am)
J. Ford Galaxie/Custom
K. 1961 Lincoln
   Continental
L. Mustang
M. Mystery Machine
N. 1960 Peugot
O. Pontiac Firebird
P. Rolls-Royce
Q. 1957 T-bird convertible
R. 1950 Woody
   station wagon

SOLUTION
1. B, 2. P, 3. J, 4. N, 5. F, 6. A, 7. I, 8. E, 9. R, 10., H, 11. D, 12. O, 13. M, 14. L, 15. K, 16. G, 17. Q, 18. C

Miami Mango Flan

It's a Miami vice.

■ This is one of my favorite recipes, which is prepared with this rich and flavorful tropical fruit. It's very popular among residents and visitors of the South Florida area.

14 ounces fresh or frozen mango
 1 14-ounce can sweetened condensed
    milk
 1 14-ounce can whole milk
 4 eggs
 4 tablespoons sugar
 1 teaspoon vanilla extract
    Caramel (recipe follows)

Preheat the oven to 350°. Purée the mango in a blender with half of the milk. Add the 4 eggs and blend for about 1 minute. Add the rest of the ingredients, except Caramel, and blend for another 2 minutes. Pour the mixture into the pan coated with the Caramel. Place the pan in a larger pan of water. Place both in oven and bake for 1 hour. Remove from oven and separate pans. Let the mixture come to room temperature in its pan and then put the pan in the refrigerator to cool. Turn over on a serving dish before serving.

Caramel:

½ cup sugar

Cook sugar over low heat, stirring constantly until it melts and is caramel colored. Spread the syrup all over the sides of the pan.

Makes 8 servings.

Donald H. Warshaw
Chief of Police
Miami, Florida

Virginia Vice Rice Pudding

a.k.a. Squad Squash Pudding

2 eggs
½ cup sugar
½ teaspoon salt
2¼ cups milk
1 teaspoon vanilla extract
2 cups rice or squash, cooked
   Dash ground nutmeg

Preheat the oven to 350°. Beat the eggs. Add the sugar, salt, milk, vanilla, and rice (or squash). Turn into a round baking dish. Sprinkle on or stir in the nutmeg. Bake for 45 minutes or until a knife inserted into the center comes out clean.

Makes about 6 servings.

Col. Allen Barley
Chief of Police
Winchester, Virginia

Dragnet, the most cited cop show in television history, was the prototype of all police programs. Its television debut was in January of 1952 after three years on radio. Pictured here are Jack Webb and Harry Morgan as *Dragnet's* officers Joe Friday and Bill Gannon.

Scott Hylands (right) portrayed real-life policeman turned best-selling author Joseph Wambaugh (left) on the *Police Story* anthology series (1973–77), which Wambaugh created and for which he served as production consultant.

"Golden Orange" Siren Sauce

1   cup firmly packed brown sugar
½   stick butter
2   oranges, peeled (removing all pulp), seeded, and diced
3   ounces Grand Marnier
    Vanilla ice cream

Melt the sugar and butter in a microwave on high for 2½ minutes, removing after each 30 seconds to stir. Add the diced oranges and microwave on high for 40 seconds, removing once to stir. Add the Grand Marnier and microwave on high until it bubbles, approximately 15 seconds. Serve warm over vanilla ice cream.

Makes 6 servings.

Joseph Wambaugh

POLICE, DETECTIVE, CRIME, AND MYSTERY FILMS THAT HAVE COPPED AN ACADEMY AWARD

1929–30: *The Big House:* writing, sound recording

1940: *Northwest Mounted Police:* film editing

1944: *Laura:* black-and-white cinematography

1948: *Key Largo:* Claire Trevor, best supporting actress

The Naked City: cinematography, film editing

1950: *Panic in the Streets:* writing

The Third Man: cinematography

1952: *The Lavender Hill Mob:* story and screenplay

1955: *To Catch a Thief:* story and screenplay

1958: *The Defiant Ones:* story and screenplay, black-and-white cinematography

1967: *In the Heat of the Night:* Rod Steiger, best actor; writing, sound, film editing

Cool Hand Luke: George Kennedy, best supporting actor

1968: *Bullitt:* editing

The Thomas Crown Affair: "The Windmills of Your Mind," music

1971: *The French Connection:* best picture; Gene Hackman, best actor; William Friedkin, director; writing, film editing

Klute: Jane Fonda, actress

Shaft: "Theme from Shaft," music

1972: *The Godfather:* best picture, Marlon Brando, actor; writing

1973: *The Sting:* best picture; George Roy Hill, director; story and screenplay, art direction/set decoration, scoring, film editing, costume design

1974: *The Godfather Part II:* best picture; Robert DeNiro, supporting actor; Francis Ford Coppola, director; screenplay, art direction/set decoration, original dramatic score

Murder on the Orient Express: Ingrid Bergman, supporting actress

Chinatown: writing

1975: *Dog Day Afternoon:* writing

1978: *Death on the Nile:* costume design

1985: *Prizzi's Honor:* Anjelica Huston, supporting actress

Witness: original screenplay

1987: *The Untouchables:* Sean Connery, supporting actor

1988: *The Accused:* Jodie Foster, actress

1990: *GoodFellas:* Joe Pesci, supporting actor

1991: *The Silence of the Lambs:* best picture; Jonathan Demme, director; Anthony Hopkins, actor; Jodie Foster, actress; screenplay adaptation

Thelma and Louise: original screenplay

1993: *The Fugitive:* best picture; Tommy Lee Jones, supporting actor

1994: *Bullets Over Broadway:* Dianne Wiest, supporting actress

Pulp Fiction: original screenplay

1995: *Dead Man Walking:* Susan Sarandon, actress

The Usual Suspects: Kevin Spacey, supporting actor; original screenplay

1996: *Fargo:* Frances McDormand, actress

Director's Choice Velvet Cream

■ This recipe has been in Jim's family for several generations. We serve it every Thanksgiving and Christmas.   —Suzanne (Mrs. Jim) Woolsey

1 pint whipping cream
1 envelope unflavored gelatin
½ cup water
4 egg yolks
1 cup sugar
1 teaspoon vanilla extract

Whip the cream until stiff and set aside. Soak the gelatin in 2 tablespoons of cold water. Add water to make ½ cup. Microwave for 30 seconds or until bubbly. Beat the egg yolks until they are lemon colored. Add the sugar gradually and then drizzle in hot gelatin mixture slowly while continuing to beat. Fold in the whipped cream and add the vanilla. Refrigerate. Stir once before the mixture sets (about 15 to 20 minutes). Serve with strawberries or other fruit.
    Makes 4 servings.

Jim Woolsey
Director, 1993–95
Central Intelligence Agency

Detective Briscoe's Tough Guys Dessert

■ Since my wife does all the cooking in the family, here's my simple recipe for something unusual and surprisingly delicious.

Vanilla ice cream
A shot of Scotch whiskey
Black pepper (to taste)

To a dish of vanilla ice cream add Scotch whiskey and sprinkle with pepper. Believe it or not!

Jerry Orbach

Chocolate Ice Crime

Freeze!

3 eggs
1 cup sugar
1 quart half & half
1 pint whipping cream
1 cup chocolate syrup
1 tablespoon vanilla flavoring
3 cups milk

Beat the eggs until frothy. Slowly add the sugar and beat until lemon colored and thick. Slowly add the half & half, whipping cream, chocolate syrup, and vanilla. Pour into a 3-quart (or larger) ice cream freezer and then pour in the milk. Freeze and serve.
    Makes about 2½ quarts

Richard L. Garner
Special Agent in Charge,
Field Division
U.S. Treasury Department
Bureau of Alcohol, Tobacco, & Firearms

He has been Det. Lennie Briscoe on *Law & Order* in the 1990s, but Jerry Orbach also played Boston private eye Harry McGraw in 1987 on *The Law and Harry McGraw* after his character made several appearances on *Murder, She Wrote.*

Brothers in blue on *In the Heat of the Night* include (left to right) David Hart as Sgt. Parker Williams, Randall Franks as Deputy Goode, and Alan Autry as Capt. Bubba Skinner. *Photo courtesy of Lynn Lockwood.*

Bubba's Chocolate Gravy

1¼ cups sugar
  3 heaping tablespoons Hershey's cocoa
  3 heaping tablespoons flour
  1 stick butter
  2 cups milk

Mix sugar, cocoa, and flour. Stir in a half cup of the milk. Set aside.

Heat remaining milk and the butter until butter is melted. Stirring constantly, add the cocoa mixture. Stir until the mixture thickens. Serve over hot biscuits.

Makes about 3 cups.

Alan Autry

> *"My dad once gave me a few words of wisdom which I've always tried to live by. He said, 'Son, never throw a punch at a redwood'."*
>
> —Thomas Magnum
> *(Magnum, P.I.)*

> *"Just remember: The eagle may soar, but the weasel never gets sucked up into a jet engine."*
>
> —Rick Simon
> *(Simon & Simon)*

Bomb Squad Hot Fudge

It's dynamite!

■ This is very good. Dad says Mom won his love with this one.

2 cups sugar
2 squares unsweetened chocolate
1 cup milk
1 tablespoon butter
1½ teaspoons vanilla extract

In a saucepan over medium heat, mix together the sugar, chocolate, and milk. Stir until thickened and remove from heat. Add the butter and vanilla and beat until thickened. When you put it on ice cream, it will harden slightly, like candy.

Makes about 3 cups.

Jeff Bridges

Jeff Bridges played the leader of a Boston police bomb squad in the 1994 film *Blown Away*. He was also an ex-cop in the 1986 films *The Morning After* and *Eight Million Ways to Die*.

George's Famous Fudge

Nonstick cooking spray
2 cups sugar
½ cup cocoa
¾ cup whole milk (or low-fat milk, not non-fat)
2 tablespoons butter
1 teaspoon vanilla extract

Spray a large, heavy pot with cooking spray. Over medium heat, combine sugar, cocoa, and milk with a wooden spoon or whisk until the sugar and cocoa are dissolved.

Clip a candy thermometer to the side of the pot. Make sure it rests in the mixture without touching the bottom of the pot. Bring cocoa mixture to a boil—when the temperature reads 212°. Continue to cook the mixture, stirring only if necessary to prevent burning, until the temperature reaches a soft boil or 238°.

Remove from heat and, without stirring, add the butter.* Cool the mixture by immersing the bottom of the pot in cool water. When cooled, add vanilla extract. Beat mixture until just creamy, and as it thickens, spread into a lightly buttered 8x8x2-inch pan. Cut into squares before it hardens.

Enjoy! Share this fudge with someone you love!

George Peppard
Submitted by Laura (Mrs. George) Peppard

*Note: At this point, stir in the butter to make the mixture a perfect hot-fudge sauce for ice cream.

George Peppard starred as Polish-American private eye Thomas Banacek, a smooth, cool detective who lived in Boston's Beacon Hill, in *Banacek*, one of the rotating segments of *The NBC Wednesday Mystery Movie* from 1972 to 1974. Peppard also played cop or detective roles in the movies *Pendulum* and *Newman's Law* and in the television movie *Man Against the Mob*.

Aiding and abetting Judge Wapner on *The People's Court* is Bailiff Rusty Burrell, whose famous line was "Remember, when you get mad, don't take the law into your own hands. Take 'em to court." Burrell served with the Los Angeles County Sheriff's Department for thirty-two years, and his son Larry followed in his footsteps to serve twelve years with the same department.

Tell It to the Judge Fudge

1½ sticks margarine
3 cups sugar
1 5-ounce can evaporated milk
1 12-ounce package semisweet chocolate chips
1 7-ounce jar marshmallow creme
1 teaspoon vanilla extract

Lightly grease a 9x13-inch pan. Microwave the margarine in a 4-quart microwavable bowl for 1 minute or until melted. Add the sugar and milk; mix well. Microwave on HIGH for 5½ minutes, stirring after 3 minutes. Gradually stir in the chips until melted. Add the remaining ingredients and mix well. Pour into the prepared pan. Cool at room temperature. Cut into squares and enjoy!

Makes approximately 3 pounds.

Rusty Burrell

Nick Knight's Chocolate Pizza

1 uncooked pizza dough, divided in half
8 ounces mascarpone cheese
6 ounces bittersweet chocolate, frozen and then grated
¼ cup nuts (any variety), finely chopped
2 ripe bananas, thinly sliced
Cinnamon
Whipped cream
1 tablespoon nuts

Preheat the oven to 375°. Roll out both halves of dough to fit the pizza pan. Lay 1 half on a baking sheet. Spoon the cheese evenly onto the dough, leaving a 1-inch border. Sprinkle evenly with the chocolate and nuts. Add the banana slices. Place remaining dough on top and pinch the edges together. Bake for 20 to 25 minutes. Top with a dusting of cinnamon, a dollop of whipped cream, and nuts.

Makes 4 servings.

Geraint Wyn Davies

Geraint Wyn Davies starred as Det. Nicholas Nick Knight in *Forever Knight,* one of the few police/supernatural dramas. Knight was a nearly eight-hundred-year-old vampire who drove a 1962 Cadillac while working the night shift as a homicide detective. The CBS production went to first-run syndication in 1994.

The son of a police officer, Arnold Schwarzenegger (seen here with pal Sylvester Stallone, left) has played characters on both sides of crime and law enforcement. One of his most endearing roles was as a detective and teacher in the 1990 hit film *Kindergarten Cop*. He also played an antiterrorist expert in 1994's *True Lies* with Jamie Lee Curtis; and he was a Soviet cop in 1986's *Red Heat*, in which his American counterpart was a Chicago detective played by James Belushi.

Mom's Apple Strudel

They'll be back for more.

    5 sheets phyllo dough (19x29 inches)
    1½ sticks butter, melted
    1 pound of pound cake crumbs
    6 ounces cinnamon sugar

Apple Filling:

    15 ounces sliced Granny Smith apples
     5 ounces crushed pineapple
     5 ounces pineapple syrup
     6 ounces cinnamon sugar
     5 ounces apple juice
     2 ounces cornstarch
     4 ounces raisins
        Chopped pecans or walnuts (optional)

Procedure for Making Filling: In a saucepan over medium heat, cook the apples, crushed pineapple, syrup, and cinnamon sugar for 15 minutes. Meanwhile, mix the apple juice and cornstarch together, blending well. At the end of the 15 minutes, add the cornstarch and apple juice mixture to the apples along with the raisins (and nuts, if desired). Cook for 5 minutes. Remove from heat.

Procedure for Assembling Strudel: Lay out a large piece of baker's parchment on a clean work table. Lay the first sheet of phyllo dough on top of the parchment paper, being careful to keep a moist towel over the other pieces of phyllo to prevent their drying out.

With a large pastry brush, sprinkle generously with melted butter. Do not brush as you may tear the phyllo. Sprinkle a fourth of the available crumbs over that sheet. Sprinkle a fourth of the available cinnamon sugar over that sheet.

Lay the second and third sheets of phyllo on top of this. Sprinkle with melted butter, a fourth of the crumbs, and a fourth of the cinnamon sugar. Lay the fourth and fifth layers of phyllo on top of this. Sprinkle with melted butter and a fourth of the cinnamon sugar.

With the remaining crumbs, make a bed about 3 inches wide across the sheet about a quarter of the way up from the bottom. Arrange the apple mixture on this bed all the way across the sheet. Using the parchment paper to lift and pull with, roll the sheets into a tight strudel. *Note:* After rolling, make sure to crimp the ends so that the filling does not come out the ends.

Brush the strudel with the remaining butter and sprinkle with the last of the cinnamon sugar. Bake or freeze immediately. Bake in a 325° oven for 20 minutes.

Makes 1 strudel.

Arnold Schwarzenegger

It's a Plane! Peaches Flambé

It's super, man!

    ¼ cup apricot jam
    3 tablespoons sugar
    ½ cup water
    4 large fresh peaches, peeled and sliced
    1 tablespoon lemon juice
    ¼ cup brandy
    1 quart vanilla ice cream
       Whipped cream (optional)
       Slivered almonds (optional)

Combine the jam, sugar, and water in a medium saucepan or chafing dish. Simmer over low heat for 5 minutes or until syrupy. Add the peaches and continue cooking over low heat for about 3 minutes or until tender.

Heat the brandy. Pour over the peaches and ignite. Let the flames die down. Stir well before serving. Spoon the peaches and syrup over each serving of ice cream. Add whipped cream and slivered almonds if desired.

Robert Shayne
Submitted by Elizabeth (Mrs. Robert) Shayne

Ed Harris co-starred as Det. Seth Frank in the 1997 Clint Eastwood film *Absolute Power*, which also starred Gene Hackman. Harris also played a persistent FBI agent in the film version of *The Firm*, starring Tom Cruise and Gene Hackman.

Darin' Man's Mandarin Orange Dessert

■ I got this recipe by way of my mother, Margaret Harris. It was passed down to her from my grandmother, Annie Abernathy Harris.

1 **14-ounce can sweetened condensed milk**
  Juice of 2 lemons
1 **6-ounce can mandarin oranges with juice**

Vanilla wafers
1 **cup whipped cream or nondairy whipped topping**

In a bowl, blend the first 3 ingredients by hand. In a buttered 8-inch-square oven-proof glass dish, place a layer of vanilla wafers. Cover the wafers with the orange mixture. Add a second layer of vanilla wafers. Cover with whipped cream or nondairy whipped topping. Sprinkle crushed vanilla wafers crumbs on top. Cover and refrigerate for 24 hours.

Makes 6 to 8 servings.

Ed Harris

Don Knotts won five Emmy Awards for his portrayal of Mayberry Deputy Barney Fife on *The Andy Griffith Show*, which finished every season in the top ten during its prime-time run on CBS (1960–68). Don Knotts continued his crime-fighting ways in two movies, *The Ghost and Mr. Chicken* in 1966 and *The Private Eyes* in 1980 with Tim Conway.

Barney's Chocolate Moulage

Don't worry about the calories; it all goes to muscle.

- 4   whole eggs
- 2   egg whites
- 2½ cups sugar
- ⅔   cup all-purpose flour
- 4   tablespoons cocoa
- 1   stick butter
- 2   teaspoons vanilla extract
- 1¼ cups chopped pecans
    Chocolate syrup (optional)
    Ice cream

Preheat the oven to 300°. Beat the eggs, egg whites, and sugar with a mixer for 10 minutes. Sift the flour and cocoa together then add, along with the butter and vanilla, to the egg mixture. Add the nuts. Pour the mixture into a greased 12x15x2-inch baking pan. Place the pan in a pan of water. Bake for 55 to 60 minutes. (Bake 5 minutes longer if using a slightly smaller and deeper pan.) Drizzle with chocolate syrup, if desired, before serving. Serve with your favorite ice cream (also drizzled with chocolate syrup).

Makes about 10 servings.

Don Knotts

Barney never really needed the single bullet Sheriff Andy Taylor let him carry in his shirt pocket. He just made his whole body a weapon.

This rendering of the Mayberry Deputy is the quick-draw work of Deputy Sheriff Rod Sadler, who specializes in forensic illustration with the Eaton County Sheriff's Department in Charlotte, Michigan. In his spare time, Rod is leader of Mayberry, Michigan chapter of The Andy Griffith Show Rerun Watchers Club.

R. SADLER 1997

The bridges and *Streets of San Francisco* belonged to Det. Lt. Mike Stone (Karl Malden).

Partners

INDEX OF POLICE CHIEFS
AND OTHER LAW ENFORCEMENT CONTRIBUTORS

Agents and Organizations

Index of Celebrity Cops

Rap Sheet

GENERAL INDEX

Greta Garner-Hewitt, a former licensed private investigator, is married to a detective sergeant and SWAT team member and is the daughter of television and movie actor James Garner. She lives in Nashville, Tennessee.

Ken Beck and **Jim Clark** are the authors or co-authors of *The All-American Cowboy Cookbook, Mary Ann's Gilligan's Island Cookbook, Aunt Bee's Mayberry Cookbook,* and *Goober in a Nutshell.* Ken Beck lives in Watertown, Tennessee, and is an editor and writer for the *Tennessean.* Jim Clark is a freelance writer who lives in Nashville, Tennessee.